ENTERPRISE
RESOURCES PLANNING
AND
BEYOND
Integrating
Your Entire
Organization

The St. Lucie Press/APICS Series on Resource Management

ENTERPRISE RESOURCES PLANNING AND BEYOND

Integrating Your Entire Organization

GARY A. LANGENWALTER
CFPIM, CIRM

The St. Lucie Press/APICS Series on Resource Management

St. Lucie Press
Boca Raton • London
New York • Washington, D.C.

The Educational Society for Resource Management

APICS
Falls Church, Virginia

Library of Congress Cataloging-in-Publication Data

Catalog record is available from the Library of Congress

© 2000 by St. Lucie Press
St. Lucie Press is an imprint of CRC Press LLC

No claim to original U.S. Government works
International Standard Book Number 1-57444-260-0
Printed in the United States of America   3 4 5 6 7 8 9 0
Printed on acid-free paper

Contents

Preface

The purpose of this book is to assemble, in one volume, all the components of Enterprise Resources Planning (ERP) and its extensions and to discuss how to choose, install, and successfully use ERP systems. There are many excellent books on the individual functions. The focus of this book is on the relationships *between* each of the functions. However, it also covers the basics of each function, so that a reader who is not familiar with that function can understand it well enough to appreciate how it affects the other areas.

This book can be used as reference by a seasoned practitioner at any level of an organization or for an introduction to ERP by a person who is new to the concepts. It is particularly helpful for project teams that are selecting or implementing ERP systems because it discusses how some manufacturers achieve greater than 100% ROI on their entire ERP investment (compared to the norm of 25% to 50%)

We introduce the acronym *TEI*, for Total Enterprise Integration, to represent information flow through an entire manufacturing company, customers, and suppliers. TEI is a superset of ERP, as shown in Figure 1.2; it includes all of ERP, adding extensions in several key areas.

The book is organized by major function within a manufacturing company, then by subfunction within those major functions. Each of these functions is briefly introduced below. To assist the reader in further exploration of the topics, each chapter ends with many references, both books and periodicals, and each chapter contains footnotes on key concepts.

Throughout this book, we use the terms "customer," "manufacturer," and "supplier" as follows:

- *Customer* — the downstream customer of the manufacturer. The customer might be another manufacturer, or it might be a distributor or retailer, or a government or institution.
- *Manufacturer* — the central focus of this book; the company that is running the TEI system. This manufacturer is a supplier to its customers, and a customer to its suppliers.
- *Supplier* — the upstream provider of raw materials, components, and services to the manufacturer.

Executive Support

ERP and TEI systems are the means of communicating executive direction throughout the company; they also provide information that enables executives to get better answers to questions, and to project more accurately the probable business results of their decisions. The functions in this area include the following:

- Strategic planning — the foundation of any manufacturing enterprise's long-term success and the basis on which day-to-day decisions should be made. The book includes:
  - A kite diagram, which shows how each of the major strategic areas interfaces primarily to two others
  - A circle of activities from strategic planning, through tactics, through execution, to strategic plan
- Marketing — this section includes the concepts of:
  - Voice of the Customer
  - Market research (with the new product idea database)
  - Quality Function Deployment, and how to translate customer requirements into executable, detailed specifications within a manufacturing company
- Sales and operations planning — reconciling actual sales, forecasts, capacity constraints, and materials availability, and then communicating those decisions throughout the organization quickly, efficiently, and effectively.
- Financial planning — showing how the Sales and Operations Plan directly feeds the financial plans and projections.
- Executive decision support — three tools that forecast the results of alternative strategic and tactical decisions. The tools include:

- Decision support simulation that shows the projected impact of decisions on the P&L statement, such as changing model mix, outsourcing or insourcing functions, adding or removing resources, and/or accepting additional customer orders
- Warning systems that alert an executive if a factor crosses a predefined threshold (such as inventory values exceeding a certain amount)
- Business process modeling tools
■ Measurement systems — classic measurement systems do not actively support continuous improvement or flexibility. This section proposes adding three new metrics to the traditional standard of profitability:
  - Time, including time to market, time to customer, and velocity
  - Quality
  - Company spirit
■ Supply chain management integration — a supply chain study shows substantial improvement in key performance indicators for best-in-class supply chain companies. We propose that supply chain is most effective when it is designed into the ERP or TEI system from the start, instead of being added on later. A graphic shows the major information flows that are internal to a manufacturer, its customer, and its supplier, and the major information flows that integrate customer with manufacturer, and manufacturer with supplier. The book presents the five key dimensions of supply chain:
  1. Strategy
  2. Infrastructure
  3. Process
  4. Organization
  5. Technology
■ The book also discusses the implications on a TEI system in each of the five stages of supply chain:
  1. Open market
  2. Cooperation
  3. Single level coordination
  4. Multi-level coordination
  5. Full collaboration

Customer Integration

The concept of *customer relationship management* assumes and requires integrating all functions that affect the customer. Areas of customer-focused information that are integrated with the rest of a TEI system include the following:

- Full sales support, including:
  - Assisted selling (in which the customer interacts with salespeople, whether inside the company or in the field)
  - Unassisted selling (including sales via Web sites)
  - Collaborative selling, a radical, customer-centric approach, based on how buyers buy
  - Sales force automation
- Forecasting integration, including:
  - Two types of forecasts (judgmental and quantitative), and the inherent flaws in each
  - How forecasts integrate with the rest of an ERP system
  - Three approaches to reducing forecast errors:
    1. Decreasing response lead times
    2. Increasing visibility with the customer
    3. Monitoring forecast errors
- Order generation — all methods of getting orders from a customer to the manufacturer, including:
  - Vendor-Managed Inventory/Continuous Replenishment
  - Electronic commerce, such as EDI and Internet commerce
  - Customer phone calls, faxes, and mail
  - *Kanbans* and other manual signals
  - Distribution Resources Planning (DRP)
- Order entry — the book discusses various alternatives and capabilities involved in actually entering orders in an ERP system, including multiple order types; handling large volumes of order line items; pricing and promotions; multiple units of measure; product substitution rules; product allocation and reservation rules; multiple sourcing options for each order line; fully integrated credit checking; and forecast coordination.
- Quoting and promising deliveries — including the three fundamental elements of a quotation: configuration, price, and delivery date. TEI systems can link the customer's computer directly to the supplier's

computer, so that the supplier's system can quote prices and delivery dates of stocked items and even legal combinations of configurable items. In advanced TEI systems, these delivery quotes fully integrate with logistics and transportation systems, routing the items from the most appropriate warehouse or factory to the customer's desired location using the lowest total cost shipping method.

- Demand management — demand can be prioritized by a new process known as "Rough-Cut Value Analysis," which ranks demand by how it fits the manufacturer's business objectives. The process has three steps:
  1. Determine demand value
  2. Determine resources required
  3. Rank by relative value
- Logistics and distribution — Value Added Logistics integrates the logistics chain to lower the total costs (inventory, material handling, and transportation) and to increase service levels. TEI can group shipments by destination, filling a truck for multiple stops (even in multiple cities), meeting customer due dates as the lowest possible cost, using the truck ship date as the internal due date for manufacturing. Warehouse management systems (WMS) increase efficiencies and accuracy of the warehouse functions.
- Field service — manufacturers that make capital equipment, both consumer and industrial, need to fully integrate field service information with their customer resource management, quality, material planning, inventory management, and accounting systems.

Engineering Integration

Approximately 90% of a product's total cost is a determined during the design cycle; its quality characteristics are also fundamentally determined during product design and process design. The book presents how to integrate the entire engineering process with the rest of the company, including:

- The design process — the book covers all seven stages of the design process. It emphasizes Concurrent Engineering, which dramatically reduces the elapsed design time and allows a company to bring its product to market much more quickly. The seven stages include:

1. Initial concept/proof of technology
2. Design optimization
3. Marketing effort (in parallel with Step 2)
4. Pilot production
5. Product launch
6. Follow-up
7. Engineering changes

- Product phase-out — a product at the end of its life cycle requires special attention.
- Product Data Management — PDM and ERP/TEI overlap in product and process definitions and in controlling engineering changes. TEI systems and PDM systems can interface or integrate in five different ways.
- Integrating with customers — including getting direct answers from the customer with respect to their true needs, and receiving supply specifications that are sufficiently detailed that the manufacturer can design and make a product that fits the customer's needs.
- Integrating with suppliers — building a solid relationship; single sourcing as a matter of policy; inviting the suppliers to participate in designing new products and redesigning existing products, and working collaboratively with supplier to jointly develop the best alternatives to delight the customer; providing specifications in a format that the supplier can readily use, and communicating and controlling engineering changes.
- Integrating with the rest of the company — an engineering department can be proactive or reactive with the rest of the company, and can view itself as a service or a supplier
- Project management — for growing manufacturers, managing construction projects is as important as managing the flow of materials through the plant. TEI integrates project management with the rest of the company's planning and analysis systems:

Manufacturing Integration

Although this area is the design center and traditional strength of ERP systems, complete integration across the entire area was virtually nonexistent in TEI systems in early 2000. The book includes the following functions:

- Material and Capacity Planning — this section includes explanations for how each of the following functions works, then shows where each function integrates with the rest of a company's systems:

- – Master Production Scheduling (MPS)
- – Rough-Cut Planning
- – Material Requirements Planning (MRP)
- – Capacity Requirements Planning (CRP)
- – The perpetual inventory system
- ■ Manufacturing Execution Systems, including:
  - – Planning system interface with MRP, CRP, cost accounting, inventory control, and product data management
  - – Work order management and process control
  - – Workstation management
  - – Inventory tracking and management
  - – Material movement management
  - – Data collection
  - – Exception management
- ■ JIT — the book discusses the inherent conflict between ERP and JIT, because ERP is a "push" system, and JIT is a "pull" system. The book shows how the best TEI and ERP systems can support JIT pull systems and *kanban* execution on the shop floor, and display actual production and quality data. The section includes the capabilities required in TEI systems to support JIT.
- ■ Advanced Planning and Scheduling — APS systems are replacing the older, hierarchical MPS/MRP/CRP/PAC systems. The book:
  - – Shows how an APS system integrates with forecasting, customer order promising, purchasing, costing, shipping, and the shop floor
  - – Presents a more advanced type of APS system, called a "Supply Chain Execution" system, and a very advanced type that integrates manufacturers directly with suppliers' plants and with customers' plants or warehouses
  - – Discusses the special needs and technology for strategic, tactical, and operational APS systems
  - – Presents the approach, advantages, limitations, and application for the basic APS technologies:
    - - Network
    - - Finite capacity schedulers
    - - Optimizers
- ■ Supplier Integration — this section addresses three fundamental topics:
  - – How purchasing integrates internally with other key functions of the company

- How purchasing can become a commercial liaison between the company and its suppliers
- Different ways of integrating with suppliers, and the environment in which each is the most appropriate
- Quality Management Systems — after presenting ISO concepts, the book discusses:
  - Laboratory information management systems (LIMS)
  - Integration field service and maintenance
  - Integration with engineering
- Maintenance — the book presents all three modes of maintenance (reactive, preventive, and predictive) and shows how they must integrate with the company's planning and analysis systems.

Support Service Integration

Support services are those functions that do not directly touch the manufactured items or meet with the customer, but that are required for a company to operate, such as:

- Accounting — accounting systems were first integrated with MRP to form MRP II systems in the 1970s. The challenge to accountants as they implement TEI and ERP systems is to think of new and creative ways to achieve the necessary level of controls, while eliminating or minimizing the paperwork and human effort. Accounting systems can use workflow technologies to track electronic paperwork. The section discusses the following functions, including their interfaces to the rest of the company, customer, suppliers, and the government:
  1. Accounts Payable, which can use a TEI system to eliminate most paperwork and pay suppliers automatically
  2. Accounts Receivable, which can use a TEI system to invoice correctly and fully integrate credit checking
  3. General Ledger, which includes projected profit and loss (P&L) statements and flex budgeting
  4. Payroll, fully integrated with the rest of the company
  5. Fixed Assets, fully integrated with purchasing and maintenance, as well as the P&L and general ledger

- Costing — including:
  - Standard costing, with overhead allocation example and variances
  - Activity-based costing, with cost drivers and a real-world example
  - Life-cycle costing
  - Target costing
- Human Resources, with integration with the rest of the company and outside the company.
- Environmental, including Environmental, Health, and Safety systems, their basic and advanced functions, and their interfaces, both internal and external.

Technical Considerations

In nontechnical terms, the book presents six technical topics that warrant attention by practitioners, executives, and others outside the IT organization. For each of the six, advantages and disadvantages are presented.

- Work flow — performs the same function for information as a routing does for a work order. Work flow tells the worker who has a task what to do and where to send the job next.
- Object orientation — including the concepts of object classes, encapsulation, and inheritance.
- Client/server — including the three primary strategies for implementation:
  - 2-tier
  - 3-tier
  - Internet/Intranet
- E-commerce / Internet commerce — including:
  - EDI, with a table that lists EDI transaction types
  - Simple e-commerce using the Internet, following a sample purchase order through the process
  - Sophisticated e-commerce, which includes selecting configurations and options while placing an order, then confirming price and delivery
  - Advanced e-commerce, which ties customers and suppliers together so tightly that a customer's computer can perform real-time, constraint-based planning

- Data warehousing — contrasting OLAP and OLTP.
- Internet — potential competitive uses for the Web, citing several examples.

Other Topics

All ERP systems are NOT alike! Each ERP system on the market was designed with a "typical" or "target" company in mind. Some were designed for large, multi-division, multi-plant, multi-national companies; others for smaller companies. Some were designed for engineer-to-order; others for process. Before selecting a system, executives should compare the design center of the chosen system to their own company's current and projected future operations. The book presents the variations and adaptations of ERP and TEI, including the functionality required to properly support:

- Multi-plant
- Multi-division
- Multi-national
- "Nontraditional" industries, including:
  - Engineer-to-order
  - Repetitive, identifying how repetitive differs from job shop and process, and the changes to each area in the organization when repetitive is implemented
  - Process, including process flow scheduling, with its fundamental principles:
    - Process structure guides scheduling calculations
    - Choosing between processor-dominated scheduling and material-dominated scheduling
    - Scheduling based on reverse flow scheduling, forward flow scheduling, or mixed-flow scheduling
  - Hybrid, including how to create focused factories.

System Selection

Although selecting a new ERP system looks relatively straightforward, it is deceptively difficult, because the system selection process itself constrains the eventual **return on investment** (ROI) that a company will receive on its entire investment. The ten steps to system selection that yield the highest ROI are:

1. Create a vision, which is challenging, comprehensive, clear, crisp, and compelling. This step forms the foundation for a high ROI. Unfortunately, most companies bypass this step completely, or give it a quick review.

2. Create the software feature and function list, which supports the vision in Step 1.

3. Create the list of 20 to 25 potential software candidates who are the best strategic fit for the software requirements, then narrow the list to about 12.

4. Narrow the field to 3 to 5 serious candidates, by asking each supplier 30 to 40 difficult questions based on the vision and software features and functions. No supplier should be able to answer "yes" to all these questions.

5. Create and send a Request For Proposal, using the feature/function list from Step 2 as the technical content, and adding sections for supplier response format, projected schedule, decision criteria, etc. Invite each supplier to visit the company for half a day to take a plant tour, meet the selection team, and ask questions.

6. Receive the proposals. When the proposals arrive, each team member reads the sections that pertain to his or her functions.

7. Select three finalists based on the proposals, plus other information the team and/or an outside counselor provides. Invite each of the three to demonstrate their product at the company location. You can ask each finalist for a best and final offer.

8. Participate in demonstrations. Before the demonstrations, have each selection team member call their counterparts at reference sites provided.

9. Select a winner. Visit a reference site. Negotiate, keeping the runner-up available just in case.

10. Plan the implementation, at a high level. This plan provides the time phasing for the benefits, which are part of the justification package submitted to the capital appropriation committee.

Successful Implementation

The way it implements its new ERP system determines a company's final return on investment. Most companies realize returns on investment (ROIs) in the 25% to 50% range, which is not bad, but they probably could have achieved 50% to 100% or higher if they had implemented with high ROI as their constant goal. Realistic ROIs for ERP systems range from 25% to 100%, depending on the capabilities of the existing systems and how well the new system is implemented.

System implementations are times of long hours, high stress, and chaos. They are also the opportunity to dramatically improve how the company operates on a day-to-day basis, by taking advantage of the capabilities in the new system. The 12 steps to a successful implementation are as follows:

1. Organize the project. Appoint the project team and leader; review and refine the vision (Step 1 of the selection).
2. Define the vision-based performance measures for the new system, which should reflect the ROI justification.
3. Create the project plan. Add substantial detail to the initial plan from Step 10 of the selection process. Look for overcommitted resources; revise until relatively realistic.
4. Educate the project team and other key individuals.
5. Assess the integrity of the existing data base; plan to address any critical issues.
6. Install any new hardware.
7. Install the software and any modifications; perform the computer room pilot.
8. Educate the critical mass.
9. Define and refine procedures for the new system in the conference room pilot.
10. Insure that all data bridges are sufficiently robust.
11. Bring the first module/product/plant live; refine and adjust. Repeat for other modules/products/plants.
12. Improve continually.

The People Side of TEI

Technology, including TEI, can succeed only if the people involved want it to succeed. This chapter explores the human side of the organization, with special emphasis on the creative spirit that characterizes a well-functioning team or group.

Companies that embrace values and vision beyond maximizing profits outperform competitors that are purely profit-oriented. Approximately 80% of working people dislike their work; they find their life's meaning, purpose, and greatest rewards outside the workplace. However, they spend most of their waking hours at work.

Companies can implement and operate TEI systems with a framework that either ignores the spiritual side or embraces it. Unleashed spirit is the most powerful force in business today, even when compared to all our modern technology. Spirit is the genius that creates technology. Spirit is the power that causes groups to dream the impossible dream and then achieve it.

This chapter discusses the seven aspects of a fundamentally healthy organization, one in which the people will embrace the TEI systems and use them to the fullest:

- Spirit — recognizing that spirit is the underlying fabric of any business, and being willing to articulate that vision and the possibilities it can create.
- Joy — deliberately designing our jobs to create joy in the job-holder,
- Creativity — imbuing each person with not only the right, but the urgency, to be fully creative at work.
- Organizing — organizing for cultivation of spirit.
- Learning — creating an environment that supports continual learning.
- Integrity — being in integrity.
- Respecting — respecting each individual.

The chapter closes with a case study of KEEPER® Corp., which has successfully unleashed the spirit of creativity, genius, and power throughout its organization.

Summary

TEI systems are the communications foundation for an entire manufacturing enterprise, linking all functions internally and linking to customers, suppliers, and other business partners externally. When properly implemented and utilized, these systems can provide an almost insurmountable competitive edge by dramatically reducing lead times and waste throughout the supply chain.

Acknowledgments

This book is a direct result of the steadfast encouragement that my company, family, and friends have provided during its creation. I wholeheartedly thank each of them for their assistance.

My wife, Janet, cheerfully endured the loneliness of being a "book widow" for 6 months. No author could ask for a more understanding or supportive spouse.

Linda DeStasi, my office manager, professionally and calmly managed the myriad details required in making this book a reality. She remained calm, cool, focused, and efficient, even under intense deadline pressure, which I truly appreciated.

David DeStasi, at the age of 13, spent evenings and weekends converting my hand-scrawled images into the professional graphics that appear throughout the book.

A few colleagues contributed substantial content, greatly enriching the book:

- Eliot Sherman provided the basic content for the Strategic Planning section of Chapter 2 and excellent advice concerning accounting and financial topics.
- Steve Desirey created the material from which the Demand Management section in Chapter 3 was written.
- Jody Tirinato and Joe Rogers created the foundation for the product design section of Chapter 4.
- Mike McClellan provided the understanding of Manufacturing execution systems (MES) that appears in Chapter 5.
- Charles Martin wrote the Client/Server and Object Orientation sections of Chapter 7.

I am indebted to Ken Porter and Doris Obsharsky at KEEPER® Corp. for allowing me to include the case study of their organizational metamorphosis from traditional command-and-control to a truly empowering, creative orientation.

Karen Jones provided excellent comments throughout the book which have improved it substantially.

Many colleagues reviewed various drafts, providing invaluable insight and feedback: Michael Atkinson, Larry Casey, Joe Bruno Celkupa, Elaine Cornick, Arthur Daltas, Steve Desirey, Norm Fuss, Mike Harding, Phil Helle, Dan McCarthy, Mike McClellan, Robert McKosky, Ed Miller, Poppy Pearson, Frank Pechinsky, Joe Rogers, Teg Rood, Eliot Sherman, and Jay Varrone.

And special thanks to Chris Andreasen and Drew Gierman at CRC Press LLC and to Mike McClellan for introducing me to Drew. Without Drew, this book would not exist.

The Author

Gary Langenwalter has more than 25 years' experience assisting companies to successfully transform themselves. He is founder and president of Manufacturing Consulting Partners, International, Inc., a firm with 25 consultants who have an average of 20 years' experience in helping manufacturers achieve their full potential. He has designed MRP II systems, led ERP education for 25 years, and selected and successfully implemented several systems both as an in-house project leader and as an external consultant. His personal experience includes:

- Leading clients to create a compelling company vision
- Planning strategy and tactics which empower the people to achieve their vision
- Cultivating the creative spirit that exists in organizations,
- Selecting and implementing new systems
- Educating people at all levels

Mr. Langenwalter helps organizations unleash the creative spirit latent in virtually all employees. He builds teams and reduces barriers to communication with his non-threatening, people-supportive approach. He interacts effectively with persons at all levels of an organization, from president to first-line supervisor to order entry clerk to hourly employee. He encourages people to release outdated assumptions and instead collectively strive toward a comprehensive new vision. He assists people to see the potential benefits that could result from changing and then helps them realize those benefits.

He has authored *White Paper on Repetitive Manufacturing Methodologies* (1999), and co-authored the *Handbook of Material and Capacity Requirements Planning* (1993). He is the lead author of the *Repetitive Scheduling Training Aid,* published by APICS in 1998. For the APICS E&R Foundation, he created a survey that documented the true costs and benefits of implementing ERP systems.

Mr. Langenwalter has assisted clients in a wide range of industries including:

Manufacturing: agricultural chemicals, cast iron pipe, casters, centrifuges, computers, cookies and crackers, commercial laundry equipment, container machinery curtains, electronic connectors, electronic test instruments, electronics, endoscopy equipment, fragrances, high-tech medical equipment, leather goods, metal and cloth window treatments, metal fatigue test equipment, microscope slides, military vehicle modifications, mops and brooms, paper, paper products, pigments, plastic film, plastic injection molded consumer package goods, portable ventilation equipment, replicated diskettes, roll-to-roll conversion, screen printing machinery for electronics, solar film for windows, steam turbines, tie-down straps, truck bodies, wire and cable

Distribution: LTL trucking, retail marine supplies, mops and brooms

Printing: software documentation, printed plastics

Prior to founding MCP in 1988, Mr. Langenwalter held positions with:

- Coopers & Lybrand — Manufacturing Systems Consulting Manager
- KPMG Peat Marwick and KMG Main Hurdman — Manufacturing and Systems Consulting Manager
- Faultless Caster Corp. — MIS Manager and MRP II Project Manager, resulting in a $700,000 per year saving and increased market share
- Burroughs Corporation (now Unisys) — Manufacturing Software Development Manager, Educator, and Consultant
- Andersen Consulting — Programmer/Analyst

Mr. Langenwalter has taught at Nichols College and guest-lectured at Clark University (both graduate and undergraduate Operations Management courses), Suffolk University, Bryant College, and Worcester State College. He leads APICS certification review courses. He earned his M.B.A. from Michigan State University in Production Management (Beta Gamma Sigma) and a B.A. from the University of Oregon in Industrial Management. He studied international business at the Nederlands Opleidings Instituut voor het

Buitenland, in Breukelen, the Netherlands, during his junior year in college and became reasonably fluent in French.

Mr. Langenwalter is extremely active in professional societies. He is a frequently invited speaker at international, regional, and local conferences and meetings. He was certified as a Fellow in Production and Inventory Management by APICS in 1977 and was in the first group of professionals to be Certified in Integrated Resources Management by APICS in 1993. He is on the international steering committee of the APICS Process Industry SIG. He previously served on the international steering committee of the APICS Repetitive Manufacturing SIG for 4 years, and edited the Repetitive Manufacturing newsletter for 2 years. He co-leads APICS repetitive classes nationally. Mr. Langenwalter is active in the Worcester County Chapter of APICS and has been an officer and board member of several chapters including Detroit, Northern New Jersey, and Worcester (MA). He is a member of the Association for Manufacturing Excellence and the Association for Quality and Participation.

He is listed in *Who's Who in America, Who's Who in the East, Who's Who in the World,* and *Who's Who in Finance and Industry.*

About APICS

APICS, The Educational Society for Resource Management, is an international, not-for-profit organization offering a full range of programs and materials focusing on individual and organizational education, standards of excellence, and integrated resource management topics. These resources, developed under the direction of integrated resource management experts, are available at local, regional, and national levels. Since 1957, hundreds of thousands of professionals have relied on APICS as a source for educational products and services.

- **APICS Certification Programs**—APICS offers two internationally recognized certification programs, Certified in Production and Inventory Management (CPIM) and Certified in Integrated Resource Management (CIRM), known around the world as standards of professional competence in business and manufacturing.
- *APICS Educational Materials Catalog*—This catalog contains books, courseware, proceedings, reprints, training materials, and videos developed by industry experts and available to members at a discount.
- *APICS—The Performance Advantage*—This monthly, four-color magazine addresses the educational and resource management needs of manufacturing professionals.
- *APICS Business Outlook Index*—Designed to take economic analysis a step beyond current surveys, the index is a monthly manufacturing-based survey report based on confidential production, sales, and inventory data from APICS-related companies.
- **Chapters**—APICS' more than 270 chapters provide leadership, learning, and networking opportunities at the local level.

- **Educational Opportunities**—Held around the country, APICS' International Conference and Exhibition, workshops, and symposia offer you numerous opportunities to learn from your peers and management experts.
- **Employment Referral Program**—A cost-effective way to reach a targeted network of resource management professionals, this program pairs qualified job candidates with interested companies.
- **SIGs**—These member groups develop specialized educational programs and resources for seven specific industry and interest areas.
- **Web Site**—The APICS Web site at http://www.apics.org enables you to explore the wide range of information available on APICS' membership, certification, and educational offerings.
- **Member Services**—Members enjoy a dedicated inquiry service, insurance, a retirement plan, and more.

For more information on APICS programs, services, or membership, call APICS Customer Service at (800) 444-2742 or (703) 237-8344 or visit http://www.apics.org on the World Wide Web.

Testimonials

Enterprise Resources Planning and Beyond: Integrating Your Entire Organization *is a "must read" for every manufacturing manager or executive who is seeking to maximize the benefits of ERP in their company.*
— Norman Fuss
   Senior Manager, Business and Technical Solutions, BDO Seideman, LLP

This book is an excellent addition to the body of knowledge on manufacturing systems. It should be on the list of recommended readings for certification programs. This book is right in pointing out that manufacturing systems need to continue to provide more integration and additional functionality. A great contribution!
— Phil Helle
   Principal, Helle Associates

This book is an impressive document. I enjoyed reading it. One of the first things that caught my eye was Figure 1.3. That is the clearest description I have seen of what ERP is and how it relates to other areas. Great job!
— Sam Tomas
   Adjunct Faculty Member, University of Phoenix, and President, Agility Training

Enterprise Resources Planning and Beyond: Integrating Your Entire Organization *collects all of the organization improvement techniques that have been touted over the past couple decades from MRP to TEI. The book does a nice job of weaving all of these concepts together into a whole. While the book may be targeted at organizations taking on the task of "doing" a TEI implementation, it could be used by any organization that is just looking for improvements in their operations. The bullet style text provides a convenient format for companies to put together their own plan for organization improvement.*
— Chad Coullard
   IT Manager, Barco Inc./South Windsor

1 Introduction

Winning in today's business climate requires more than just providing high-quality, low-cost products to customers, when and how the customers want them. Customers and suppliers also require information that is fully integrated throughout the supply chain, or value chain. And executives in manufacturing companies require the integration of their strategies and tactics into all facets of their companies, so that all people throughout the organization make the best decisions and take actions that consistently move toward achieving the corporate objectives.

Competitive pressures frequently force manufacturers to decrease prices, in spite of the fact that their internal costs continue to rise. These two forces combined can quickly eliminate any profitability and can threaten a company's ability to survive. One way to reduce costs is to eliminate the waste caused by poor communication and coordination throughout the manufacturing company, and between the company and its suppliers and customers. We have created a term, **Total Enterprise Integration** (**TEI**), to describe the process of integrating all information and actions required to fully support a manufacturing company and its supply chain. TEI also incorporates the people, as well as the technology.

This book focuses on what a fully integrated system can do *for* a manufacturer. The power of TEI is not in the rich functionality of any individual function (although that rich functionality can help the practitioner perform his/her job better). These islands of functionality have existed for years. The power of TEI is in creating ***strategic advantage,*** rather than just improving operating efficiencies.* It is in the ***integration*** across the entire manufacturing company, and out through the supply chain to customers and suppliers, as

---

* Callahan, Charles V., and Nemec, Joseph, Jr., "The CEO's Information Technology Challenge: Creating True Value," *Strategy and Business,* First Quarter, 1999, p. 78.

1

illustrated in Figure 1.1. It is in the *communication,* letting everyone know the full ramifications of a new customer order that was just received, or a supplier shipment that will be late, or a quality hold on an outgoing shipment, or unscheduled maintenance on a given machine. It is the intelligent use of work flow to push responsibility lower in the organization to the most appropriate decision makers, while maintaining proper budgetary and operational controls. It is in the entrepreneurial *spirit* of the workforce, dedicated to continuous improvement.

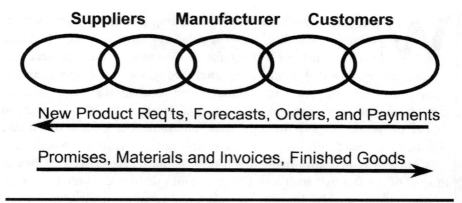

Figure 1.1 Supply Chain

This book shows how each function of a fully integrated system can support a thriving manufacturer, and how each function connects with the others inside the company and with customers, suppliers, and other outside organizations. It also integrates the people aspects of TEI systems. Figure 1.2 illustrates a high-level overview of how each of the functions integrates with the others. Figure 1.2 is admittedly complex because the reality that it represents is extremely complex. Each of the boxes, with expanded linkages, is the subject of a section or subsection in this book. The boxes have existed in manufacturers for years; TEI's difference is in improving the communications through the arrows. The figure groups the functions by the chapter in which they are discussed.

The systems component of TEI is the fourth generation of systems that started in the late 1960s with **MRP** (**Material Requirements Planning**). MRP was superseded in the 1970s by **MRP II** (**Manufacturing Resources Planning**), which integrated material planning, accounting, purchasing (of materials for

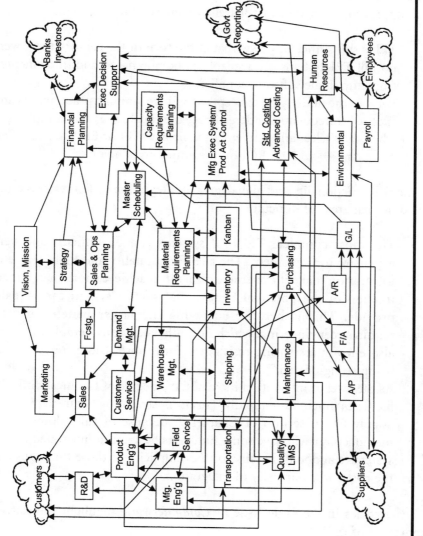

Figure 1.2 Total Enterprise Integration

production), and the shop floor. MRP II, in turn, evolved into **ERP** (**Enterprise Resources Planning**) in the 1990s, integrating many more functions. **TEI** is the final stage of that evolution. The comparison between the functionality of MRP, MRP II, ERP, and TEI is illustrated in Figure 1.3.

Because TEI is the next evolution of ERP, rather than a completely different approach, there are two apparently contradictory problems:

1. TEI is still sufficiently new that at the turn of the century there were no full TEI systems yet available to be purchased and implemented from any single software supplier.
2. Because the underlying concepts of TEI are familiar, practitioners and executives frequently underestimate the capabilities and complexities when they select and implement their new TEI or ERP systems. This can cost 25% to 50% ROI on the entire investment.

The rich functionality and high degree of integration in TEI systems cause two additional areas of difficulty:

3. The most complete TEI/ERP systems can be difficult and very expensive to implement. The rich functionality and high degree of integration make it extremely difficult to achieve more than a mere fraction of the potential benefit that such a system can actually provide. This is because achieving the larger benefits usually requires reengineering, which not only takes considerable time, but also encounters strong resistance from those whose functions are being reengineered.
4. As the level of integration increases, the degree of technical difficulty increases much more rapidly. This is illustrated by Figure 2.17, in the Supply Chain section of Chapter 2. Because of this, almost every manufacturer will have some functions best left unintegrated from a systems standpoint because of the simplicity of those functions and the cost and complexity of integration.

Two articles in the same issue of *Computerworld* highlight the stategic importance of ERP.

■ Motts North America, a juice and applesauce maker, is "one of the users leading the charge to wring more strategic business value — and higher paybacks — out of their enterprise resource planning

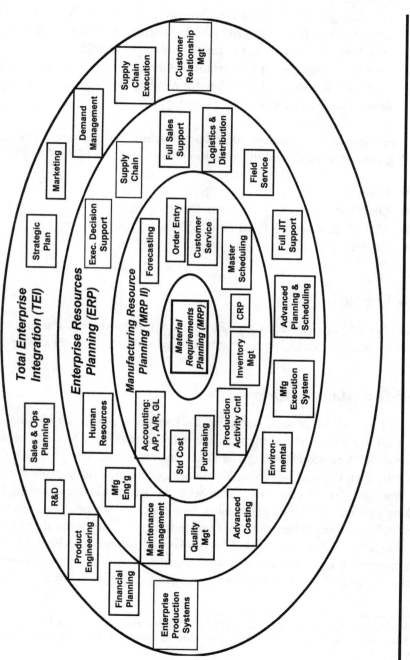

Figure 1.3 MRP, MRP II, ERP, and TEI Functionality Comparison

systems. ..."* Motts is adding an integrated advanced planning and scheduling with the intent to improve customer service. It is also improving its financial systems to help senior executives better measure how different products contribute to profitability.

■ ERP can "help deliver important, intangible benefits such as better customer service, and it's a key foundation for high-payback applications such as supply-chain planning." **

Weyerhaeuser's door factory has achieved substantial business gains from its integrated, Internet-based information system in 4 years (1995–1999):***

■ Production volume — up 100%.
■ On-time deliveries — up from 40% to 97%.
■ Market share — up from 12% to 26%.
■ Return on Net Assets — up from 2% to 27%.

Two Scenarios

What does TEI actually do? Can TEI help a company thrive? The following scenarios illustrate the difference that true integration can make in a company.

Half-Fast Manufacturing

The calendar said "Thursday," but to Pat, the president of Half-Fast Manufacturing, it felt more like another Monday. *Every* day seemed like a Monday, because Pat could feel Greased Lightning Manufacturing exceeding them in sales, for the first time ever. Greased Lightning had long since become more profitable. Pat was absolutely frustrated — no matter what he did or said, his company kept making mistakes. All kinds of mistakes — big expensive ones, little annoying ones, and everything in between. And these mistakes were slowly but surely killing the company. They weren't caused by people who wanted to deliberately hurt the company or its customers; they were mistakes caused by lapses of communication or lack of information. For example, in just the last month:

*   Stedman, Craig, "Motts Turns ERP Up a Notch," *Computerworld*, April 5, 1999, pp. 1, 16.
**   Stedman, Craig, "Survey: ERP Costs More Than Measurable ROI," *Computerworld*, April 5, 1999, p. 6.
*** Stepanek, Marcia, "How an Intranet Opened up the Door to Profits," *Business Week e.biz*, July 26, 1999.

- The last-minute change in specs from their most important customer failed to make it to the shop floor before the order was assembled, packed, and shipped. They diverted a unit intended for a less-important customer (causing that customer's shipment to be late) and air freighted it to the first customer where it arrived later than the promised date. Rather than thanking them for their efforts above and beyond the call of duty, the customer told the salesperson that this was the last mistake they would tolerate from Half-Fast.
- A customer had started paying later and later, so the Credit Manager put them on hold. Knowing that the system only checked credit on incoming orders, the Credit Manager even told the assembly supervisor to hold all orders for that customer. Unfortunately, while the assembly foreman was on a 2-week vacation, the assembly department assembled, tested, and shipped a unit to the customer. Slow-Pay declared bankruptcy a week later. And when Pat became angry with the assembler, the assembler retorted, "Just last week, you told us to make sure that shipments went out on time. I was only doing what you told me. Make up your mind!" Pat was predicting privately that one or two people would finally quit over the angry silence that had enveloped the assembly department since that heated discussion.
- Salespeople were making their quotas, but the company's profits were steadily declining. Pat was slowly becoming convinced that their standard costing system was not telling him the real truth about costs. Each time that his staff discussed costs, the discussion quickly degenerated into a finger-pointing exercise about overhead allocations.
- Customers were increasing pressure on Half-Fast to link much more closely with them to reduce lead times and costs. They wanted Half-Fast's engineers to participate in their design processes, to jointly work on design documents by exchanging them electronically, and to even bring in Half-Fast's key suppliers. Then, when the design was finished, the engineers were supposed to be able to "push a button" and have the designs translated directly into the materials planning and manufacturing systems!
- Half-Fast can't seem to ship orders on schedule easily, quickly, and efficiently. The materials and manufacturing people are constantly fighting shortages, capacity problems, supplier problems, and quality problems. Just 2 weeks ago they had to air freight a product to a customer to make the promised dock receipt date. That incident was caused by capacity problems in plating. The week before, it was caused by a key supplier. Two weeks before that … it was all lost in a blur

of crises and late nights and strong coffee. Half-Fast's current MRP II system assumes that suppliers can meet the schedules and reschedules until and unless the supplier calls with a different date. And even when suppliers do that, Half-Fast's planners don't have enough time to assess the full impact of the changed schedule, nor do they have the proper tools to determine the best options.

Three months earlier, Pat had taken his executive staff off-site for a 2-day strategic planning meeting. The meeting had been extremely successful; at least, that's what everybody said. But the strategies had apparently not filtered down into the day-to-day decisions and activities of the company. This repeated the pattern of prior years — the decisions from strategic planning meetings in earlier years had also failed to impact daily operations.

Pat was not convinced that the decisions that the executives made were as good as they could have been. He sensed that the executives, including himself, were not able to fully grasp all the interrelationships and tradeoffs at a sufficiently detailed level to make the best possible decisions. For example:

- Their salespeople would periodically discover an opportunity to sell a quantity of items at a reduced price. Should Half-Fast submit a quotation?
- Their materials manager was trying to convince the company to reduce setups, reduce lead times, and reduce inventories. It sounded promising, but the savings in inventories alone did not appear to justify the effort and change. And besides, it also required turning over responsibility for day-to-day detailed decisions to the workers — the same ones that kept making mistake after mistake after mistake.

Half-Fast sells configure-to-order products to other manufacturers. The salesforce has to call the office for quotations for many products because of the large variety of potential configurations. Customers are saying that the Greased Lightning salesforce is now creating quotes on their laptops at the customer's office, and inviting the customers to link their computers directly to Greased Lightning's computer, for real-time quotation and delivery information.

Field service has its own stand-alone system, deployed on a network of PCs, which they developed themselves using a popular PC database tool. They get paper copies of the assembly sheets from manufacturing so they can enter the serial numbers of the specific components that make up a final, as-shipped, product. They would like to try to recover warranty reimbursement from their suppliers when they replace a supplier's part in the field. However, neither their field service system nor the main MRP II system maintains that information. When field service technicians repair machines in the field, the system doesn't always bill the customer for the full amount, because the system is not always clear about what replacement parts or services are covered by the customer's warranty or service agreement, and which are not.

Half-Fast's stand-alone quality system is not bad, but it doesn't provide data to the rest of the company's systems. It does not receive data from field service, so the quality people review potential problems based on verbal complaints and anecdotal evidence from the field.

The Engineering Department's product data management system and the MRP II system each use the same key information. They do not integrate, so an engineering intern has to enter the changes from the PDM system into the MRP II system to insure that it remains in synch. And the product design process is still basically sequential, such that it takes 9 to 12 months from concept to production. The new product ideas that the Marketing Department keeps on file contain very few actual specifications. When Engineering starts to design a new product, Marketing is not very clear on the details of what the customers really want. So Engineering does the best it can with the information available.

Accounting systems are still paper-oriented. The computer does a three-way match to pay suppliers based on the receiving report. An accounting clerk enters each supplier's invoice as a voucher. If a supplier calls Purchasing to ask when an invoice will be paid, Purchasing has to call Accounting for the answer. Those calls have been increasing recently, because Half-Fast is delaying supplier payments an extra week or two to help its cash flow. Manufacturing is more concerned about shipping the product to the customer than they are about accuracy of paperwork. So another accounting clerk spends 50% of his time trying to find out what the actual configuration was on each product shipped. This delays the invoices going out to customers a few days, and sometimes he makes an honest mistake.

An increasingly large percentage of Half-Fast's business has been winning bids that require extensive engineering efforts compared to the direct labor involved. On paper, the company should be making money. But Half-Fast's actual profits have been steadily declining for the last 3 years, mostly because it has had to hire more engineers. The additional engineers drove the overhead rates up, causing Half-Fast to lose more of its bread-and-butter business, which had higher direct labor content.

EPA and OSHA have been requiring additional reports ever since that accidental chemical spill a year ago. An engineering intern works 2 days per month just to compile the information in a PC and then create the reports.

Most paperwork throughout the company is still manual. If someone wants to find out where a document is sitting, waiting for approval or waiting to be processed, they have to physically hunt it down. Purchase requisitions sometimes get lost in the approval process, so requisitioners have learned to keep copies of all submissions and to follow up every 1 to 2 weeks.

In short, Half-Fast Manufacturing is operating about as well as many manufacturers; there are some who are less efficient and effective, and some who are more efficient and effective.

Greased Lightning Manufacturing

Unfortunately for Half-Fast Manufacturing, one company that is operating substantially more efficiently and effectively is its arch-rival, Greased Lightning Manufacturing. They pulled even with Half-Fast Manufacturing's sales last year (but had three times the profits), and they expect to be 20% larger this year by taking sales from Half-Fast and other less responsive competitors. Five years ago, Greased Lightning was a relatively small company and was experiencing operational and financial difficulties. A partner at one of the large consulting firms decided to buy it and turn it around. As the new owner, Chris called a company meeting to share her excitement about the possibilities of the company and to assure each person that they would be valued and listened to. She also told them that she wanted them to own half the company. Naturally, the employees were somewhat skeptical, but when they found Chris living up to her word, they started sharing her excitement and enthusiasm. As she empowered them and removed the previous impediments to their effectiveness and decision-making, the employees became passionate about improving *their* company. They started focusing on reducing waste, reducing lead times, and dramatically improving profitability. One major project in their drive to dramatically improve their competitive edge was selecting and implementing an integrated TEI system.

New System Selection

To start the selection process, Chris called Juan, the president of a regional consulting firm that specialized in systems selections and implementations for mid-sized manufacturers. Juan suggested a vision-based selection process, because it would:

- Harness the creative vision that was latent in the employees.
- Create a substantial competitive advantage, and therefore
- Return at least 100% ROI.

Chris asked Juan and his company to guide Greased Lightning through the selection and implementation process. Based on his advice, she asked her VPs to identify the constructive complainers, the people who were not satisfied with the status quo and were willing to embrace change. She called a meeting in which she invited them to participate in the selection and implementation. After they agreed, Juan outlined the process and gave them each a sample vision as a basis for creating their own radical vision of the new Greased Lightning. When they met again 3 days later, most of the team members were clearly excited about the possibilities that they had created for their departments and for the company. Juan challenged their assumptions and encouraged them to stretch even farther, and to ask for ideas from others who shared the same commitment to change. By the end of the second week, the vision of the new Greased Lightning, radical as it was, was beginning to look achievable. It included:

- Reducing order-to-ship time from 12 weeks to 8 work days.
- Eliminating most paperwork throughout the company, including on the shop floor, and with most suppliers.
- Fully automating the quotation process, to provide accurate price quotations and delivery schedules on-line directly to customers via computer-to-computer links, and to the field sales force on their laptops while they are meeting with customers.
- Reducing inventories by 80% by implementing repetitive/flow/lean techniques throughout the company.
- Fully integrating design engineering and process engineering with materials planning and field service.
- Integrating quality with shop floor data and the design process.

Deborah, Juan's consultant, fleshed the vision into specific features and functions, then reviewed this list with the team and revised it. Deborah called 12 potential software suppliers with a two-page questionnaire that asked the difficult questions. The consultant and Juan presented the strengths and weaknesses of the top eight respondents to the team, which agreed on six suppliers that should receive the Request For Proposal. They met with each of the suppliers, sharing the vision and answering their questions. After reading the proposals, the team met and narrowed the list to three, guided by Juan and Deborah. The team called the suppliers' references and created a high-level script for the demonstrations. During each two-day demonstration, the team asked questions based on the supplier's proposal and reference checks. Juan led the decision meeting, in which the team eliminated one potential supplier, but could not decide between the other two. So the team invited the two remaining suppliers to address their questions and concerns, along with best and final proposals. One week later, the team achieved consensus on their choice of software packages. They visited a reference site, which further strengthened their decision.

Deborah worked with the team to create a high-level implementation plan that outlined the time-phased resource requirements and the time-phased projected benefits of the system. The team presented the plan to the executive staff, which reviewed the commitments, especially the projected savings and increases in sales, then approved wholeheartedly. The executive staff asked the team to make the presentation to a local bank for funding for the system. The loan committee was extremely impressed by the team's thoroughness and commitment to the success of the project; the bank quickly approved the financing.

System Implementation

Greased Lightning engaged the regional consulting firm to guide the implementation. Chris opened the project kick-off meeting for all employees, praising the work of the selection team. Chris assured each employee that their paycheck was secure; however, many tasks and jobs would change (usually for the better). She asked each person to support the new system wholeheartedly as a key foundation toward Greased Lightning's future success. Karl, the selection team leader and materials manager, presented the implementation plan and the justification. Chris asked Karl to lead the implementation because of his outstanding results with the selection team.

When the new software arrived, the IT department had already created a "war room" for learning the new system and had installed six networked PCs. The software supplier led a 1-week hands-on overview of the software for the implementation team, Deborah, and a few other key individuals. During that week, the implementation team entered demonstration data into their new system that would serve as the foundation for educating the rest of the company, and then the conference room pilot. They refined their intended performance measures. They decided which functions to leave non-integrated. They also revised the implementation schedule, working with the Steering Committee to resolve resource constraints and conflicts. They tentatively selected their Vanguard product line for the initial implementation, because it was relatively self-contained, and because the people who worked in that area were enthusiastic about the new system.

Team members and Deborah attended training classes at the software supplier's education center. Although the travel expenses and cost in time by these key individuals seemed high, the team and the Steering Committee recognized that extensive education was essential for them to achieve their objective of using the new system as effectively as possible.

Deborah and Karl educated virtually all of the company's employees on TEI concepts. The education process was designed to accomplish two objectives:

1. Provide initial introduction to the concepts and operating style of the new system
2. Encourage the participants to understand and embrace the changes that would be happening throughout the company

To accomplish these objectives, the sessions included a hands-on simulation of how Greased Lightning could operate most effectively, contrasted against their current operating methods. The initial two groups of employees were somewhat skeptical about the new system, but they really became enthusiastic about the new system during the hands-on exercise. Their enthusiasm spread quickly throughout the company. At the end of each education session, Karl asked each participant which topics they wanted to be trained on and filled in a training matrix with topics and dates.

The implementation team members started assessing data integrity and availability in their current system, deciding what to do for each suspect or missing data element, and planning to correct or collect data that was critical to initial implementation success. To support the implementation schedule, the IT department brought in some temporary programmer/analysts to create data bridges between the old system and new system. IT also contracted to upgrade Greased Lightning's internal network.

The team, aided by Deborah, spent several hours a week in the war room, designing new procedures that implemented the initial strategic vision that they had developed during the selection process. These new procedures used the work flow and other capabilities inherent in the new system to gain a competitive edge by:

- Maximizing speed and throughput of information and materials throughout the company.
- Minimizing response time to customers, suppliers, and decision makers throughout the company.
- Pushing decisions to the lowest appropriate level in the organization, using work flow to ensure adequate controls.
- Maximizing the information available to decision-makers at all levels of the company.
- Integrating directly into the supply chain.

When they felt the new procedures were sufficiently robust, the team invited other key individuals to participate in testing the procedures by simulating the company's cycles (e.g., order to shipment to cash, idea to design to product). After 2 months, the team felt sufficiently confident that they started training the professionals on the new system with the intent to implement the system in the first product line a month later.

Prior to implementation, the team invited all Greased Lightning employees and a few key suppliers who directly affected, or were directly affected by, the Vanguard product line to a day-long hands-on demonstration of the new system, and to start learning the new procedures. That day was followed by several other days as participants played "what-if" with the new procedures and system. The team also role-played the initial cutover and subsequent operation of the company on two systems, with the old system still running the bulk of the company, while the new TEI system supported Vanguard.

Finally, the cutover weekend arrived. As Karl later remarked, "We felt like Mission Control during the launch of Apollo 11; we wanted to make sure we weren't launching Apollo 13." The team executed the cutover procedures with only minor problems. When they went home Saturday night, the Vanguard product line seemed ready to roll on Monday. People were at work more than an hour before their normal starting time on Monday, just to see the new system. The implementation team was supported by Deborah and consultants from the software supplier, the hardware supplier, and the local computer networking firm. Monday was almost anticlimactic; no major surprises occurred, and the system ran relatively smoothly.

After Vanguard's first month end, the team created a time-phased implementation schedule for the rest of Greased Lightning to be fully on the new system within 4 months. They achieved their goals, on schedule and on budget. At the congratulations banquet, Chris presented each team member with a bonus check for their contributions to the future success of Greased Lightning, then challenged each person to live up to the potential of Greased Lightning by using the new system to its fullest.

TEI System Impact

Due to the new TEI system and the implementation of the Repetitive/Lean methodologies, salespeople started reducing lead times to customers, first to 9 weeks, then 8, then 7, down to 3, and then finally 2. Customers responded by calling Greased Lightning first for quotations. The word spread quickly that Greased Lightning delivered on schedule in their very short promised lead times, at prices equal to, or even slightly lower than, the competition.

The on-line quotation system was based on the new costing system, which allocated overhead according to the activity that caused the overhead. Thus, jobs that required a lot of engineering compared to the direct labor were quoted higher. Greased Lightning still got several of those because of its ability to ship quickly. And they started getting almost all the jobs that had lower engineering content, because their quotes were 10% to 20% lower than the competition, with substantially shorter lead times. The new costing system helps them quote on special opportunities as well.

Orders flow directly through the system, with electronic "paperwork" and decisions guided by the work flow capabilities of the system. Most of the real paperwork is gone. A person can quickly find out the status of anything in the system, from a customer order to a purchase requisition. Because of the accurate and timely reporting from the shop floor, based on the new bar code scanning system, the invoicing system automatically generates accurate invoices to customers within hours after a shipment leaves the dock. And that same shop floor data, showing "as-built" with serial numbers, is now available to Field Service.

The new procedures made possible by the new system substantially reduced effort throughout the company. The very short lead times virtually eliminated customer changes; the few times that a customer requested a change in specification, the system immediately communicated that change throughout the company and to the suppliers.

The new advanced planning and scheduling system is not fully operational yet, but the Master Scheduler is looking forward to using it. The Master Scheduler monitors the schedule frequently to insure that capacity constraints are not violated at Greased Lightning or its key suppliers.

The new data from Field Service and Manufacturing helped the Quality Department pinpoint some chronic problems that had previously defied analysis. The data showed R&D where to change the designs to eliminate the problems in future products. And Field Service now knows, automatically, when an item is covered by the warranty to the customer. Furthermore, the system notifies the Field Service technician of any component with a supplier's warranty, so that the failed component can be replaced at no charge to Greased Lightning.

Suppliers are extremely happy with Greased Lightning's new payment system. Greased Lightning sends deposits directly into all key suppliers' bank accounts weekly, for all items that have been received more than 14 days earlier. No invoice required, no PO match, no follow-up phone calls to find out when they will be paid.

Product design process time has been substantially reduced, using concurrent engineering approaches. And Marketing now keeps new product ideas in a common database, which can be added to by salespeople in the field, Field Service technicians, and anyone else with an idea. Design Engineering is also keeping a database of "Lessons Learned" in the entire process, to provide the wisdom of experience for future design teams.

The radical reduction in inventory provided a substantial boost to cash flow and profitability, enabling Greased Lightning to pay generous year-end bonuses to all its employee-owners. The employees' excitement was contagious — Greased Lightning became the employer of choice in the area, then the region.

The differences between Half-Fast and Greased Lightning are summarized in Table 1.1.

One of the most important benefits of the new system was intangible. The company's spirit of teamwork, first fostered by Chris, then focused by Juan in the vision-setting meetings, proved to be a major competitive advantage for years to come. Greased Lightning quickly earned a reputation as a "can-do" organization that was a pleasure to work with for customers, employees, and suppliers alike.

**Table 1.1. Performance Measurements of Full TEI
vs. Average Company**

Characteristic	Half-Fast	Greased Lightning
Lead time to customers	10 weeks	2 weeks
On-time shipments	75%	98%
Errors in finished product sent to customers	5%	<1%
Ability to respond to customer change request	A committee has to meet to decide	Done by customer service over the phone
Price to customers	Normal	Slightly lower
Quotations	Based on standard cost	Based on Life Cycle costing
Profitability	Modest, and declining	Robust, and increasing
Inventory turns	3	10 and increasing
On-line information to customers?	No	Yes
On-line information to suppliers?	No	Yes
Days to pay suppliers	45, and increasing — invoice required	15 straight into the bank — no invoice required
Employment candidates	Run of the mill	Best and brightest

Multi-plant, Multi-division, Multi-national Manufacturers

The scenarios above used single-plant manufacturers, because their relative simplicity helped contrast the differences between the two examples. As companies increase their complexity by adding plants, divisions, and transnational capabilities, well-implemented TEI systems become even more essential for survival. The more robust TEI systems can perform true interplant materials planning and logistics.

Other Industries

Manufacturers in virtually all industries can benefit from the enhanced integration offered by TEI systems. Customers in some industries, such as automotive manufacturing and retail, are requiring increased integration as a condition of remaining a supplier.

For a manufacturer of consumer packaged goods, integration with the customer's system is absolutely critical, as is the ability to support Vendor-Managed Inventories. Additionally, manufacturers who sell to large retailers often have very complex quoting and pricing structures, with special deals, store-opening promotions, end-cap displays, and some rebates based on semiannual or annual volume.

Summary

TEI systems are the communications foundation for an entire manufacturing enterprise, linking all functions internally and linking to customers and suppliers externally. When properly implemented and utilized, these systems can provide an almost insurmountable competitive edge by dramatically reducing lead times and waste throughout the supply chain, and by empowering individuals at all levels to substantially improve the quality of their decision making. The implementation process itself can contribute significantly to the team spirit of an organization, further increasing the competitive advantage.

References

Callahan, Charles V., and Nemec, Joseph, Jr., "The CEO's Information Technology Challenge: Creating True Value," *Strategy and Business*, First Quarter, 1999.

Stedman, Craig, "Motts Turns ERP Up a Notch," *Computerworld*, April 5, 1999.

Stedman, Craig, "Survey: ERP Costs More Than Measurable ROI," *Computerworld*, April 5, 1999, p. 6.

Stepanek, Marcia, "How an Intranet Opened up the Door to Profits," *Business Week e.biz*, July 26, 1999.

2 Executive Direction and Support

Total Enterprise Integration (TEI) systems are the means of communicating executive direction throughout the company; they also provide information that enables executives to get better answers to questions, and to project more accurately the probable business results of their decisions. TEI's contribution is not the individual underlying systems; most of them have been successfully used for many years. The power of TEI is in creating *strategic advantage*, rather than just improving operating efficiencies.* TEI's difference is its *integration* of those systems throughout the company, and in the quick and accurate *communication* of decisions and events throughout the company. Finally, it is in the entrepreneurial *spirit* of the workforce, empowered by information, and dedicated to continuous improvement. TEI contrasts with ERP by integrating many executive systems that fall outside of typical ERP systems.

Executive functions include:

- Strategic planning
- Marketing
- Sales and operations planning
- Financial planning
- Executive decision support
- Measurement systems
- Supply chain management integration

---

* Callahan, Charles V., and Nemec, Joseph, Jr., "The CEO's Information Technology Challenge: Creating True Value," *Strategy and Business,* First Quarter, 1999, p. 78.

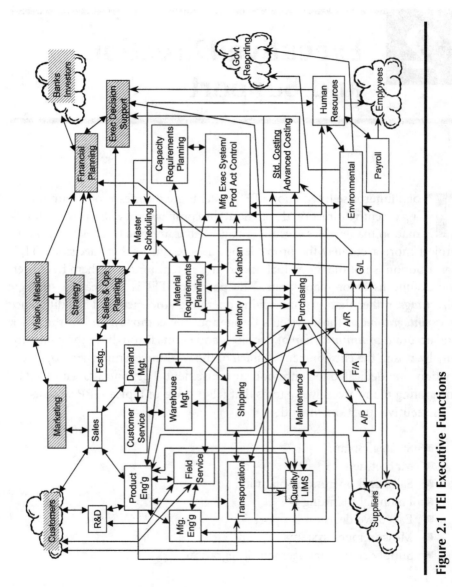

Figure 2.1 TEI Executive Functions

These functions are highlighted in Figure 2.1, which shows the relationships between these functions and the rest of a Total Enterprise Integration system.

Strategic Planning

In 1990, APICS, the Educational Society for Resource Management, became very concerned because many manufacturers who were using, or at least trying to use, the best available techniques such as JIT and MRP II were going out of business. APICS asked top practitioners and consultants to determine the missing ingredient(s) in its body of knowledge, so that manufacturers who used its education, tools, and techniques would prosper and thrive. The research found a lack of effective strategy and an even greater lack of coordination between the corporate strategy and departmental objectives and day-to-day decisions. For example, the Sales and Marketing Department might be enthusiastically responding to its customers' requests for unique, special products (sensing a true competitive opportunity), while Manufacturing is still organized to make the same standard products again and again.

Lack of a vision-based, well-communicated strategy can cause the following conditions:

- The company's vision is implicit or unknown.
- The business strategy is developed solely on the basis of analyzing the competition.
- The business strategy is defined as quantitative projections based on historical data.
- The company attempts to compete against all competitors in the industry.
- Decisions on whether to pursue opportunities are made on projected monetary gain or risk avoidance.
- Decisions move the company in conflicting directions.
- There are too many active projects, with constantly shifting priorities.

Contrary to popular belief, the most successful companies pursue goals that are at least equal to, if not more important than, profit alone. In a recent study of 18 pairs of matched companies (identical industry, comparable size), the companies that have "been more ideologically driven and less purely profit-driven than the comparison companies were more successful in seventeen out of the eighteen pairs."*

The process of communicating strategy and implementing it successfully in all levels and functions of a company is illustrated in Figure 2.2.** The figure shows that while strategy starts with corporate vision, the vision and the resulting strategy are affected by the results of executing the strategy, tactics, departmental goals, and objectives. Instead of being linear with a one-time goal to achieve, the strategic planning and implementation process is circular; it continues as long as a company remains in business.

Figure 2.2 Strategic Implementation Loop

* Collins, James C., and Jerry I. Porras, *Built to Last: Successful Habits of Visionary Companies,* HarperBusiness, New York, 1994, p. 55.
** Developed by Eliot H. Sherman and Burton Widener as part of Executive Visioning Conference offered by Manufacturing Consulting Partners, Inc., Bolton, MA.

In Figure 2.2, the outer circle lines depict information flowing in both directions. In reality, there are also lines between every pair of nodes in the circle; these additional lines were omitted from the diagram to aid legibility.

One way to illustrate the high-level relationships between each of the six major functions in a manufacturing company, called a "kite chart," is shown in Figure 2.3.

Top management works with all areas in a company. From a strategic standpoint, however, top management's primary focus has to be on the future. Thus, it focuses on new products for its customers (R&D) and new capabilities for its people (Human Resources). Top management also monitors sales and production. Externally, it answers to the owners, who invest capital and expect a return on their investment.

Sales and Marketing focuses on finding and keeping customers. It concentrates on defining new products (R&D) and on ensuring that customer orders will be shipped right and on time (Operations). The horizontal line that connects Sales and Marketing with Operations is the company's internal section of the supply chain, which connects customers with suppliers.

Operations focuses on acquiring materials from suppliers and manufacturing finished products, on time and on budget. It concentrates on meeting customer demand (Sales), and scheduling and deploying the work force to meet ever-changing conditions (Human Resources).

Human Resources focuses on attracting, training, and retaining a qualified work force. It concentrates on ensuring the availability of the right types of workers for future needs (Top Management), and for current requirements (Operations).

Research and Development focuses on creating new products. It concentrates on current and projected customer needs (Sales and Marketing), and on products that can create a strategic advantage for the company (Top Management).

Finance and Accounting is the language with which the rest of the company communicates. It receives production expense data from Operations, and sales revenue data from Sales and Marketing. It provides the measurement framework for decision-making (for example, capital budgeting and investment analysis) and keeps score of the results (for example, the profit and loss report, the cash flow report, and the balance sheet).

A company's strategic focus determines the areas in which its TEI systems must excel. For example:

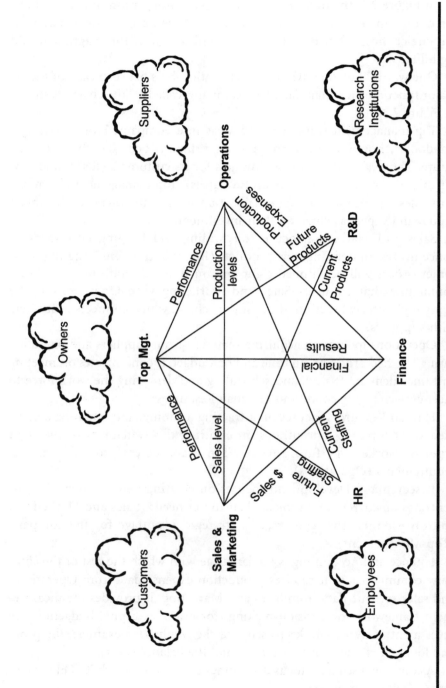

Figure 2.3 Relationships Between Major Functions in a Manufacturing Company

- Top management and the finance and accounting function are comfortable communicating results and plans using financial numbers. While it seems obvious that the TEI system must provide information for each critical area in a form and format that helps those functions support the corporate objective, many TEI systems actually have great difficulty in projecting the effect to the company (especially on the bottom line, or in market share, or customer satisfaction) of a decision that an individual or department is making while it is being made.
- If a company is going to emphasize quick response, its TEI systems must support quick and accurate information flow throughout the sales, order entry, and customer service functions. They must also be designed to empower manufacturing and materials to respond quickly.
- If a company's strength is engineering, its TEI system must integrate the manufacturing, materials, and accounting functions with its engineering systems, as discussed more fully in Chapter 4.
- For communicating and managing achievement of strategic and tactical objectives, software systems now exist in which an executive can create an ultimate goal or objective, then break it down into smaller objectives and assign each of those to a person or team. That person or team can report back on progress, using their PCs attached to an internal network or through the Internet. These goals can be specific and measurable, such as "win contracts from at least two new customers per quarter."

Marketing

Marketing fills the space between strategic planning and selling the products. Marketing creates the environment in which the customer decides to buy. This includes defining new products and services that the customer wants, and providing the means for the customer to understand how the products benefit *their* business. Marketing also decides the customers to whom the products and services will be offered, and how to price and position the offerings for customer value. Two techniques that can be successfully applied to determine what the customer actually wants are Voice of the Customer and market research. A third technique, Quality Function Deployment, helps management determine how best to satisfy the array of sometimes competing customer wants. Marketing can also maintain the new product idea database and is frequently responsible for competitive strategy.

Voice of the Customer (VOC)

Voice of the Customer (VOC) is a proven methodology for quickly and economically determining, ranking, and quantifying the needs, wants, and expectations that drive customer decision-making. A Voice of the Customer audit involves selecting and interviewing key executives from selected customers. The results are best when the interviews are conducted by a neutral outside firm, with anonymity guaranteed, because:

- The customer will tell an outsider things that they would never tell an employee of the supplier.
- The outsider can listen much more objectively — they will hear the customer's words without the filters and expectations that an insider invariably interjects.

The results of a VOC audit include:

1. Ranked customer expectations and performance metrics
2. Customer perceptions of performance
3. Trend analysis
4. Supply chain process flow analysis
5. Gap analysis — customer expectations vs. the company's performance
6. Gap analysis — customer perceptions vs. the company's perceptions
7. Customer quotes

VOC information forms the basis for designing the TEI system integration with each customer, which is discussed more fully in the Supply Chain section of this chapter and in the Quoting and Promising Deliveries section of Chapter 3 . And each customer can be integrated into a manufacturer's TEI system in a different way. For example, some customers might require the manufacturer to manage inventories at the customers' distribution centers (possibly using Vendor-Managed Inventory); others might want the manufacturer to respond to their needs using more classic JIT techniques such as bread man or *kanbans*; still others might want to place their own orders using EDI as the communications medium.

VOC information also is the basic input into Quality Function Deployment (QFD).

Market Research

Market research is the process of continually reviewing the marketplace to maintain the 4 Ps, for potential products, for the company's own offerings, and for current and future competitive products. The 4 Ps are:

- Product
- Price
- Promotion
- Place (distribution)

It is this data that drives the new product development process, discussed in Chapter 4.

As Marketing listens to customer desires, sees current competitive products, and hears about potential new competitive products, they can file those ideas in a new product database. R&D or Product Engineering also contributes to this database as they visit customers to see how the customers are using the company's existing products. R&D uses this data as a primary source as they develop new products.

Quality Function Deployment (QFD)

QFD is a method of translating higher-level objectives into concrete actions and metrics. It was originally developed by the designers of Japanese automobiles to prioritize, on the basis of customer needs, wants, and expectations, the many and often-competing features that they could potentially include in their products. With this prioritization, they could select the array of product features that would deliver the highest overall customer satisfaction.

In the context of TEI, QFD tools are similarly used to determine what aspects (features) of a company's *total* product offering (including the products, plus services, ease of doing business, total cost of ownership, etc.) that will maximize *total* customer satisfaction. With this insight, management can then focus its TEI capabilities on those aspects that will have the greatest impact on total customer satisfaction.

QFD can benefit greatly from using the information about customer needs, wants, and expectations from Voice of the Customer as one vital input. QFD can also use data from other sources, including market surveys, operational assessments, and management insight.

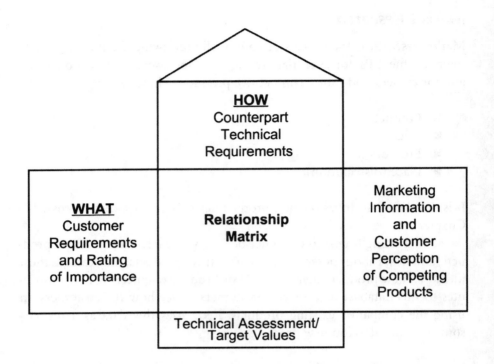

Figure 2.4 Quality Function Deployment

QFD can be illustrated by Figure 2.4. The data in a QFD "House of Quality" matrix is defined, created, and used as follows:

1. Define customer requirements in the left square. These requirements could come from a VOC audit or any other source. Make each customer requirement a row.
2. Establish a priority for each customer requirement. One way of establishing the final priority for each customer requirement is to determine the following:
   a. Importance to the customer.
   b. Current satisfaction by the customer of the manufacturer's performance.
   c. Planned satisfaction by the customer that the manufacturer would like to achieve.
   d. Improvement factor, which is "c" above, divided by "b" above.
   e. Willingness of the customer to pay (ranging from "must have and will pay," to "not willing to pay").

  f. Relative weight, which is (importance) × (improvement factor) × (willingness to pay), or item (a) × (d) × (e).

  g. Percentage weight, calculated by adding up all the relative weights, then making each relative weight a percentage of the total of all relative weights. This percentage weight can go in the Priority column. Alternatively, the matrix can be expanded to show as few or as many of the weighting factors as desired.

3. Create columns that list "how" the customer requirements might be satisfied, such as a feature or function of a product, or a service that the company can provide to its customers. For example, if a customer wants immediate answers to its requests for product availability information, one potential "how" would be to give the customer on-line access to the company's database. The top of each column defines the "how"; the bottom of the same column provides a metric, such as 2-second response time.

4. After all the rows and columns are defined, put a "+" sign into each cell (intersection of rows and columns in the center square) in which a "how" satisfies a customer requirement. Put an "x" in a cell in which a "how" dissatisfies a customer requirement.

5. In the square on the right, for each of the customer's requirements, rank the company's products or services against those supplied by the major competitors, with the worst on the left, and the best on the right. This is illustrated using a kitchen broom as an example in Figure 2.5.

6. When the "House of Quality" has been defined in enough detail at the first (top) level, cascade it down to more specific levels by taking the target values from the bottom of the initial QFD chart and making them the customer requirements of the next set of charts, then repeating the entire process of determining how to satisfy those requirements. This lets a company break down high-level customer requirements into specific functions and features (Figure 2.6).

Neither VOC nor QFD are modules in an ERP package, because neither is transaction-based, and neither uses the ERP database. However, the information they create is integral to TEI. The results of VOC help a company create strategy and tactics. The results of QFD typically affect the design of products. Additionally, the QFD approach can be used just as easily to break down customer satisfaction objectives, such as on-time and right shipment, or quick response by customer service professionals (or access to data directly by the customer).

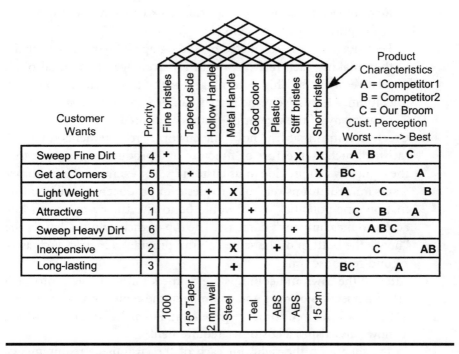

Customer Wants	Priority	Fine bristles	Tapered side	Hollow Handle	Metal Handle	Good color	Plastic	Stiff bristles	Short bristles	Product Characteristics A = Competitor1 B = Competitor2 C = Our Broom Cust. Perception Worst -------> Best
Sweep Fine Dirt	4	+						X	X	A B C
Get at Corners	5		+						X	BC A
Light Weight	6			+	X					A C B
Attractive	1					+				C B A
Sweep Heavy Dirt	6							+		ABC
Inexpensive	2				X		+			C AB
Long-lasting	3					+				BC A
		1000	15° Taper	2 mm wall	Steel	Teal	ABS	ABS	15 cm	

Figure 2.5 Quality Function Deployment Example

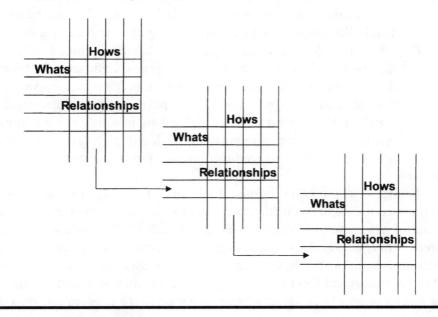

Figure 2.6 QFD Cascade

PC-based software products can be useful in deploying and tracking detailed departmental objectives based on the company's overall objectives (such as those which result from VOC or QFD). These tools monitor and adjust the lower-level objectives based on changes to the higher objectives and actual accomplishments in each department.

Once a company has decided how it will delight its customers, and what each functional area in the company must do to actually achieve the corporate objectives, it has created its TEI objectives.

Sales and Operations Planning

Sales and operations planning (S&OP) links the annual business plan (which is based on corporate strategy) to ongoing tactical and operations plans. The integration of sales and operations planning to the rest of the company is illustrated in Figure 2.7.*

Sales and operations planning is a process that brings together all the plans for the business (sales, marketing, development, supply chain, manufacturing, and financial) into one integrated set of plans. It is performed at least once a month and is reviewed by management at an aggregate (product family) level. The process reconciles all supply, demand, and new product plans at both the detail and aggregate level and tie to the business plan. The Sales and Operations Plan is the definitive statement of the company's plans for the near to intermediate term.** The planned production levels by product line drive the Master Production Schedule and determine staffing requirements. The expected sales by product line can form the basis for the more detailed sales forecasts.

Full supply chain management integration means partnering with customers and suppliers with the intent to maximize responsiveness and flexibility, while eliminating paperwork, waste, and cost throughout the supply chain. Manufacturers constantly balance alternatives strategically and tactically to continue to meet continued changes from customers and suppliers. These alternatives include:

---

* Adapted from material developed by Richard Ling, as used in "Sales and Operations Planning — The Integrator of the Business Planning Process," *1998 International Conference Proceedings*, APICS, Falls Church, VA, 1998.
** Adapted from *Dictionary, 9th Edition*, APICS, Falls Church, VA, 1998.

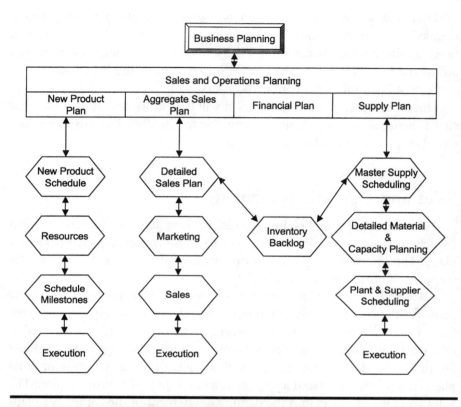

Figure 2.7 Sales and Operations Planning Integration

- Adjust inventory levels
- Adjust capacity
- Use alternative sources of supply
- Vary the lead time to the customer
- Introduce new products
- Bring in work currently performed by suppliers
- Outsource some current work to suppliers
- Purchase semifinished raw materials, rather than doing the initial processing ourselves

This continual adjustment of the balance between competing demands and resources is the essence of the S&OP process. Thus, virtually all manufacturers perform the S&OP process in some manner, whether they call it S&OP or some other term, and whether they meet monthly or decide in some other manner.

Achieving excellent results from S&OP requires that a manufacturer use it as a continuous process rather than a monthly meeting. Before the monthly meeting, executives refine:

- New product plans (release dates and sales forecasts)
- Demand plans (projected sales levels for existing products)
- Supply plans (from all sources, internal and external)

At the meeting, the executives reach consensus on the best overall solution to the various competing pressures and requirements on the company, creating an Integrated Plan of Execution (illustrated in Figure 2.8). Sales and Operations Plans can be managed using a spreadsheet like the one in the Figure 2.9, showing one product family.

The outputs of the S&OP meeting are as follows:

- New product release schedules, which tell Marketing and Sales when they can launch new products and forms the basis for coordinating the activities of all other supporting departments.
- The Master Production Schedule for existing and new products, which becomes the primary input to the MPS module of the TEI system.
- Revised supply rates from key suppliers, which Purchasing communicates to the suppliers and gains their consensus.
- Planned inventory levels, by major product line, which are computed automatically as a result of the starting inventory levels, subtracting sales and adding production for each period.
- Planned cash flow, which can be estimated based on sales and production levels, so that the Finance Department can support the cash requirements of the business.

For companies in industries that are highly capital intensive and that require longer lead times to achieve any significant capacity changes, such as the process industries, the S&OP process should have a minimum target of 18 months' visibility.

Financial Planning

The financial and accounting system is the medium of communication and measurement in a manufacturing company. Virtually all activities within a

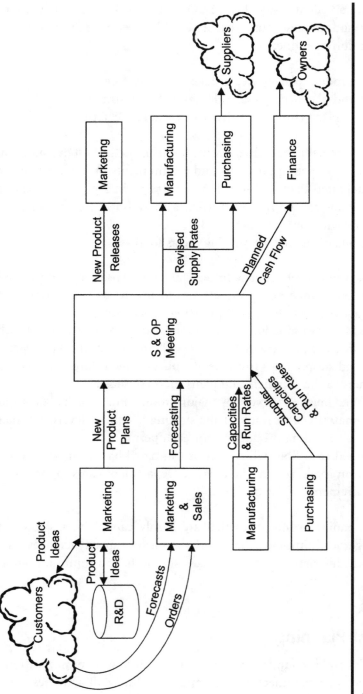

Figure 2.8 S & OP Process

Family - G-8 Carriers - March

Sales Plan	Last Dec	Last Yr Total	Mon Avg. Sales	Jan actual	Feb actual	Mar	Apr	May	Jun	Jul	Aug	Sep	Oct	Nov	Dec	Total Year, Proj.	Mon Avg.
Prior Year	2445	31052	2588	2539	2537	2914	3149	3049	3325	1949	2748	3472	3022	3416	2683	34803	2900
Budget	3075	45400	3783	2941	2910	2977	3400	3348	3524	2675	3260	2880	3569	3525	2936	37945	3162
Current	2936	36969	3081	3312	3313	4037	3469	3420	3524	2675	3260	2880	3569	3525	2936	39920	3327
Proposed	2683	34805	2900	3193	3417	4640	3455	3437	3538	2190	3260	2880	3569	3525	2936	40040	3337
Deviation	-253			-119	104												
Cum. Dev.	-2153			-119	-15												

Production Plan	Last Dec	Last Yr Total	Mon Avg Prod	Jan actual	Feb actual	Mar	Apr	May	Jun	Jul	Aug	Sep	Oct	Nov	Dec	Total Year, Proj.	Mon Avg.
Prior Year	2131	32296	2691	3584	3201	3743	3394	3458	3683	2188	2372	2804	2658	2178	2285	35548	2962
Budget	3680	45401	3783	2980	2970	3410	3380	3500	3800	1500	3450	3130	3300	3200	3400	38020	3168
Current	2519	35206	2934	3453	3267	4015	3604	3428	3607	1460	3678	3512	3682	3540	3390	40636	3386
Proposed	2202	35268	2939	2777	3063	3829	3517	3528	3798	1640	3678	3512	3682	3540	3390	39954	3330
Deviation	-233			-676	-204												
Cum. Dev.	146			-676	-880												
Spare Parts	84			49	9	48	50	56	79	40	72	68	68	60	60	659	

Inventory Plan	Last Dec	Last Yr Avg Inv.	Avg Turns	Jan actual	Feb actual	Mar	Apr	May	Jun	Jul	Aug	Sep	Oct	Nov	Dec	Total Year, Avg Inv	Avg Turns
Prior Year	3493	2540	12.2	4541	5205	6034	6279	6688	7046	7285	6909	6241	5877	4639	4241	5915	6.0
Budget	3985	3442	13.2	4024	4084	4517	4497	4649	4925	3750	3940	4190	3921	3596	4060	4179	9.1
Current	3938	5643	6.6	4170	4124	4102	4237	4245	4328	3113	3531	4163	4276	4291	4745	4110	9.9
Proposed	4029	5826	6.0	3613	3259	2448	2510	2601	2861	2311	2729	3361	3474	3489	3943	3050	13.1
Deviation	91			-557	-865												
Cum. Dev.	78			-557	-1422												

Capacity	Last Dec			Jan actual	Feb actual	Mar	Apr	May	Jun	Jul	Aug	Sep	Oct	Nov	Dec	Total	Avg
Work Days	20			20	19	23	21	20	22	12	22	21	21	20	20	241	20.1
Sat/Sun worked	0			3	3	3	3	4	4	2	4	4	5	5	3	43	3.6
Total Days/Mo	20			23	22	26	24	24	26	14	26	25	26	25	23	284	23.7

Figure 2.9 S & OP Plan Example

TEI system are directly connected with the financial system. Therefore, the financial impact of each function is described in the section for that function in this book.

A two-dimensional representation of the information and decision flows in a manufacturing company (as illustrated in Figure 2.1) is extremely limiting. One way to picture the integration of financial planning with the rest of the company is to imagine a three-dimensional picture of the company, in which the financial functions exist on a different plane and are tied to each of the nonfinancial functions. Such a picture might look like Figure 2.10.

The Sales and Operations Plan forms the basis for a top-level financial plan for the next 12 to 18 months or longer, which informs the financial executives of projected profitability and cash flow.

The TEI system contains the detailed plans and data necessary to calculate the top-level financial plan, including:

- Current customer orders and forecasted sales (from which the system can compute projected invoices to customers and subsequent cash receipts).
- Contracted and projected material acquisitions (from which it can compute projected payments for supplier invoices).
- Contracted and projected labor, including overtime (from which it can compute projected payments for payroll and payroll taxes).
- Projected inventory levels, including finished goods in all distribution areas, work in process, and raw materials.

The financial planning system can then combine these projections of cash outflows and inflows with other financial data, such as:

- Other contracted and projected income (rent, royalties, interest)
- Other contracted and projected payments (e.g., rent, advertising, etc.)

to create detailed financial projections. This process is illustrated in Figure 2.11.

Traditional MRP II systems have included standard accounting functions for years, but have usually lacked assistance in the treasury function or financial planning.

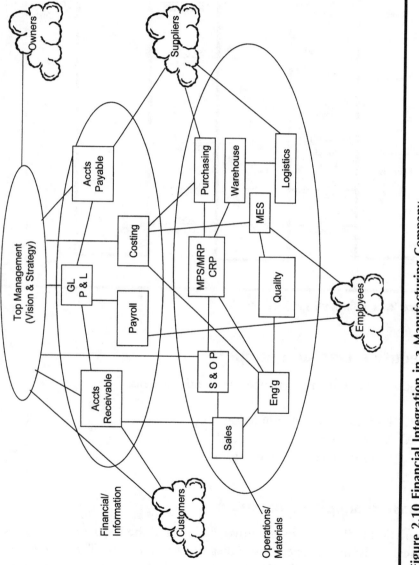

Figure 2.10 Financial Integration in a Manufacturing Company

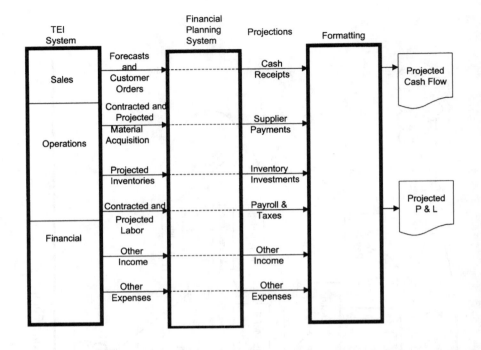

Figure 2.11 Financial Projections

Executive Decision Support

Executive decision support encompasses three areas:

1. Decision support simulation
2. "Alert" warning systems
3. Business process modeling

Decision Support Simulation

Simulation tools can help executives understand the impact of strategic and tactical decisions on operating indicators and the P&L. These tools utilize data from throughout the TEI system to project answers to questions such as, "What would be the impact on operations and my P&L if we:

- Changed our model mix by discontinuing one or more products, and/or adding one or more products? What if that impacted the prices for which we sell those products?
- Accepted a hot customer order that requires capacity in our bottleneck work center?
- Opened an additional warehouse in location *x*, or location *y*?
- Brought additional work in that we are currently letting our suppliers perform?
- Outsourced some current work to suppliers?
- Purchased semifinished raw materials, rather than doing the initial processing ourselves?
- Added an additional shift in a bottleneck work cell?
- Accepted a customer order for less than our desired selling price?"

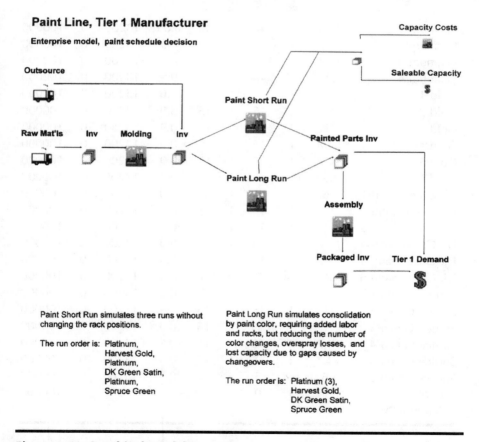

Paint Short Run simulates three runs without changing the rack positions.

The run order is: Platinum,
Harvest Gold,
Platinum,
DK Green Satin,
Platinum,
Spruce Green

Paint Long Run simulates consolidation by paint color, requiring added labor and racks, but reducing the number of color changes, overspray losses, and lost capacity due to gaps caused by changeovers.

The run order is: Platinum (3),
Harvest Gold,
DK Green Satin,
Spruce Green

Figure 2.12 Graphical Model Example

These tools are relatively inexpensive to acquire and easy to operate. The best ones use a graphical display to represent the business model and spreadsheet-like tables to enter and modify data. They easily receive data from the company's TEI system. The best tools also tell the executive which constraints should be examined, and the relative value of loosening each of the constraints. Examples of the graphical model and underlying tables of this type of tool are shown in Figure 2.12 and Tables 2.1 and 2.2.

Table 2.1 Decision Support Tool Tables

Process	Units/Hr.	Rate Adj.	Inputs	Input Adj.	Outputs	Yield Adj.	Cost/ Hr.	Min. Prod'n	Max Prod'n
Platinum 1	3.43	1	48	1	48	0.85	13200	0	100000
Platinum 2	3.43	1	48	1	48	0.9	13200	0	100000
Platinum 3	3.43	1	48	1	48	0.9	13200	0	100000
Platinum 4	3.43	0.9	48	1	48	0.9	13200	0	100000
Gold 1	66	1	5	1	5	0.6	13200	0	100000
Gold 2	11	1	15	1	15	0.9	13200	0	100000
Gold 3	11	1	15	1	15	0.9	13200	0	100000
Gold 4	14.7	1	15	1	15	0.9	13200	0	100000
Gold 5	14.7	1	15	1	15	0.9	13200	0	100000
Gold 6	66	0.4	5	1	5	0.9	13200	0	100000
Dk Green Satin 1	66	1	5	1	5	0.6	13200	0	100000
Dk Green Satin 2	11	1	15	1	15	0.9	13200	0	100000
Dk Green Satin 3	11	1	15	1	15	0.9	13200	0	100000
Dk Green Satin 4	14.7	1	15	1	15	0.9	13200	0	100000
Dk Green Satin 5	14.7	1	15	1	15	0.9	13200	0	100000
Dk Green Satin 6	66	0.4	5	1	5	0.9	13200	0	100000
Spruce Green 1	66	1	5	1	5	0.6	13200	0	100000
Spruce Green 2	11	1	15	1	15	0.9	13200	0	100000
Spruce Green 3	11	1	15	1	15	0.9	13200	0	100000
Spruce Green 4	14.7	1	15	1	15	0.9	13200	0	100000
Spruce Green 5	14.7	1	15	1	15	0.9	13200	0	100000
Spruce Green 6	66	0.4	5	1	5	0.9	13200	0	100000
Feet of Opportunity	660	1	0	1	1	1	0	0	100000

Table 2.2 Decision Support Tool Recommendations

Description	Price/Unit	Min. Units	Max Units	Recomm'd Prod'n	Opportunity Value	Total Revenue
Platinum Package	1500	48	64	48	0	72000
Gold Package	4000	5	6	5	−5	20000
Dk Green Package	4000	5	6	6	68	24000
Spruce Green Package	4000	5	6	6	68	24000
Total	140000					

Figure 2.12 illustrates a decision about how to maximize production and profitability through a paint line. The chain that carries parts through the paint line is 1000 feet long and runs three complete cycles per 8-hour shift. The company has two basic alternatives:

1. Leave the racks in place on the line for several cycles, with spaces between each set of racks to allow for changing colors. This is a classic Just-In-Time (JIT) approach, painting whatever color the customer wants within a few hours of receipt of the order. However, it causes a high number of changeovers, which have three costs:
   - Gaps between racks to prevent overspray during a color change
   - Paint in the lines, which must be flushed
   - Lower quality of the parts on the first rack of the new color being painted (due to latent overspray, paint lines not running cleanly, etc.)
2. Change racks with each complete cycle of the paint chain. This alternative increases the quantity of items painted at one time to the total quantity required for a shift, or a day. It increases expense by requiring the company to hire two more people to remove and attach racks, and to invest in additional racks and the storage space for those racks.

The types of data that the modeling tool can use are illustrated in Table 2.1. To model this environment, the business analyst translated data concerning the width of each rack and the number of specific parts that fit on each rack, plus a yield factor to reflect quality losses on the first rack of a new color due to overspray, bubbles in the paint line, etc. The analyst added an extra row for "feet of opportunity" to be able to report the quantity of unused feet on the paint line chain, so that marketing would be aware of the additional capacity that they could sell.

Table 2.2 shows the results of one run of the simulator in the simulator's sales table. The company groups four platinum parts (described in Table 2.1 as Platinum 1, 2, 3, and 4) into a platinum package, and likewise groups each of the other colors of items as packages. Their customers require at least 48 platinum packages and at least 5 each of the other packages per day. Customers are willing to buy up to 64 platinum packages and 6 each of the other packages per day. In the Recommended Production column, the modeling tool suggests that the company make only 48 platinum packages, 5 gold packages, 6 dark green packages, and 6 spruce green packages to maximize profits within the predetermined constraints. In the Opportunity column, the modeling tool is telling management that the company is losing money on the final unit of production of the gold package, breaking even on the last unit of the platinum package, and could increase profits if they could sell at least one additional unit of the dark green and spruce green packages.

Using such a tool involves four steps:

1. Developing the initial business model:
    a. Developing the initial computer model
    b. Setting up the initial data
    c. Testing the model to insure that it accurately represents processes and work flows
2. Benchmarking the model using existing data:
    a. Running the model against known data, such as a previous week's or month's operation, to prove the validity of the model
    b. Insuring that the model is correct in all aspects of the company's operation, including its financial predictions
3. Assessing the opportunities using initial data:
    a. Optimizing the model, to identify the cost/profit of one additional unit (of work, product, material, etc.) Although the optimization run is a complete solution of the model, the solution is merely the starting point for management analysis
    b. Analyzing the results of the optimization run, and then conducting several additional such runs before deciding on a particular set of results that will be the foundation for the next step

4. Refining the model; reassessing the opportunities:
   a. Running a number of simulations with the model; each run involves a specific set of assumptions or changes in the values of certain data elements, and shows the resultant impact of those assumptions and values on operations and profitability
   b. Defining an appropriate set of process and work flow rules to help achieve the optimum operations and profitability

Once a relatively accurate business model has been created, the value of the simulation tool continues to increase. Each subsequent use refines and enriches the model and the data in one or more areas.

"Alert" Warning Systems

"Alert" warning systems in TEI systems alert executives when the system detects that threshold value that has been set for a particular attribute has been exceeded. For example, a VP of Operations could set a threshold for yields in a given manufacturing plant; if the actual yields for a given period fall below that threshold, the TEI system would automatically notify the VP. A CEO could set a threshold for minimum profitability for sales of a product group, by region.

This can be a very powerful tool for upper and middle management. Senior management can set thresholds for each of the attributes that are keys to financial and operational performance, such as gross margin, production volumes, and yield. They can also set thresholds for the attributes on which they are measured by their customers, such as on-time shipments. Middle management can set thresholds for the items for which they are responsible, such as on-time performance, yield, operating efficiencies, or sales by region by product line.

Business Process Modeling

Several PC-based tools allow a company to model its business processes and to simulate throughput and bottlenecks visually, watching the queues build behind bottlenecks. These tools can be extremely useful in modeling current and proposed businesss processes in a variety of circumstances, including plant layout, information flows, and TEI implementations (especially in the Conference Room Pilot, which is described in Chapter 10). A sample of such a flow is shown in Figure 2.13.

Process Order - System Dynamics Model

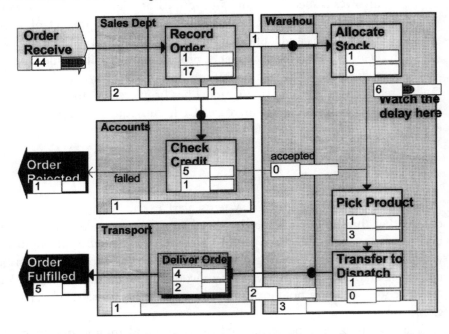

Figure 2.13 Business Processing Modeling Example

Measurement Systems

Jack Welch, CEO of General Electric, says that businesses tend to go wrong because they focus on predictability of operations. Instead, businesses must be flexible to meet the needs of the marketplace. Additionally, long-term relationships between companies must be based on flexibility, rather than today's market or specific volumes.

One of biggest obstacles to flexibility is the behavior that is reinforced by current accounting systems, which are based on predictability rather than flexibility. For example, departments and departmental managers are measured on performance against budget; budgets are created a year at a time, with the budgeting process starting 3 to 6 months before the year in question actually starts. Thus, at the end of a budget year, the original budget being used as a standard is 15 to 18 months old. Additionally, standard costs for the year are determined during the budgeting cycle. If a department can keep costs at or below the standard cost, the department is rewarded for meeting goals.

The basic problem that arises from a system that is based on predictability and standards is that more and more markets are moving faster than traditional measurement time frames. For example, in 1999 the life cycle of a PC model is 3 to 4 months, and the life cycle of a CPU chip model is 9 months. The other major problem with such systems is that they actually discourage continuous improvement.

We propose instead a new measurement system that recognizes that everything is temporary — products, customers, workers, and processes. It should base its approach on the assumption that all products have life cycles, and should have four key metrics: profitability, time, quality, and company spirit. It should also require continuous improvement.

Profitability

Profitability has traditionally been the primary measure of a company's performance. However, we propose that companies measure each department and function on contribution to profit for the entire life cycle of the product. This contrasts directly with current practice, in which departmental goals are often in conflict with each other. Some proposed departmental goals might include:

- Sales — contribution to margin, rather than gross revenues. Under this system, weaker and unprofitable products would be eliminated quickly.
- Manufacturing and materials — total life cycle cost of producing the product, including acquiring and converting the materials. Purchasing should be part of a manufacturing unit, which has P&L responsibility for its product line, rather than a corporate function.
- Engineering — designing products that make money over the product's life cycle (they share in the contribution to margin of the products they design); all warranty services are charged to Engineering under the assumption that they were probably caused by the product's design, rather than by the manufacturing workers or suppliers.
- All other functions (such as HR, IT, and cost accounting) have to sell their services to the three departments above, at a price the departments are willing to pay.

Time

Standard measurement systems ignore time, even though time is a more important measure of process than money. Time can have at least three dimensions: time to market, time to customer, and velocity.

- *Time to Market* — The right product at the wrong time is the wrong product. Several studies have shown that time to market is much more important for long-term product profitability than staying on budget. For example, a McKinsey study found that a 6-month delay in entering a market (to avoid budget overruns) would result in a 33% reduction in after-tax profit over the life of the product. The 6-month delay is five times more costly than a 50% development-cost overrun, and about 30% more costly than having production costs 10% over budget.*

- *Time to Customer* — The Just-In-Time movement, which started sweeping North America in the early 1980s, has encouraged most manufacturers to radically reduce their lead times to customers. Similarly, mail-order retailers have metamorphosed dramatically. In the 1960s, a customer expected to wait 1 to 2 weeks from the date they put an envelope in the mail until they received the package. Now, most catalog retailers ship the same day, and some (especially in the PC software business) deliver the next business day even if a customer orders at midnight. American Turned Products, a manufacturer of precision-machined components and assemblies, reduced customer order lead time from 8 weeks to 2 days.**

- *Velocity* — **Velocity** can be defined as the total elapsed time consumed by a process divided by the actual value-added time contributed by the same process. For example, if the lead time, or typical total elapsed time, for an assembly process, including all paperwork, material movement, and inspection, is 3 days of 8 hours each, and the actual value-added time is 2 hours, the velocity is 24/2, which is 12. For most industries, world-class velocity is less than 2.

---

* Blackburn, Joseph D., "Time-Based Competition," in *Strategic Manufacturing: Dynamic New Directions for the 1990s,* Patricia E. Moody, Ed., Business One/Irwin, Homewood, IL, 1990.
** Eighmy, Scott, and Ken Wantuck, "Eight Weeks to Two Days: The ATP Story," *1996 Conference Proceedings,* APICS, Falls Church, VA, 1996.

Quality

Another key metric must be quality. Focusing on cost standards can easily compromise quality as well as time, because cost standards measure quality against fixed expectations, rather than insisting on continuous improvement. The specific measurables for quality should come from the TQM (or similar) effort in the company.

Spirit

The fourth fundamental metric lies totally outside most systems thinking and outside traditional technology. A company is its people. It can have customers, products, plants, and equipment, but without skilled, dedicated, knowledgeable people, it cannot function. It is the people that develop relationships with customers and suppliers and that create new products and processes. We use the term "spirit" as the attribute that symbolizes the health of the people side of the company. This idea is explored more fully in Chapter 11.

As one means of providing a greater sense of ownership to people, we propose that companies divide themselves as much as possible into focused factories, splitting not only manufacturing, but *all* support functions, including purchasing, engineering, sales, and accounting. The mini-companies can be focused on specific product lines, specific customers, or specific processes. But each mini-company should sell its product to outside customers. Each mini-company would have its own P&L responsibilities, and its own board of directors, comprised of one representative from each function, plus the workforce.

Supply Chain Management Integration

Full supply chain management integration means partnering with customers and suppliers with the intent to maximize responsiveness and flexibility, while eliminating paperwork, waste, and cost throughout the supply chain. In its ultimate form, it requires a company to source each group of materials or services with only one supplier, and for the manufacturer to be the sole source for its products for its customers. Only in that way can the supplier be held completely accountable for fully supporting its customers, and can all interim paperwork and administration be completely eliminated. Likewise, only in that way can the manufacturer have the incentive to invest the time and resources into working closely with its customer, to co-develop new processes and products, and to divulge proprietary information. While this practice initially appears unrealistic in many industries, those companies that have implemented it have gained a substantial competitive edge.

Some writers differentiate between supply chain and **demand chain,** as follows:

- Supply chain starts with the initial supplier, and has five steps:
  1. Buy raw materials
  2. Make finished product
  3. Move goods to market
  4. Sell through retailers
  5. Receive returnables from retailers or collection points
- Demand chain contains the same basic steps, but reverses them using a pull philosophy:
  1. Receive returnables from retailers or collection points
  2. Sell customized product
  3. Move to delivery based on consumption
  4. Make only those products for which there is known demand
  5. Buy raw materials as needed to support production*

While we completely support the pull concepts that "demand chain" evokes, we will continue to use the term "supply chain" throughout this book to denote the second approach, as well as the first, in keeping with the wide acceptance of the term.

What are the results of industries that are moving toward supply chain? One result is lower inventories, as documented in a study performed by the Kellogg Graduate School at Northwestern University (Table 2.3)** More impressive results are documented in a 1997 supply chain benchmarking study performed by PRTM (Pittiglio Rabin Todd & McGrath).*** The study compares results of best-in-class companies with median companies in areas shown in Table 2.4. "For a company with annual sales of $500 million and a 60% cost of sales, the difference between being at median in terms of

---

* Lummus, Rhonda R., and Robert J. Vokurka, "Managing the Demand Chain through Managing the Information Flow: Capturing 'Moments of Information,'" *Production and Inventory Management Journal,* First Quarter, 1999, p. 17.

** *Global Supply Chain Study,* J. L. Kellogg Graduate School of Business, Northwestern University, 1997.

*** Mistry, Prafal, "1997 Benchmarking Study Shows Dramatic Reductions in Costs Using Best Practices for Supply-Chain Management," *Insight* (PRTM, Weston, MA), Winter 1997.

Table 2.3 Inventory as a Percentage of Gross Sales

Industry	1996	1997	2000 [a]
Automotive	19.6%	15.9%	14.2%
Chemicals	16.8	17.2	13.4
Consumer electronics	24.1	19.3	15.3
Consumer products	14.2	13.5	11.8
Food and agriculture	11.8	11.2	10.1
Industrial products	17.6	16.9	13.3
Pharmaceuticals	18.0	17.2	14.9
Retail	16.2	15.4	3.6

[a] Forecast.

Table 2.4 Key Performance Indicators, Best In Class vs. Median Performers

Metric	Median	Best-In-Class	% Diff.
Total supply-chain management cost (% of revenue)	11.6	6.3	46
Inventory (Days of Supply)	66	34	48
Cash-to-Cash cycle time	87	31	64
On-Time Delivery to Customer Request Date (%)	81	94	16
Upside Production Flexibility (days to implement an unplanned 20% increase in end-product supply)	26	4	85

performance and being in the top 20% is $44 million of available working capital," PRTM Director Mike Aghajanian noted.

TEI must not only support supply chain; it must be designed with supply chain as its center. In the past, supply chain was viewed as merely an arrangement that secured the lowest price for the customer, while assuring adequate supply. **Supply chain management** as used in this book is much more; it is a process for designing, developing, optimizing, and managing the internal and external components of the entire material supply and consumption system, including:

- Extracting initial materials from the ground or original source
- Transportation at each stage
- Transforming materials at each stage of manufacture
- Recycling waste materials from the production process
- Distributing finished products or services to the ultimate consumers
- Recycling nonconsumed materials to appropriate reclaiming processes

Further, the process must be consistent with overall objectives and strategies. Figure 2.14 illustrates a **supply web**, which recognizes that each manufacturer has many suppliers (who have many customers) and many customers (who have many suppliers). Each of the circles in Figure 2.14 represents a separate company, each of which can have its own full TEI capabilities.

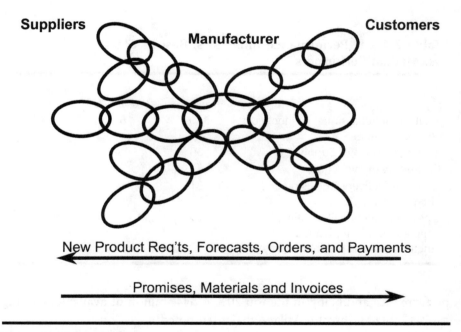

Figure 2.14 Supply Web

The essence of supply chain management is as a strategic weapon to develop sustainable competitive advantage by reducing investment while assuring customer loyalty. Since each level of the supply chain focuses on a compatible set of objectives, supply chain designers deliberately focus on eliminating or reducing redundant activities and duplicated efforts. Successful supply chains require the open sharing of information on the basis of trust and mutual benefit so that all companies can achieve their objectives. Supply chain strategy requires understanding and managing sourcing strategy, information flows (internal and external), new product coordination, concurrent procurement, teaming arrangements, commodity/component strategies, long-term requirements planning, industry collaboration, and staff development, all with the focus on providing the best product and service, at the lowest total investment, to the ultimate customer. The TEI communications required to support a supply chain are illustrated in Figure 2.15.

Inside each of the three companies shown in Figure 2.15 (in the nonoverlapped portions of the circles), we show the major internally focused TEI functions in 3 major groups:

- Executive and support functions, including human resources, executive decision support, and environmental.
- Customer responsiveness and manufacturing functions, including Sales and Operations Planning, Master Production Scheduling, Materials Requirements Planning, Capacity Requirements Planning, Advanced Planning and Scheduling, Manufacturing Execution Systems, Just-In-Time, engineering, inventory management, maintenance management, and quality management.
- Financial functions, including financial planning, costing, and accounting.

At the intersection between customer and manufacturer, and manufacturer and supplier, we show the three major groups:

- Customer-to-supplier product and order information, including Vendor-Managed Inventories, customer orders, forecasts, inventory status, quality standards, and product design requirements.
- Supplier-to-customer information, including promises (such as ship date, quantity, and quality), shipments, and quality information.
- Financial information, including payments from customers and invoices to customers.

Designing and implementing supply chain involves much more than just TEI. The five key dimensions include:*

---

* Copacino, William C., "Get the Complete Supply Chain Picture," *Logistics Management & Distribution Report*, November, 1998.

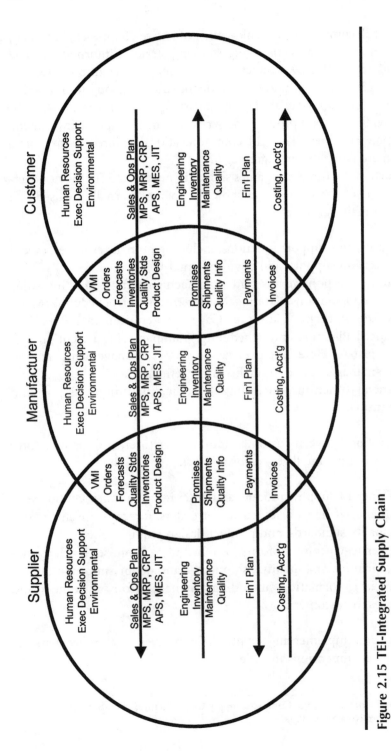

Figure 2.15 TEI-Integrated Supply Chain

1. **Strategy** — aligning supply chain strategies with the overall business direction.
   - What is required to align the supply chain with the business strategy?
   - What level of customer service must be provided to each customer and customer segment to compete most effectively?
   - Which distribution channels best meet our goals and our customers' needs?
2. **Infrastructure** — affecting cost/service performance and establishing the boundaries within which the supply chain must operate.
   - How should the physical network of plants and distribution be structured?
   - How should the current network be rationalized?
   - What transportation services can best link the facilities in the network?
   - What activities should be outsourced, such as manufacturing and logistics?
3. **Process** — achieving functional excellence and integration across all major processes.
   - What are the core supply chain processes driving the business?
   - How can the best-in-class methodologies be adapted most successfully to the core processes (e.g., manufacturing, integrated demand planning, procurement, cycle-time compression)?
   - How can linkages be best built and improved with suppliers and customers?
4. **Organization** — providing the critical success factors of cohesion, harmony, and integration across organization entities.
   - What level of cross-functional integration is required to manage core processes effectively?
   - How can cross-company skills and abilities be leveraged?
   - What performance measurement and reporting structure can best help achieve our objectives?
5. **Technology** — empowering the supply chain to operate on a new level of performance, and creating clear competitive advantages for those companies able to effectively harness it.
   - Do the information technology platform and core applications support world-class supply chain management? If not, can they?
   - Where will advanced decision-support capabilities have the greatest impact on business performance?

- What data and applications are required to manage the core business processes outlined above?
- How can advanced communications (e.g., Intranets and the Internet) provide a competitive edge in the supply chain?
- How can enhanced visibility of customer demand and other key operating parameters be leveraged for competitive advantage?

Since TEI is the primary information foundation for supply chain, increasing supply chain integration requires increases in both the degree of information integration and the amount of information. Unfortunately, the difficulty of integrating information increases at an accelerated rate with respect to the degree of supply chain integration, as shown in Figure 2.16.

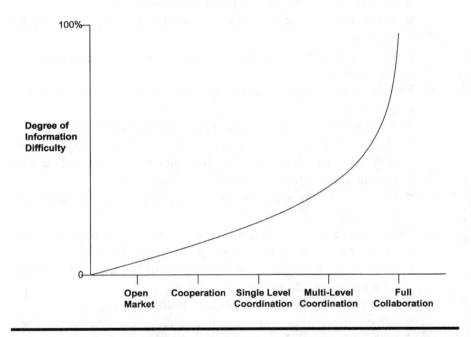

Figure 2.16 Degree of Information Difficulty vs. Supply Chain Integration

This increasing difficulty is caused by the increasing complexity within each system, and by the requirement to integrate disparate systems (which have been designed without the intent to be integrated together) running in different operating environments. This lesson has been learned by many companies that have decided to replace separate divisional and functional systems with a single, completely integrated TEI system, throughout the entire company. Such implementations normally cost far more and take far longer than originally anticipated because of the business integration issues involved. But these examples are still within the same company, which has the authority to make whatever changes and decisions are required. Fully integrating a supply chain across multiple companies is substantially more difficult.

Let us examine implications for an TEI system at the manufacturer in each of the five stages of supply chain shown in Figure 2.17:

1. **Open Market** — This is characterized by mistrust and animosity between customer and manufacturer, and manufacturer and vendor (the term "supplier" implies at least some cooperation). The manufacturer negotiates with many vendors for required items, keeping the vendors at arm's length.
   - On the supply side, the TEI system should provide forward visibility of future requirements to assist Purchasing in negotiating quantity discounts and securing sufficient capacity.
   - On the demand side, the TEI system should provide excellent capabilities in quoting, contact management, contract management, and forecasting.

2. **Cooperation** — This is characterized by the beginning of a partnership attitude between customer and manufacturer, and manufacturer and supplier. The customer has narrowed the supplier base and is starting to share more information with the remaining suppliers and to award longer-term contracts.
   - On the supply side, the TEI system provides MRP reports to provide greater visibility to the suppliers. Inventory buffers are starting to be reduced; the due dates are becoming "real."
   - On the demand side, the TEI system uses customer forecasts as a primary input, in addition to the internal forecasting capabilities from Stage 1, above.

3. **Single-Level Coordination** — This is characterized by "single source" long-term commitments, with direct electronic sharing of inventory planning data. The supply partner is starting to function as an extension of the customer partner's plant.
   - On the supply side, the TEI system provides EDI (or e-commerce), or the execution system provides *kanban* signals to the supplier. Alternatively, the supplier might use a "bread man" automatic replenishment system. The invoice step can be eliminated; the manufacturer can pay the suppliers for the computed amount of the supplier's items used based on the manufacturer's actual pro-

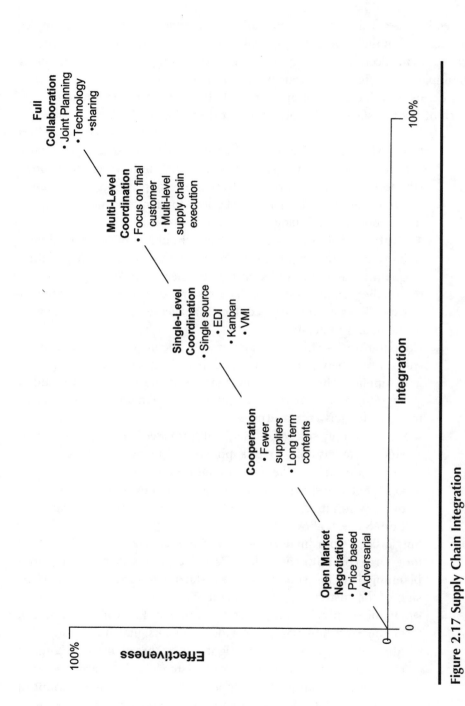

Figure 2.17 Supply Chain Integration

duction. The supplier's computer updates the manufacturer's computer with current schedules and actual production.

- On the demand side, the TEI system supports Vendor-Managed Inventories and links directly with transportation systems and carriers. (The TEI system also supports all the capabilities in the supply side.)

4. **Multi-Level Coordination** — This is characterized by a multi-level supply chain focused on maintaining the loyalty of the final customer, and designed to function as one entity.
   - On the supply side, the manufacturer's advanced planning and scheduling system is linked electronically with the supplier's TEI system (preferably an Advanced Planning and Scheduling module). Alternatively, tiers are linked by *kanban*-style execution systems, so that when the customer consumes a product, the entire supply chain reacts almost immediately. Inventory buffers are very small, and are closely monitored.
   - The demand side has the same capabilities as the supply side.

5. **Full Collaboration** — This is characterized by full partnership across all functions of the business, including joint long-range planning, sharing of technology, and joint development of new products.
   - On the supply side, the engineering functions are electronically linked throughout the supply chain, to support multicompany design teams. Quality systems are likewise linked.
   - The demand side has the same capabilities as the supply side.

Depending on the industry, supply chain efforts can also be known as:

- **Efficient Consumer Response (ECR)** — for manufacturers serving some retail industries
- **Quick Response (QR)** — for manufacturers serving some retail industries
- **Efficient Foodservice Response (EFR)** — for manufacturers serving the foodservice industries, both institutional and restaurant
- **Synchronized Consumer Response (SCR)** — for manufacturers serving retail industries.

As an example of these types of supply chains, Efficient Consumer Response targets five supply chain efficiencies in which the supplier and retailer work together:

1. Efficient Product Introduction — Developing new products and planning product launches to reduce the failure rate of new product introduction.
2. Efficient Promotion — Planning and/or implementing promotions to reduce excess costs and improve the results of promotion.
3. Efficient Replenishment — Ensuring provision of the right product, to the right place, at the right time, in the right quantity, and in the most efficient manner possible.
4. Efficient Store Assortment — Defining store assortment to maximize efficiency and profitability of space.
5. Efficient Store Merchandising — Optimizing category and space allocation, with frequent monitoring of category and item space at the store level.*

References

Bowersox, Donald J., Closs, David J., and Hall, Craig T., "Beyond ERP — The Storm Before the Calm," *Supply Chain Management Review,* Winter 1998.

Brunell, Tom, and Mahaffey, Ron, "Managing a Multi-Company Supply Chain," *1998 Conference Proceedings,* APICS, Falls Church, VA, 1998.

Burnham, John M., Natarajan, R., Nat, and Bapst, Gerald W., "Delivering Products and Services — Strategically!" *1998 Conference Proceedings,* APICS, Falls Church, VA, 1998.

Callahan, Charles V., and Nemec, Joseph, Jr., "The CEO's Information Technology Challenge: Creating True Value," *Strategy and Business,* First Quarter, 1999.

Collins, James C., and Porras, Jerry I., *Built to Last: Successful Habits of Visionary Companies,* Harper Business, New York, 1994

Copacino, William C., *Supply Chain Management, The Basics and Beyond,* St. Lucie Press, Boca Raton, FL, 1997.

Copacino, William C., "Get the Complete Supply Chain Picture," *Logistics Management & Distribution Report,* November 1998.

Greene, Alice H. "Looking Beyond ERP for Supply Chain Advantage," *Managing Automation,* January 1996.

Hamel, Gary, and Prahalad, C. K., "Strategy as Stretch and Leverage," *Harvard Business Review,* March-April 1993.

Hammer, Michael and Champy, James, *Reengineering the Corporation,* Harper Business, New York, 1993.

Jutras, Cindy, "Virtually Vertical Manufacturing: Transforming the Supply Chain," *Midrange ERP,* July/August, 1998.

---

* Carlberg, Ulf Casten, "Integrated Order Fulfillment as ECR's Enabling Application," *1998 International Conference Proceedings,* APICS, Falls Church, VA, 1998.

Kaplan, Robert S. and Norton, David P. , *The Balanced Scorecard,* Harvard Business School Press, Cambridge, MA, 1996.

Kinni, Theodore, *America's Best —* Industry Week's *Guide to World-Class Manufacturing Plants,* Wiley, New York, 1996.

Kotler, Philip, *Marketing Management Marketing Management: Analysis, Planning, Implementation, and Control (9th ed.),* Prentice-Hall College, Englewood Cliffs, NJ, 1996.

Levitt, Theodore, *The Marketing Imagination,* Free Press, New York, 1986.

Ling, Richard C., "Sales and Operations Planning: the Integrator in the Business Planning Process," *1998 International Conference Proceedings,* APICS, Falls Church, VA, 1998.

Lummus, Rhonda R. and Vokurka, Robert J., "Managing the Demand Chain through Managing the Information Flow: Capturing 'Moments of Information,'" *Production and Inventory Management Journal,* First Quarter 1999.

McHugh, Patrick, Merit, Giorgio, and Wheeler, William A., III, *Beyond Business Process Reengineering,* Wiley, New York, 1995.

Mistry, Prafal, "1997 Benchmarking Study Shows Dramatic Reductions in Costs Using Best Practices for Supply-Chain Management," *Insight* (PRTM, Weston, MA), Winter 1997.

Nagaraj, Varun, and Nooyi, Raj, "Configuring Your Supply Chain to Provide Your Customer's Total Solution," *PRTM's Insight,* (PRTM, Weston, MA), Spring 1998.

Poirer, Charles C. and Reiter, Stephen E., *Supply Chain Optimization, Building the Strongest Total Business Network,* 1996,

Reichheld, Frederick F. and Teal, Thomas, *The Loyalty Effect: The Hidden Force Behind Growth, Profits, and Lasting Value,* Harvard Business School Press, Cambridge, MA, 1996.

Robert, Michel, *Strategy Pure and Simple,* McGraw-Hill, New York, 1993.

Skinner, Wickham, *Manufacturing: the Formidable Competitive Weapon,* Wiley, New York, 1985.

Spekman, Robert E., Kamauff, John W. Jr., and Myhr, Niklas, "An Empirical Investigation into Supply Chain Management: A Perspective on Partnerships," *International Journal of Physical Distribution & Logistics Management,* Vol. 28, No. 8, 1998.

Smith, Douglas K., *Make Success Measurable,* Wiley, New York, 1998.

Stalk, George, Jr. and Hout, Thomas M., *Competing Against Time,* Free Press, New York, 1990.

Stalk, George, Evans, Philip, and Shulman, Lawrence E., "Competing on Capabilities: The New Rules of Corporate Strategy," *Harvard Business Review,* March-April 1992.

Stein, Tom, and Sweat, Jeff, "Killer Supply Chains," Supply Chain Council, AMR Research, http://www.supply-chain.com.

Treacy, Michael and Wiersema, Fred, *The Discipline of Market Leaders,* Addison-Wesley, Reading, MA, 1995.

Wallace, Bob, "Ford Suppliers Get Call to Design," *Computerworld,* March 10, 1999.

Weiss, Marc S., "Does Your Company Have a Business Strategy?" *1995 International Conference Proceedings,* APICS, Falls Church, VA, 1995.

3 Customer Integration

I ntegrating with customers is absolutely essential for a business to thrive. The concept of "customer relationship management" assumes and requires integrating all functions that affect the customer. Areas of customer-focused information that are integrated with the rest of a TEI (Total Enterprise Integration) system include:

- Full sales support
- Forecasting integration
- Order generation
- Order entry
- Quoting and promising deliveries
- Demand management
- Logistics and distribution
- Field service

(Marketing is discussed in Chapter 2.) Figure 3.1 shows how these customer-focused functions integrate with the rest of a TEI system.

Full Sales Support

Sales functions can be divided into the following categories:

- Assisted selling — involves the interaction between salespeople and consumers, and can occur either:
  - Outside the company (using salespeople in the field)
  - Inside the company (using telesales or customer service representatives)

61

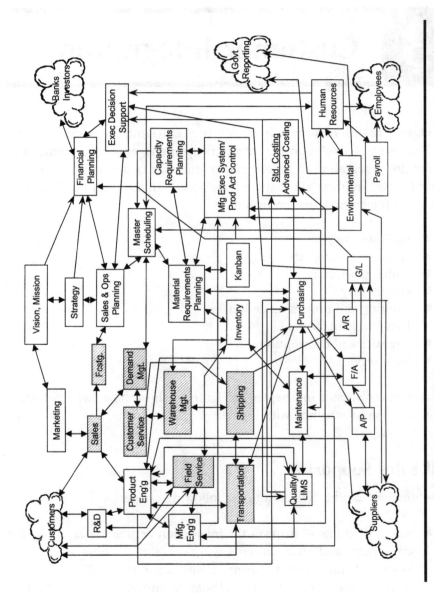

Figure 3.1 TEI Customer Functions

- Unassisted selling — includes sales via Web sites and kiosks at customer sites

"Sales force automation" normally refers to assisted selling, outside the company. MRP II systems were extremely weak in supporting salespeople in the field. However, virtually all of these capabilities are also required by inside salespeople. A fully integrated TEI system needs to permit a field salesperson with a laptop to have full access to all TEI functionality no matter where he or she happens to be. Sales force automation software should primarily assist the *salesperson* in the field and in the office, rather than focus on administrative tasks and management reporting. This software should help the salesperson delight the customer. Salespeople really want four basic capabilities:*

1. More and better sales information — especially accurate, advance knowledge of customer sales opportunities, competitive threats, and service problems
2. Better value proposition, business case development, and sales presentation knowledge and tools
3. Better and more straightforward ways to manage orders, agreements, and contracts
4. Simpler ways to communicate with the customer, marketing, service, shipping, each other, and alliance partners

"Collaborative" selling is a radical, customer-centric approach (rather than the traditional manufacturer-centric approaches) that involves:

- Understanding how their buyers buy, and how to enable the buyer to buy more easily. Then designing *those* capabilities into the marketing and sales support system.
- Focusing on ways to enable buyer and seller collaboration, especially around problem solving and solution design. Effective collaboration builds value and enduring relationships.
- Enabling buying and selling work to be aided by data-rich communications tools. Using those tools, a person can track and report work

---

* Parke, Shep, "Avoiding the Unseen Perils of Sales Technology," *Sales & Field Force Automation,* November 1998.

automatically, thereby eliminating the "after-the-fact typing and reporting" burden.

The following hypothetical example illustrates this:

XYZ Manufacturing makes consumer plastic products that it sells through large retailers and grocery stores. Early one morning, Chris, the sales manager, gets messages from the Internet and e-mail. A filtered news service to which XYZ subscribes announces that its biggest customer, MegaStores, is purchasing Regional Stores East, which has been stocking a competitor's products.

Chris asks an assistant to research the number of stores, and square feet per store, of Regional Stores East, and to suggest the proper amount of aisle footage for displaying XYZ's products at each of the Regional Stores based on their size.

Two hours later, the assistant provides the data to Chris, who creates a proposal for MegaStores, outlining the XYZ program for each of the Regional Stores. The VP of sales and marketing and the president are on the road visiting customers in another state. Chris e-mails the proposal to the VP and president, then calls their voice mail and leaves an urgent message for them to check their e-mail and get back to him.

The VP calls in for messages after lunch, accesses e-mail, and reviews the proposal with the president. They call Chris to ask questions and make suggestions, then approve the revised proposal and praise Chris for being so customer-focused.

Chris e-mails the proposal to the buyer at MegaStores. The buyer receives the e-mail, reviews it, and calls Chris with some suggestions and questions about the product mix, pricing for stores in one region, and logistics. They reach agreement. Chris incorporates the changes into the proposal and e-mails the revised proposal to the buyer, who forwards it to the VP at MegaStores.

That afternoon, the filtered news service informs Chris that state regulators are forcing MegaStores to sell several stores in specific cities to competitors. Chris revises the proposal and e-mails the revised proposal to the buyer. The buyer e-mails Chris a thank-you.

Two days later, the buyer e-mails Chris a purchase order for the products for the Regional Stores East stores that MegaStores will be retaining, with a proposed timetable for stocking each store with XYZ's product line.

This hypothetical example contrasts starkly with a more typical way of gathering information, reviewing proposals with upper management, proposing to customers, and negotiating the final agreements. The traditional approach would take 2 to 3 weeks, or longer, to accomplish the same result, allowing competitors precious time to encroach in the customer base.

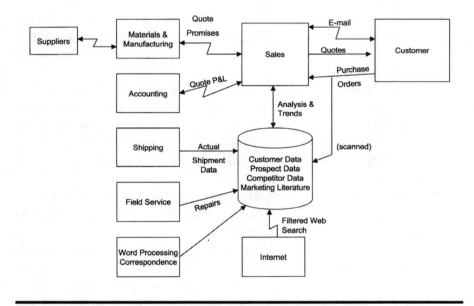

Figure 3.2 Sales Support System Integration

Sales force information integrates with many different departments and functions, both inside and outside the manufacturer, as shown in Figure 3.2. The best sales force automation is that which gets the sales process out of the way of the salesperson, and allows the salesperson to focus on the needs of the customer. Some of the functions of sales force software include:

- Support for team selling, allowing team members to work jointly and/or individually on common documents, and to easily exchange intelligence on customer requests and concerns.

- Customer and prospect data mining tools to help salespeople easily identify and move on opportunities. This should include filtered news search and powerful Web access.
- Access to marketing literature and competitor data.
- Ability to generate and modify quotes, with accurate delivery dates (as an integral part of the quoting system rather than a separate system). The accurate delivery dates could be from an Available To Promise feature in a traditional Master Production Scheduling package, or from an Advanced Planning and Scheduling system, or another type of scheduling system:
  - Reference management system, which tracks references by products and models used, problems encountered, type and size of company, etc., and ensures that references do not get called too frequently
  - Integrated with tools that produce a customer business case
- Ability to configure products, using the Product Configurator that is integrated with the engineering system (for acceptable configurations and options), the material planning system, potentially an Advanced Planning and Scheduling system, costing, and pricing (to create a customer-specific price).
- P&L impact of sales proposals, integrated with the accounting system, which shows not only the increase in revenues, but the probable gross margin from each possible sale.
- Customer sales trends and exceptions (e.g., changing buying patterns).
- Integrated contact management system, which:
  - Replaces the old-style call reports by providing detailed data about past meetings and phone calls with each person at a customer's or prospect's company
  - Is fully integrated with the word processing program
  - Is searchable by company, individual being called upon, and customer problems and issues
  - Tracks leads, and integrates with accounting systems that determine the cost of each sales campaign, so that the actual results of a lead-generation campaign can be computed
- Automated salesperson expense reporting system (possibly integrated with the contact management system and sales call reporting system).
- Probability-weighted sales cycle tracking system, integrated with the forecasting system and/or financial systems, to predict which prospects will close, by date.

- ■ A single "face" by which salespeople can easily access any and all information about a customer, by document type, date, or key word, including:
  - – Customer orders (current and shipped), payments, credit status
  - – Copies of scanned documents, including letters from the customer, customer PO's, signed Bills of Lading, freight invoices, and customer remittance advices
  - – Any and all correspondence sent to the customer, from the word processing system
  - – Field service and repair incidents, by symptom, from the field service system, including both warranty and out-of-warranty service
- ■ Integration with Personal Digital Assistants (palmtop computers).

Forecasting Integration

For many manufacturers, forecasting is still more of an art than a science, because it needs to blend intelligence from the field with actual past sales to create the most accurate forecast available. For example, Customer "A" is planning to open 50 new stores next year; Competitor "L" is bringing out a new product that might cause our sales to plummet; Supplier "X" has a new technology that can give us a competitive edge. Forecasts drive capital decisions, both plant and equipment, material volume (and even supplier choice) decisions, staffing decisions, and financial plans. In many companies, the marketing and sales department forecasts in dollars (currency) by time period, and the manufacturing or materials function translates that to product forecasts. In other companies, the various departments fail to agree on a single forecast.

Even when a forecast has been accepted, most companies have great difficulty in communicating the impact of forecast adjustments on each affected area unless the forecasts are part of a fully integrated ERP or TEI system. There are two basic types of forecasts: qualitative and quantitative (statistical).

Qualitative Forecasts

Although **qualitative forecasts** are often perceived as "last resort" techniques (because there are not enough "hard data" to create a statistically valid forecast), qualitative methods can frequently provide very accurate forecasts.*

---

* Chase, Charles W., "Selecting the Appropriate Forecasting Method," *Journal of Business Forecasting*, Fall 1997.

The most widely used qualitative techniques are independent judgment, committee consensus, sales force estimates (also known as "sales force composites"), and juries of executive opinion. The best qualitative forecasts also include commitments from customers. For example, a customer can commit to the manufacturer for a total volume of jeans that will be sold for a year, with some expectations about colors and styles. The qualitative forecast can break those expected sales by region, because some colors and some styles might sell better in some regions than in others.

Qualitative forecasting methods have several advantages:

- Low cost to develop the forecast.
- Executives and others understand the assumptions that drive the forecasts and how the forecasts were determined.
- Small time commitment required.

They also have several disadvantages:

- Inherent bias by the group that develops them.
- Not consistent over time due to their subjective nature.
- Not well suited for companies with a large number of products.

Companies that utilize qualitative forecasting methods must manually enter the resulting forecasts into their TEI systems.

Quantitative Forecasts

Quantitative forecasts operate on the assumption that the future can be predicted from past data. The data can come from two basic sources:

1. **Intrinsic** — internal to the company, such as shipments of finished goods, number of service contracts signed, MTBF (Mean Time Between Failures) on replaceable components, etc. These data normally reside in a TEI system. However, intrinsic data have three inherent flaws because they reflect the item, quantity, and date actually shipped:
   - *Item:* They show the item sold, not the item the customer originally wanted. If a customer wants a specific item or configuration that is unavailable, they have three choices: buy a substitute item,

buy from a competitor, or defer the purchase. Potential sales and sales inquiries are usually not captured in the sales database. And if they are actually captured, that data can also be misleading (a prospect can call two or three times.)
- *Date Shipped:* Potential sales that were missed because the manufacturer could not ship at the right time are normally *not* in the TEI database, and are therefore excluded from the forecast. Additionally, some older MRP II databases lack the original customer wanted date.
- *Past vs. Future:* Past data are not always a good predictor of the future. Some manufacturers that serve rapidly changing markets are finding that a 13-week history for nonseasonal business is better than 2 years of history for the same product.

2. **Extrinsic** — external to the company, such as housing starts, birth rates, weather, etc. Although these data do not normally reside in older MRP II systems, some more advanced forecasting tools also allow the user to enter extrinsic data, or to link to prespecified sources of extrinsic data.

TEI systems either incorporate or interface with a variety of forecasting packages. The statistical and modeling methodologies inside forecasting packages can range from extremely simple to complex and intricate mathematics. Table 3.1 presents some of the more common approaches, in increasing order of responsiveness.

Minimizing the Impact of Forecast Errors

By definition forecasts are inaccurate. While they are the best information available, companies that create plans based on forecasts should strive to **reduce forecast error,** and design their internal systems to **communicate changes quickly** and to accommodate the forecast errors as those errors become known. These strategies are discussed in more detail below.

Reducing forecast error is not always as difficult as it might seem. It can be accomplished by any combination of three approaches:

1. Decrease response lead times. The ultimate goal for a manufacturer is to be able to efficiently and effectively manufacture what the customer wants within the customer's lead time.
2. Increase the time period of demand visibility with the customer.
3. Increase forecast accuracy by monitoring forecast error.

Table 3.1 Forecasting Methodologies

Name	Description	Strengths	Weaknesses
"Same as last period"	The future will be just like the past	Very simple	Frequently too simple; no trend, no changes
Simple Moving Average	Average of the last "x" periods	Easy to understand	Ignores trends; dampens changes
Trend/ Regression	The future will continue on the same trend	Relatively simple; includes trend	Still relatively simple; misses changes
Seasonal	Allows for seasonal fluctuation	Includes trend and seasonal	Requires 2+ years' data; misses changes
Exponential smoothing	Weights recent data more than older data	Reflects changes; requires very little data storage	Ignores trends unless used with regression
Box–Jenkins	Combines time series and regression	Very successful	Complex

Decrease response lead times

Forecast error increases as the amount of time in the future increases. For example, a weather forecast for tomorrow is substantially more accurate than one for a week from tomorrow. This is because the longer the time period, the greater the opportunity for unanticipated events, even events that appear small or unrelated, to affect the eventual outcome. Thus, one obvious way to reduce forecast error is to reduce the amount of time in the future being forecast. For manufacturers, this means slashing the time required to make and ship customer orders. The ideal manufacturing lead time for finished goods is one that is shorter than the response time that customers require. For example, assume that a customer is delighted to receive the goods 1 week after the customer places the order. The manufacturer's cumulative lead time, starting with the longest lead time from its suppliers, is 12 weeks. This would normally mean that the manufacturer must forecast customer orders 11 weeks before they are received. However, most manufacturers would have some of the long lead time purchased items in stock and/or en route, so that the "real" lead time for the customer order could be 5 weeks.

The 5-week (25 work days, at 5 days per week) cumulative lead time is composed of the activities shown in Table 3.2. If the customer wants to receive its merchandise 1 week after it faxes the order, the manufacturer probably operates from a make-to-stock (MTS), ship-from-stock business model, depicted in the right-hand column of Table 3.2. The merchandise ships 5 days after the order is received and arrives 7 business days from the fax date. This is not really "on time," but the customer has learned to live with the extra 2 days and has added it to their lead time. Why are lead times in multiples of days? Because the older MRP II system requires nightly batch runs to produce most of the new paperwork.

Table 3.2 Lead Time Components, Normal

Step	Activity	Time Days	Total Cum Time	MTS Lead Time
1	Receive customer order by fax, enter order and check credit	2	2	2
2	Run MRP	2	4	
3	Create work order for subassemblies	2	6	
4	Make subassemblies; inspect, receive to stores	5	11	
5	Create work order for final assembly	2	13	
6	Make final assembly; inspect, receive to finished goods warehouse	5	18	
7	Cut shipping paperwork	1	19	3
8	Pull from warehouse; pack for shipment	1	20	4
9	Call trucker; ship	1	21	5
10	In transit to customer	2	23	7
11	Allowance for schedule slippage	2	25	

Unfortunately, the product lines have many features and options, such that the customers can (and do) request several different configurations. This creates an environment in which:

- Finished goods inventories are "too high" (according to the Controller).
- The requested configuration is in stock less than 50% of the time when a customer order arrives, which creates an emergency. There are three choices:
  - Ship a substitute configuration (with additional features, or higher cost options, at no charge to the customer).
  - Disassemble and reassemble an existing finished good as quickly as possible, filling out all paperwork later.
  - Create a rush order for the subassembly and assembly, causing the shipment to be at least a week late to the customer.

Each of these choices adds cost and chaos; none adds value to the customer.

How can this be changed? The manufacturer can redesign its business model, both internally and externally (the interface with the customer). Internally, the manufacturer could design for quick-turn, assemble-to-customer-order, so that the custom-assembled merchandise would leave the dock in *less than 20 (work) hours* (or 3 days, assuming a one shift/day operation) after receipt of the customer order! The customer will receive the order in 4 or 5 days, with no expediting and no crises. This is illustrated · in Table 3.3.

Table 3.3 Lead Time Components, Compressed

Step	Activity	Time, Days	Total Cum. Time, Days
1	Receive customer order by fax, enter order and check credit	.250	.250
2	Run MRP	.125	.375
3	Create work order for sub-assemblies	.125	.500
4	Make sub-assemblies	.750	1.250
5	Create work order for final assembly	0	
6	Make final assembly; inspect, receive to finished goods warehouse	.750	2.000
7	Cut shipping paperwork	0	2.000
8	Pack for shipment	.125	2.125
9	Call trucker; ship	.250	2.375
10	In transit to customer	2.000	4.375

This redesigned business model requires a TEI system that is truly on-line, with action screens letting each person know what he or she needs to do next. When the order has been entered, the system automatically checks credit, runs a mini-MRP for materials, and creates a work order for the custom subassemblies and the final assembly. The plant is highly responsive, completing the subassemblies in 6 hours, and the final assembly in another 6 hours. Shipping paperwork is ready to be printed on demand at the shipping dock; the system told the shipping clerk about the order as soon as the order arrived, so the shipper has already called for the truck.

The illustration is not unrealistic, or even unusual, in spite of the disbelief of many seasoned practitioners. Many companies have indeed achieved results like this as documented in various articles; one article documents the lead time and inventory reductions of three companies that changed from a job shop business model to repetitive,* another provides a case history of lead time reduction from 8 weeks to 2 days.**

The concept of **velocity**, which is the total lead time divided by the total value added time, is critical here. A company with a velocity greater than 2 is being forced by its own internal practices to forecast much farther into the future than it should have to. The costs of forecasting inherently include:

- High inventories
- Low customer service (on-time shipment)
- High administrative costs
  - Expediting
  - Changing priorities in the shop and with suppliers
  - Making excuses to customers for poor performance

Increase visibility with the customer

Increasing visibility into customer demand effectively increases customer lead times for the manufacturer. Customer lead times have been reducing consistently in most industries through the 1980s and 1990s, and fully expect that trend to continue. However, this does not prevent manufacturers from learning of impending customer demand earlier. Many customers are willing to

---

* Langenwalter, Gary A., "Why Use Repetitive? For the Results!" *1998 Conference Proceedings,* APICS, Falls Church, VA, 1998.
** Eighmy, Scott, and Wantuck, Ken, "Eight Weeks to Two Days: The ATP Story," *1996 Conference Proceedings,* APICS, Falls Church, VA, 1998.

help their suppliers help them, realizing that both parties will reduce cost and therefore increase profits. There are various approaches to learning about customer demand more quickly, including:

- Vendor-Managed Inventory (VMI)
- Receiving a customer's MRP run for the appropriate items
- Being on a *kanban* system (manual or electronic) with the customer,
- Providing "bread man" supply service to the customer*
- Working with the customer to help them eliminate their internal paperwork and accompanying delays, so that replenishment notification is transmitted as quickly as possible
- Using electronic communications from customer to manufacturer, such as EDI or e-commerce (eliminating printing out and rekeying that is required with faxes)

Following the lead of the Japanese, the North American automobile industry has deliberately improved communications to direct suppliers (known as "tier 1," because they supply the final manufacturers directly). The final assemblers, or OEMs, provide weekly forecasts for 5 weeks into the future, then actual releases against those forecasts. Some of the forecasts are incorrect, but they are the best information available at the time they are transmitted, and the OEMs correct them as quickly as possible.

These two concepts — reducing actual lead time and increasing visibility — are illustrated in Figure 3.3, which shows four sets of time lines: three for the manufacturer and one for the customer. The first manufacturer's time line shows the original lead times, cumulative, for making the order to customer specification if the manufacturer starts with the customer-specific subassembly. The individual steps are defined in Table 3.2. Since the customer is not willing to wait 5 weeks to receive an order, the manufacturer has chosen to stock specific configurations of finished goods, hoping that the customer will order those configurations that are in stock. The second manufacturer's time line highlights the only activities that the manufacturer performs after receiving the customer order: order entry, packing, and shipping. The third manufacturer's time line shows the compressed lead time, which has eliminated most nonvalue-added time. The Actual Customer Activities time line

---

* "Bread man" supply refers to the bread distributors that resupply food market shelves. The "bread man" arrives every 2 to 3 days to restock the shelves from the bread on the truck. The supermarket does not place orders; the "bread man" automatically resupplies all bread that has been purchased since the last visit.

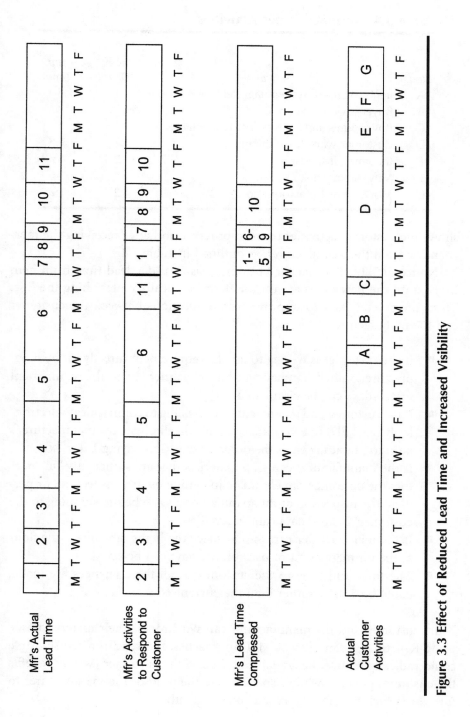

Figure 3.3 Effect of Reduced Lead Time and Increased Visibility

Table 3.4 Customer Order Activities

Step	Activity	Time, Days	Cum. Time
A	Items are used; system flags item for reorder	1	1
B	Buyer reviews report	3	4
C	Buyer prints and faxes order to manufacturer	1	5
D	Customer waits for shipment	7	12
E	Incoming inspection	2	13
F	Move items to stockroom	1	14
G	Move items to factory floor	2	16

shows the customer activities prior to ordering and after receiving the merchandise from the manufacturer, as outlined in Table 3.4.

Notice in Table 3.4 that the customer has a 16-day lead time from item usage until the new items are on the floor, physically replenishing the line. There are several ways to improve communications between the customer and the manufacturer:

- If the customer is willing to fax the requirement directly to the manufacturer, rather than having a buyer/planner review the requirement first, 3 days can be eliminated.
- If the customer and manufacturer are willing to communicate electronically (e.g., EDI or e-commerce), that will eliminate the manufacturer's need to physically enter the order information, saving 1 day.
- If the manufacturer can ship materials that are sufficiently "in spec" that the customer can eliminate incoming quality inspection, or perform the inspection at the manufacturer's site before shipping to the customer, 2 more days can be saved.
- If the manufacturer can ship or place the items directly on the floor at the ultimate point of use, 3 more days can be saved.
- The total lead time to the customer, if all these changes are made, could be 5 days, rather than the current 16.

If the customer and the manufacturer can synchronize their material flows, using Repetitive, Lean, Flow, or JIT approaches, the synchronized schedule could radically reduce the actual lead time to the customer (which benefits the customer greatly), while also eliminate the need of the manufacturer to forecast (which benefits the manufacturer greatly).

Increase forecast accuracy by monitoring forecast error

Forecasts are, by definition, inaccurate. As actual data becomes available in the TEI system, the system should compare it to the forecast and alert management when a forecast is outside of a predetermined **forecast error range** (e.g., 25% for a month, 15% for 6 months, and 10% for a year), also known as a **forecast tracking signal**. This allows management to review the assumptions underlying the forecast and to revise the forecast as appropriate. This process is illustrated by Figure 3.4.

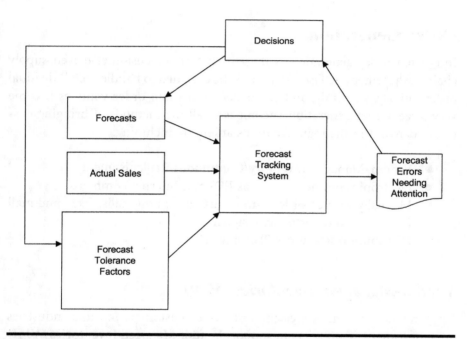

Figure 3.4 Forecast Feedback Loop

Communicate Changes Quickly

Forecasts can be changed at a sales and operations planning meeting, or the weekly planning meeting, or the daily status meeting. No matter when the forecasts change, a company has to communicate the full effect of those changes throughout its own organization and to its suppliers. A properly designed, properly implemented, fully integrated TEI system excels at this task. As soon as the change is approved, the Master Scheduler incorporates the changes into the Master Production Schedule. This MPS change provides the foundation for the TEI system to calculate the full effect of the changes on the rest of the organization and supply base, including:

- Production control
- Manufacturing
- Human resources (overtime)
- Suppliers
- Finance (cash flow projections)

Order Generation

Integrated order generation is the cornerstone of customer-driven supply chain management. A TEI system must be designed to handle each individual order quickly, smoothly, and efficiently, even when order volumes become very large. Order generation encompasses all the methods of bringing customer demand to the manufacturer's attention, including:

- Vendor-Managed Inventory/Continuous Replenishment
- Electronic commerce, such as EDI and Internet commerce
- Manually entered orders, from customer phone calls, faxes, and mail
- *Kanbans* and other manual signals
- Distribution Resources Planning (DRP)

Vendor-Managed Inventories (VMI)

Large retailers and an increasing number of customers in other industries are requiring their suppliers to support **Vendor Managed Inventories** (**VMI**) as a condition of continuing to do business with them. Another term used by retail industries is **continuous replenishment program**.

VMI moves day-to-day responsibility for management of inventories from the customer to the supplier, subject to controls that they mutually define in advance. This removes one redundant layer of planning (at the customer) in the supply chain by tightly integrating the customer and supplier, resulting in lower costs and reduced response times (Figure 3.5).

In the traditional mode, with retailers placing orders to the suppliers, the retailers sometimes wait to reorder until their stocks are very low or gone, thereby creating stockouts or expedite situations. Because the manufacturer

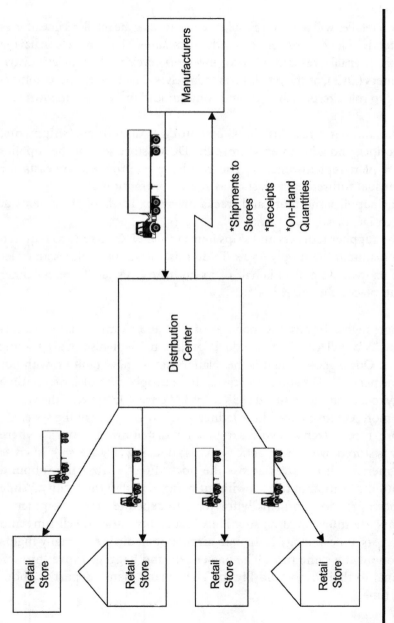

Figure 3.5 Vendor Managed Inventories

is monitoring the inventories, properly implemented VMI can increase sales through the channel, while decreasing transportation costs by avoiding premium freight.

A typical retailer will require a supplier to ensure that the retailer's inventories are consistently as low as possible, but with *no stockouts*. This can include having the manufacturer take responsibility for inventory levels in the retailer's **distribution centers (DCs)**, or the retail stores themselves. The retailer and manufacturer agree to roles, responsibilities, and communication as in the following:

- The retailer provides daily inventory transactions (shipments, receipts, and adjustments) from the DC or store so that the supplier can plan replenishments. The retailer also provides forecasts for unusual future demand, such as special promotions.
- The supplier monitors and tracks inventory levels of their items at each DC or store.
- The supplier reorders and ships items to each DC or store as required to maintain the supply levels. To do this, the supplier places an order in its own system on behalf of its customer, just as if the customer had placed the order itself.

Bob Burroughs, Tropicana's manager of EID and Continuous Replenishment, says, "We will continue to add [Continuous Replenishment] trading partners. ... Our biggest benefit is the relationship we have built up with our trading partners. ... (I)n almost all cases, those people did not have the time nor energy to look at the day-to-day SKU level. We are able to tweak the system a little bit more, cut inventory a little tighter, and take costs out of the system."*

A more recent trend involves replacing distribution centers, where inventory is stored, with the practice of **cross docking** (Figure 3.6). In cross docking, merchandise moves across the dock directly from the inbound trucks onto the outbound trucks, without being stored in the facility. While this has been practiced informally for years to expedite urgent shipments, distributors are intentionally using it to reduce inventory dwell time and handling costs. One analogy is the hub airport of an airline — many flights arrive at about the same time. The passengers and baggage move through the terminal to their outbound flights. Then many planes depart at about the same time.

---

* Bernstein, Ralph, "Premium Forecasting Cuts OJ Inventory," *Consumer Goods*, January/February 1999, p. 12.

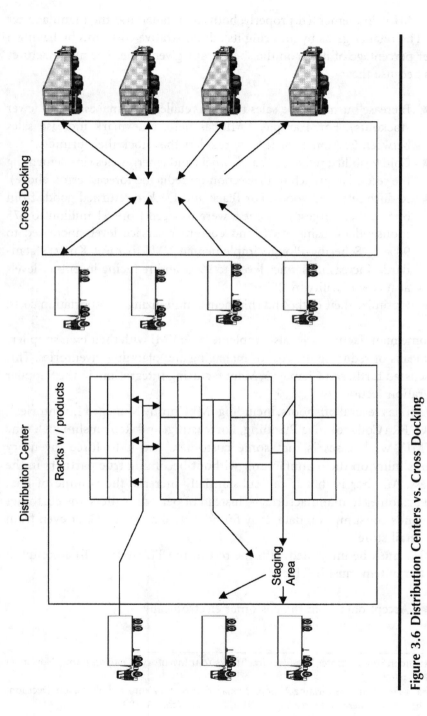

Figure 3.6 Distribution Centers vs. Cross Docking

If VMI is implemented properly, both the retailer and the manufacturer gain. The retailer gains by lowering its administrative costs and by having a higher percentage of items on the shelf at any given time. The manufacturer gains because they:

- Increase business (the sales that the retailer now makes due to fewer stockouts). For example, VMI has helped Lexmark increase sales between 5% and 12% at large retailers that stock their printers.*
- Gain visibility, reducing "rush" orders and emergencies (implementing the second approach in the section on reducing forecast error, above).
- Reduce returned goods. For Black and Decker, returned goods from one of their largest customers were reduced from $1 million to $75 thousand by using VMI, and customer service levels increased to 98%.** Schering-Plough implemented VMI to meet Kmart's standards, increasing service levels to 99%, and reducing inventory levels at its own facility by 25%.**
- Optimize their outbound shipments, minimizing transportation costs.

Some manufacturers are also implementing VMI with their own suppliers as a means of reducing the cost of managing and planning inventories. This is discussed further in Chapter 5, Manufacturing Integration, in the Supplier Integration section.

VMI has several offshoots, including JMI (Jointly Managed Inventories), and CPFR (Collaborative Planning, Forecasting, and Replenishment). One of VMI's weaknesses is that some customers use it to force inventory responsibility on the manufacturer without becoming true partners in the process. Another is that it can substantially increase the volume of data from customer to manufacturer — instead of periodic orders, the customer now sends consumption data daily for each item at each DC, or even from each retail store.

VMI must be integrated with the rest of the TEI system. To accomplish this, the system must be able to:

- Accept data from the customer electronically

---

* Alexander, Steve, "Printer Manufacturer Tracks Your Inventory," *Computerworld*, November 16, 1998, p. 67.
** Fox, Mary Lou, "Integrating Vendor-Managed Inventory into Supply Chain Decision-Making," *1996 Conference Proceedings*, APICS, Falls Church, VA, 1996.

- Track inventory levels at customer locations (with proper ownership of the merchandise for accounting systems)
- Create customer orders automatically, following predetermined rules

Electronic Commerce/Internet Commerce

This approach utilizes the capability of electronic commerce to directly enter orders into the manufacturer's computer, with the potential to dramatically reduce total order processing times. The approach is discussed in a dedicated section in Chapter 7.

Manually Entered Orders

Many customers still rely on the manufacturer to physically enter their orders into the manufacturer's TEI system. These customers primarily use phone calls and faxes to inform the manufacturer of their requirements. Order entry capabilities have been in MRP and MRP II systems since their inception; these modules can be highly robust in current systems, including the ability to predefine the customer's order (for which the system uses incoming caller ID in the phone system to bring up the customer's data and typical order onto the screen of the order entry person).

When a customer calls to place an order, the TEI system must be sufficiently responsive to allow the customer service representative to quickly and accurately enter the order while the customer is on the phone, providing a firm ship date and a total price for the order (and assuring creditworthiness in the background). This requires full integration with an Available To Promise capability in a traditional Master Production Scheduling module, or the ability to rapidly project a ship date using an APS (Advanced Planning and Scheduling) system.

Kanbans *and other manual signals*

Kanbans and other manual signals relay an authorization to ship products to a customer without any paperwork or intervention on the part of customer service. They can arrive at the manufacturer's finished goods shipping dock, where the shipping personnel ship the requested goods immediately. If the manufacturer is operating in an assemble-to-order mode, the *kanban* can be delivered directly to the final assembly area as an authorization to assemble and immediately ship that specific configuration and quantity of products.

Distribution Resources Planning (DRP)

Distribution Resources Planning (DRP) is a precursor of Vendor-Managed Inventories. It monitors the current and projected future on-hand of finished goods at warehouses, in the same way that MRP monitors the current on-hand and projected usage of inventory inside the plant. DRP predicts future shortages, by item number and warehouse, and schedules replenishment orders from the plant to avoid the projected shortages. This is illustrated in Table 3.5. Each column is one time period (e.g., a week). This presentation format is explained in greater detail in the section on Master Production Scheduling in Chapter 5.

Table 3.5: Distribution Resources Planning

	Los Angeles Distribution Center						
	OH	*1*	*2*	*3*	*4*	*5*	*6*
Forecasts		100	100	100	100	100	100
Customer Orders		120	60	30	5	20	0
Projected On-Hand	50	130	30	130	30	130	30
Replenishment Due		200		200		200	

Table 3.5 uses the following assumptions:

- Forecasted demand is 100 units/week.
- Customers sometimes give orders with future ship dates; however, most of their orders ship the same week in which the order is received.
- DRP subtracts whichever is greater, the customer demand for the week or the forecasts for the week, from the previous week's on-hand balance to determine the balance at the end of the week.
- We have specified that DRP should order 200 at a time from our plant, to minimize shipping costs.

DRP is appropriate when finished goods are stored in warehouses, because it provides visibility about future lumpy demand due to several warehouses running low on product simultaneously. It requires that the TEI system track finished goods at remote warehouses. One of the management issues is that the remote warehouses are frequently not owned by the manufacturer, which increases the difficulty of timely and accurate information reporting.

Order Entry

Order entry addresses the various options and challenges involved in accepting the demand from the customer, no matter in which form it has arrived. Some of the issues that must be addressed when a manufacturer selects and implements the order entry module of a TEI system include:

- Multiple order types
- Handling large order volumes (large quantities of order line items, rather than large quantities of finished goods being ordered)
- Pricing and promotions
- Multiple units of measure
- Product substitution rules
- Product allocation and reservation rules
- Multiple sourcing options for each order line
- Fully integrated credit checking
- Forecast coordination

Multiple order types

There are many different order types that might be required by a manufacturer, including:

- Regular, for standard items; these items will be shipped to the customer.
- Samples (no charge to the customer) for standard items.
- Samples (no charge to the customer) for prototype items.
- Replacement parts (no charge to the customer), for warranty service.
- Prospective — a high probability of an actual order in the near future (this can actually be treated as a forecast by the TEI system); the manufacturer needs to determine the extent to which resources (materials, labor, capacity) will be invested in a prospective order.
- Drop-ship — for items that the manufacturer buys from a supplier; the supplier can drop-ship these items directly to the customer (TEI systems should support this business method; some older MRP II systems have difficulty invoicing the customer, because the MRP II system did not direct the physical shipment from the manufacturer's facility).

Handling large volumes of orders

Handling a large volume of orders (line items) can stress the capabilities of a system and an order entry organization, causing increased error rates and delays in filling customer orders. Some TEI systems have been designed, both technically and ergonomically, to support large volumes of orders; many have not. The essence of system design for large volumes of orders is automating wherever possible, and streamlining the process from start to finish. When implementing a TEI system in such an environment, the manufacturer must also design the workflow of the order entry process to support large volumes.

Pricing and promotions

Manufacturers that sell to retailers have considerable difficulty in tracking promotions. Orders can arrive from stores in a specific chain for merchandise that is on promotion, but fail to mention the promotion, or fail to order the combination of items that is on promotion (e.g., buy a mop and a broom, get a mop refill and a dustpan free). Or stores can ask for the promotion price outside the time window of the promotion.

Pricing can range from relatively simple to extremely complex, depending on the customers' industry. All pricing involves payment terms, which can remain simple or get very creative. Some customers negotiate allowances (deductions off the price) for:

- Advertising
- Freight
- Defective merchandise
- New stores (for the retail industry)

These allowances can be subject to global caps, in dollars and percentages, by time period. Additionally, some customers ask for rebates based on purchase volume for one or more time periods.

Multiple units of measure

When is a unit of measure not interchangeable? When it has been defined by a customer. One customer might insist that six items be packed in a case. Another customer might insist on 8 or 10 or 12 of the same items in a case. The same scenario can hold true for palletized packages. Additionally, one customer might order the same SKU by several units of measure, including "each," bundle, carton, and pallet. Unit of measure inconsistencies are relatively prevalent in process industries.

Product substitution rules

If the requested product will not be available by the ship date, will the customer allow substitution of another product? If so, what rules have the customer and manufacturer established? The rules will be by SKU and by customer. For example, if a plastic hangar manufacturer is selling multicolored assortments of hangars, the SKU for the assortment might specify the precise quantity of each color allowed, or the SKU could merely specify that the sleeve will contain six hangars of varying colors (letting the manufacturer choose the actual color when they ship the order).

Product allocation and reservation rules

Some MRP II systems allocate finished goods to an order when the order is entered, regardless of the order ship date. This prevents an order that is entered later from using these finished goods, even if its ship date is sooner and additional goods could be procured in time to satisfy the first order. More sophisticated TEI systems do not allocate finished goods until they issue the order to pick for shipment.

Multiple sourcing options for each order line

Usually, each line item on a customer order is shipped from only one location. Most TEI systems easily allow shipment of different line items from different locations. However, a manufacturer might choose to split the shipment on a single line item, shipping partials from two or more locations.

Fully integrated credit checking

Credit checking must be fully integrated with order entry, so that when the order has been completely entered, credit is checked automatically and approved orders go directly to the next step in the customer order fulfillment process (usually shipping or assembly). If the order is being entered while the customer is on the phone, the person entering the order should be immediately notified of any orders that have not been approved for credit reasons so the customer can be informed. Some manufacturers want the TEI system to assume that orders that are on credit hold will be valid orders, and to commit resources to support those orders; other manufacturers want their system to *not* commit resources until the orders are released from credit hold.

Forecast absorption

Forecasts are usually grouped by time periods (frequently a month or quarter). If an order is entered on the first or last day of a time period, how should the manufacturer decide which forecast that order should be allocated against? There are no simple answers to this issue. However, at a minimum, the TEI system should allow the manufacturer to specify the forecast time period into which the order should be placed for forecasting purposes, which might be different from the actual shipment date, and might also be different from the financial month into which the order is credited.

What are the potential benefits of streamlining the order entry process? Reebok reengineered its global order entry and approval process, slashing lead times from 4 to 6 weeks to 24 hours. They used workflow and Internet communications to radically reduce order entry errors.*

Quoting and Promising Deliveries

Quoting and promising deliveries can be done by the salesperson in the customer's office, or anywhere else. More advanced TEI systems support this by:

- Linking the customers' computer directly (probably with e-commerce, using the Internet) to the supplier's computer.
- Providing the logic in the supplier's system so that it can quote prices and delivery dates of stocked items and even valid combinations of configurable items, with no human intervention required unless capacity or material constraints will be violated.

In extremely advanced TEI systems, these delivery quotes fully integrate with logistics and transportation systems, routing the items from the most

---

* Margulis, Ron, "Reebok Runs On a New ERP Path," *Consumer Goods*, March/April 1999, p. 12.

appropriate warehouse or factory to the customer's desired location using the lowest total cost shipping method (combining with other orders going to the same customer, and/or with other orders that can be dropped off a truck before or after the customer's order) that still fulfills the customer's requested date.

There are three important attributes to a quote:

1. *Configuration.* Some manufacturers sell standard finished goods, with little variation in those finished goods. Others can have simple to very complex sets of features and options, with highly complex relationships between some of the features and options. The more complex features and options capabilities are found in TEI packages that target make-to-order and engineer-to-order manufacturers. Consumer package goods and automotive Tier 1 manufacturers, for example, have products that are much simpler, generally requiring only a single tier of options.

2. *Price.* Quoting a price can range from very simple (item list price, less a specified discount percentage for this customer or customer class, based on volume), to extremely complex in a make-to-order or engineer-to-order manufacturer. In a relatively manual environment, where the computer calculates a suggested price quote, then the executives meet to refine it, the computer quote is a suggestion. At the other extreme, when a company allows customers to receive price quotes directly from its computer, without human intervention on its part, the quotes must be totally accurate. This implies that all the data on which they are calculated must also be accurate (such as component prices and labor standards), and that the quoting model itself must be highly refined. In a larger company, this can require the very difficult task of integrating disparate systems that might even be on different computer platforms.

3. *Delivery date.* As difficult as quoting a price can be, it is easy compared to quoting delivery. Some MRP II systems had a feature called "Available To Promise," which compared actual customer orders to scheduled production, and made unpromised production available to whichever customer wanted it. TEI systems now feature "Capable To Promise," which includes not only scheduled production for the item in question, but a calculation of when missing components can actually be made, assuming finite capacity and finite materials. In the future, we expect that "Capable To Promise" calculations will no longer be confined to an individual

manufacturer, but will also be able to include inventories and capacity available at key suppliers. "Capable To Promise" is difficult to add to conventional ERP and MRP II systems, because it uses logic that replaces the traditional MPS, MRP, and CRP. To operate most effectively, it should have been included in the TEI or ERP system when the system was designed.

The ultimate system will not only automatically quote price and delivery accurately, but it will determine the lowest total cost (or highest profit margin) way to fulfill the customer's request, by factoring in detailed plant cost and logistics and distribution information, including:

- Determining the best of the various shipping options, with the actual pickup and delivery times for each.
- Selecting the company's plant that is the best choice for actually manufacturing the item, by checking the actual total manufacturing cost at each plant, plus the availability of capacity (including additional cost for overtime, if available) and materials (and including supplier lead times for materials that need to be replenished).
- Selecting the suppliers that will actually supply the required components and materials, with transportation options.

The ultimate system performs that analysis almost instantaneously, and fully automatically, so that it can respond to an electronic inquiry from a customer or a customer's computer at any time of the day or night.

Virtually all systems allow the manufacturer to convert a quote to a firm customer order with just a few keystrokes. They also provide reminders when a quote is about to expire so that a salesperson can follow up. Most systems allow quotes to include items that are not normal "part numbers," such as engineering time, generic types of raw materials, generic machine time, etc. Quotation systems can integrate with sales and operations planning and/or forecasting and/or Master Production Scheduling to predict future demand. The better quotation management systems include a probability of receiving each order and the due date for the order. Quotations can also be analyzed using Rough-Cut Planning, to determine potential resource constraints.

For assemble-to-order manufacturers, the quoting capability should include intelligent or "rules-based" features and options, and should remember, by customer, what features and options have been previously selected.

Demand Management

Traditionally, companies have treated customer demand very simply: "All customer demand will be fulfilled!" In reality, however, not all customer demand benefits a company equally.* Demand management, therefore, is a formal approach to stratifying customer demand, so that:

- Salespeople are given incentive to increase the "best" type of demand.
- When there are resource shortages, the demand that contributes the least to the manufacturer will absorb the shortage.

The demand manager consolidates demand from *all* sources, as illustrated in Figure 3.7, including:

- Customers (both order entry and order promising, and electronic links such as EDI and e-commerce)
- Forecasts
- Sales and Marketing
- Distribution (including DRP and VMI)
- Interplant demand
- New product development

In smaller companies, the demand manager and the supply manager (the Master Production Scheduler) might be the same person. In larger companies, these positions are typically filled by different individuals.

Demand has traditionally been prioritized by the relative size of the revenue, tempered by the importance of the customer and possibly other factors. This is illustrated by Figure 3.8.** However, demand can be prioritized by a new process known as "Rough-Cut Value Analysis," *** which involves the following process.

---

* Brooks, Rick, "Alienating Customers Isn't Always a Bad Idea, Many Firms Discover," *Wall Street Journal*, January 7, 1999, p. 1.
** Unpublished Figures 3.8 through 3.11 from Stephen Desirey. With permission.
*** Desirey, Stephen and Ozatalay, Savas, "Rough-Cut Value Management: Maximizing Business Value with Supply Capabilities," *1998 International Conference Proceedings*, APICS, Falls Church, VA, 1998.

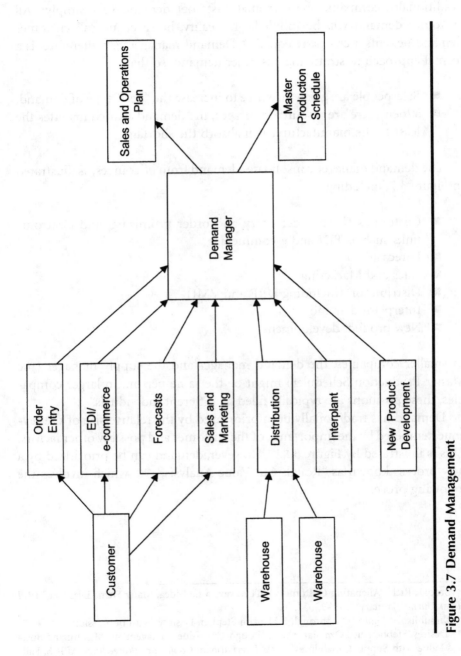

Figure 3.7 Demand Management

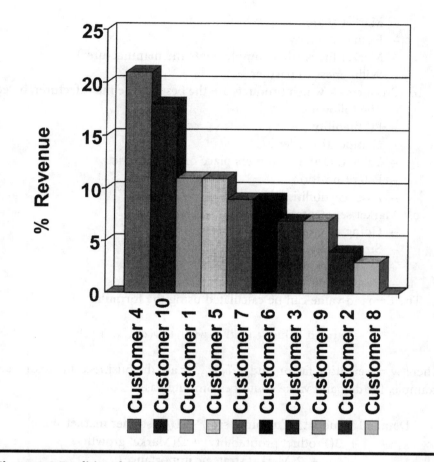

Figure 3.8 Traditional Customer Value Ranking

Step 1 — Determine Demand Value

The first step is to determine demand value for a customer, product, or market. Each of these categories has several subfactors that can be included in the demand value equation.

a. Customer classification — which customers have the most appropriate of the following attributes (to achieve the manufacturer's objectives):
   – Size
   – Technology
   – Sales

        – Market share
        – Business quality
        – Market focus (that complements the manufacturer)
        – Willingness to partner

b. Products — which products are the best for the manufacturer, based on the following:
        – Profitability
        – Competitive offerings
        – Value that the customers place on the product
        – Patent position
        – Asset capabilities

c. Market segmentation — which markets are:
        – Going to grow
        – Strategically important
        – Financially attractive
        – Responding well to the manufacturer's brands

The demand value can be calculated using the formula:

$$\text{Demand Value} = w(a) + w(b) + w(c)\ldots + w(z),$$

where w = weighting factor, and a, b, c, $\ldots$ z are the business subfactors. For example, for demand value could be computed as

$$\text{Demand Value} = .2(\text{Customer size}) + .1(\text{Customer market share})$$
$$+ .3(\text{Product profitability}) + .2(\text{Market growth})$$
$$+ .2(\text{Market strategic importance}).$$

These factors can be put into a spreadsheet. This result of this step is illustrated by Figure 3.9.

Step 2 — Determine Resources Required

The second step, after determining demand value for the customer, product, or market, is to determine the resources required for that same customer, product, or market. Resources can include the following.

a. Capacities, such as:
        – Manufacturing
        – Storage

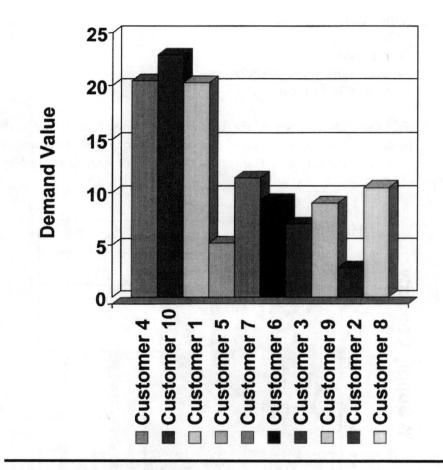

Figure 3.9 Demand Value by Customer

       – Design engineering
       – Material availability
   b. Actual costs to fully satisfy the customer, such as:
       – Manufacturing and materials costs
       – Selling costs
       – Technical support costs
       – Training costs
       – Customization costs
       – Other costs*

---

*   A more complete discussion of costing issues can be found in Chapter 6.

   c. Other constraints, such as:
- Energy
- Emissions
- Regulatory approval processing
- Capital investment

As in Step 1 above, each of the resources can be weighted, and each opportunity put into a spreadsheet to determine the total weighted value of the resources that it requires. The results of this process are illustrated by Figure 3.10.

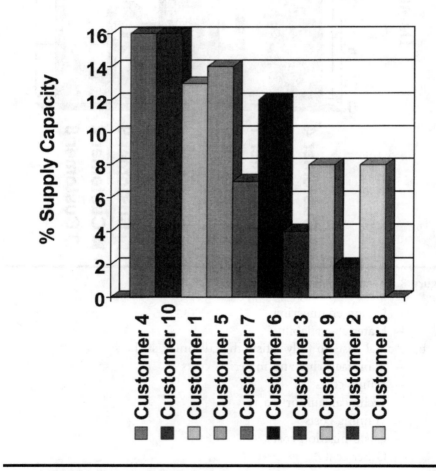

Figure 3.10 Capacity Required by Customer

Step 3 — Rank by Relative Value

The third step is to divide the demand value by the resource requirement for each customer, product, or market, giving the relative value to the manufacturer of each demand, as shown in Figure 3.11. Then rank the demand by relative value. This is illustrated by Table 3.6. Analyze the upper 20% and lower 20% to insure that the process has worked properly. The upper 20% represents the best opportunities. Plan to replace the lower 20% with opportunities with greater value.

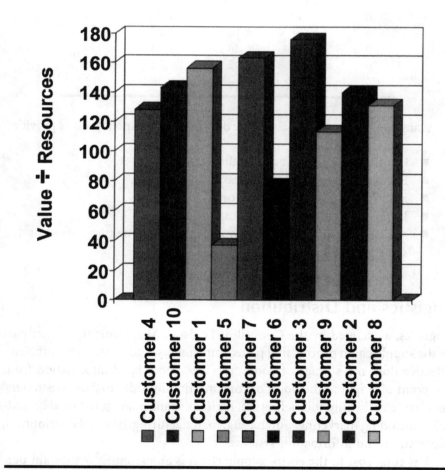

Figure 3.11 Demand Value/Resource Requirements

Table 3.6 Rough-Cut Demand Value by Customer

Customer	Demand Value	Resource Req'ts	Rough-Cut Demand Value	Cum. Resources
3	07	04	1.75	04
7	11	07	1.57	11
1	20	13	1.54	24
10	23	16	1.44	40
2	02.7	02	1.35	42
8	10.5	08	1.31	50
4	20	16	1.25	66
9	09	08	1.13	74
6	09	12	0.75	86
5	05	14	0.36	100

Using rough-cut value analysis, the demand management process provides:

- Control over product availability
- Focus on higher value business
- Smoother product introductions
- Improved ability to respond to change
- A single, integrated, unified, and optimum game plan, based on the same numbers

Logistics and Distribution

Logistics, as defined by the Council of Logistics Management, is "that part of the supply chain process that plans, implements, and controls the efficient, effective flow and storage of goods, services, and related information from the point of origin to the point of consumption in order to meet customers' requirements." Using this definition, logistics spans many functional boundaries, including marketing, purchasing, manufacturing, physical distribution, accounting, and information systems.

The **total cost to the entire supply chain** is an extremely important performance measure for the integrated logistics process. "Total cost" includes all the direct, indirect, hidden, and qualitative costs involved in the movement and storage of materials. Henry Ford created an extremely successful vertical organization that minimized total costs throughout the entire logistics chain (because he owned everything in the chain, except some of the suppliers of basic raw materials, such as rubber, and the retail automobile dealerships). Today's supply chains provide the basis for understanding, and therefore minimizing, the total cost of manufacturing and delivering what the customers want, when they want it, and where they want it.

The **total time through the entire supply chain** is the second extremely important performance measure. In some respects, time can be even more important than cost, because snow shovels just before or during a snow storm are a lot more attractive to the consumer than snow shovels a month later. United Colors of Benetton created a very lucrative market niche by being able to resupply fashion merchandise (clothes) while they were still in season. They used a strategy of providing an initial shipment of clothes of various styles and colors to each store, then rapidly replenishing those items that sold well. Other fashion retailers still typically buy and ship a full season's merchandise on speculation; when one item sells out, it is frequently not replaceable.

Value Added Logistics* (also known as "**Manufacturing Postponement**") is a concept that reorganizes the logistics chain in a more integrated way, in order to lower the total costs (inventory, material handling, and transportation) and to increase service levels. This is based on splitting production into two parts:

- Primary (parts and subassemblies)
- Secondary (assembly and/or customization), which is often combined with distribution activities

Using this concept, a manufacturer can design a distribution and logistics system to manufacture basic components in centralized plants, then assemble those components and modules into customer-specific configurations at a distribution center close to the customer. This minimizes the time to respond to a customer order while also minimizing on-hand inventories. An example might be a personal computer, with a motherboard and other electronic components manufactured in Asia, the bulky components such as the case and keyboard manufactured on each continent for local use, and final configuration assembled to customer order in distribution centers in North

---

* Verwoerd, Wout, "Value Added Logistics: The Answer to Mass Customization," *1998 International Conference Proceedings*, APICS, Falls Church, VA, 1998.

America and Europe. These concepts seem best suited to products with the following characteristics:

- High inventory carrying costs, due to
  - Short product life cycle
  - High value per volume
  - Many configurations
- Short customer lead times
- (Relatively) easy to assemble

This concept is not entirely new; it was used by Henry Ford to save transportation costs (one railcar could hold either the parts for 7 complete Model Ts, or 3 assembled Model Ts.)

A variant of Value-Added Logistics is **merge-in-transit,** which unites components of a shipment from multiple suppliers at a specified merge point located close to the end customer. It seeks to avoid traditional warehousing, in which orders are assembled from inventory in stock for direct shipment to the ultimate customer. Under a merge-in-transit system, "merge points" replace warehouses. These merge points are locations where freight from multiple suppliers is consolidated. No structural inventory is stored at these merge points, but they can provide additional services such as light assembly or inserting instruction manuals into a carton.*

Figure 3.12 shows how logistics information forms the glue that holds the entire supply (or demand) chain together. The supply chain starts with the final product being purchased by the consumer (or the returnable portion of that finished good being sent back to a collection point), back through each transportation link and each company in the process, until it reaches the raw materials as they leave the ground (for example, oil being pumped, or iron ore being mined). Logistics information includes:

- Status of the materials:
  - What stage of the processing cycle, and current owner
  - Expected completion date of that stage
  - Intended final customer or retailer (if known)
  - Anticipated delivery date to final customer, or retailer (if known)

---

* "Merge-In-Transit Yields Benefits," *Logistics Management & Distribution Report,* October 1998.

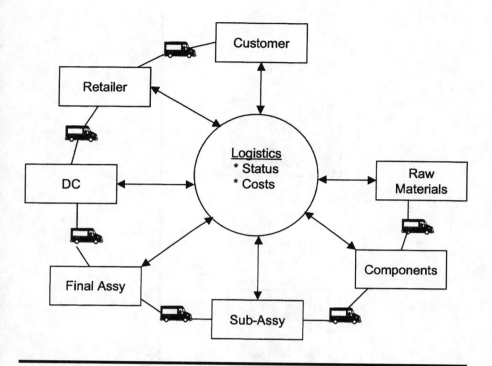

Figure 3.12 Logistics Integration in the Supply Chain

- Information about prior steps:
  - Dates
  - Companies that performed these steps (both manufacturing and distribution)
- Characteristics of materials:
  - Size and weight
  - Shipping and handling requirements
  - Any special requirements (hazardous materials, perishability, etc.)
- Costs:
  - Actual to date
  - Expected at completion

Figure 3.13 illustrates how logistics information integrates with the TEI system of a manufacturer.

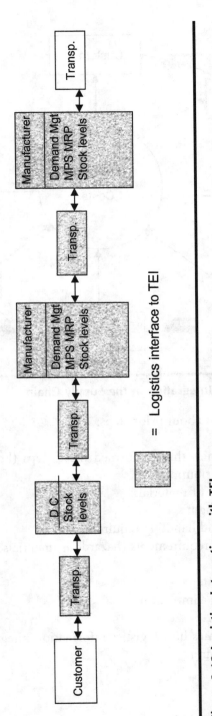

 = Logistics interface to TEI

Figure 3.13 Logistics Integration with TEI

Transportation

Until recently, MRP II and many ERP systems have basically ignored transportation, from both scheduling and cost standpoints. However, pro-active management of transportation alone contributes substantially to many manufacturers' final profit margins. The difference in cost per pound shipped between less than truckload (LTL) and truckload (TL) can be considerable. An MRP II or primitive ERP system calculates the manufacturing due date by back-scheduling from the customer on-dock due date to allow for transit time (which is generally a fixed amount of days.) A fully integrated TEI system can group shipments by destination, filling a truck for multiple stops (even in multiple cities), meeting customer due dates as the lowest possible cost, using the truck ship date as the internal due date for manufacturing. This same type of system can also plan to fill customer orders by shipping from more than one warehouse or plant, again minimizing total cost while insuring on-time delivery to the customer. Finally, a truly state-of-the-art TEI system (such as a supply chain execution system, or a fully integrated Advanced Planning and Scheduling system) compares the costs and time requirements of the various types of shipping (truck, rail, air) with capacity and current and future material availability through all locations, both plant and warehouse, to optimize the manufacturer's profits while insuring on-time delivery. Such a system can also minimize incoming freight costs as well. This type of system is illustrated in Figure 3.14.

Warehouse Management Systems

Warehouse management systems (WMS) increase efficiencies and accuracy of the warehouse functions (Figure 3.15). Swank, Inc., has achieved 100% accuracy in its orders 100% of the time with a new WMS.* It accomplished this by bar-coding the pick ticket as well as each product. When picking an item, a worker scans both the item and the order; the system immediately verifies the accuracy of the pick.

Warehouse management systems track inventories by physical location in the warehouse, by lot number; they can ensure that all inventories shipped to a customer on one order are from the same lot. They can manage order picking in a variety of ways:

---

* "WMS: More Than an Accessory for Swank, Inc.," *Material Handling Engineering,* October 1997.

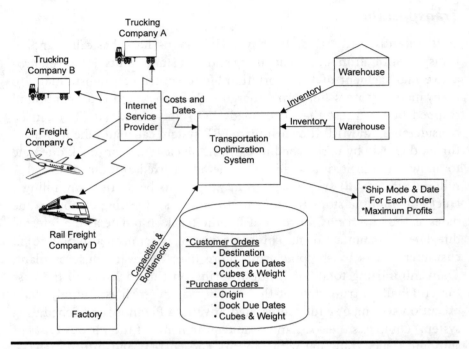

Figure 3.14 Transportation Integration

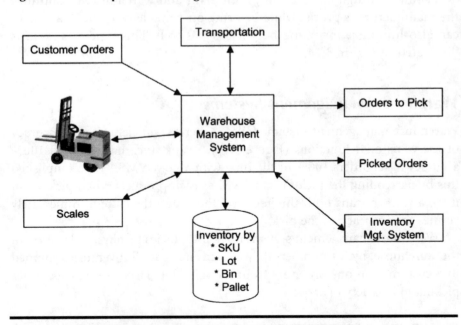

Figure 3.15 Warehouse Management System Integration

- Directing a person to the location of each item to be picked (minimizing travel time, or picking the heaviest items first so they are on the bottom of the box).

- Managing **"pick-to-light,"** by turning on a light at each location that should be picked.

- Directing an **automated storage and retrieval system (AS/RS)** to deliver the items required for a given customer order.

- Directing **"wave picking,"** in which all the items for many outgoing customer orders are pulled from the finished goods shelves in a wave, then sorted into the individual customer orders at a central sorting location.

- Incorporating **checkweigh scales** to weigh each box after picking is complete, and routing any boxes that are more than x underweight or overweight compared to a system-calculated weight to a manual quality check station.

Additionally, warehouse management systems can track each individual pallet by **"license plate,"** track each individual case that is on that pallet, and track each item that is in each case, so that when a pallet moves, the WMS knows the identity and quantity of each SKU that was moved with that pallet.

Radio frequency (RF) terminals are frequently used for communications with the warehouse workers. RF devices can be mounted on fork trucks or pallet jacks, to inform the operator where to go next to put a pallet away or to retrieve a pallet. During the put-away process, the operator can scan the bar code of the receiving location to tell the system where the pallet is being placed; during a pick, the operator can scan the bar code of the location being picked from so the system can verify that the right items and lot numbers are being picked.

Finally, some warehouse management systems incorporate truck loading and traffic routing capabilities, which they use to prioritize loading and to minimize transportation costs. Others interface with transportation software.

As for tailoring the warehouse management system to fit the individual company, newer systems allow the user to define the company's business rules using "natural language," or sentences, or fill out attribute tables; older systems sometimes required lines of code to be written to tailor the software to the using company.

Field Service

Manufacturers that make most consumer products don't need to provide field service. However, those that make capital equipment, both consumer and industrial, need to fully integrate field service information with the entire organization through their TEI system to:

1. Provide accurate and responsive promises to the customer, including:
   - When a service technician will be on-site
   - When the equipment should be repaired, tested, and available again
   - The probable total cost of the repair (if the equipment is not covered by warranty)
2. Ensure optimal customer support by customer service representatives and salespeople, both in the field and in the office. The "front line" of a manufacturer needs to have all customer-related information at their fingertips (and even receive alerts when critical information becomes available) so that they can best serve the customer. If a particular machine has been having problems, the customer will expect the field salesperson or customer service rep to know about the problems and to provide access to the necessary resources to insure that the problems are completely eliminated. If a salesperson calls on the customer and is not aware of field service issues, the salesperson (and the manufacturer) are in very poor position for partnering with the customer. To appease the customer, the salesperson may feel obligated to give away services or something else of value, thereby lowering the company's profits.
   The level of excellence of field service dramatically affects the probability of follow-on sales of additional equipment to the customer, as well as the level of sales of spare parts and maintenance services.
3. Provide maximum communication from salespeople and customer service to the field service organization and technicians. Sometimes salespeople will hear customer comments about reliability, performance, etc., of a machine from someone in the customer's organization, when the customer has not informed the field service organization.
4. Ensure an optimal supply of parts for the field service organization without cannibalizing parts for production and/or other customer service. Field service uses many of the parts, subassemblies, and assemblies that are used in production, which can cause shortages of those parts in production if they are used for repairs (or else cause

customer equipment to be down "waiting for parts," if production keeps the parts).

Field service should be its own independent demand in MPS and MRP, based on the number of pieces of equipment in the field. Some modules inside equipment fail at random intervals, such that demand will be relatively constant over time throughout the life of the equipment in the field. However, other components and modules have a relatively predictable life span, which can be illustrated by a bell-shaped curve (as shown in Figure 3.16). For these components, the manufacturer can be much more proactive in predicting and preparing for future requirements for replacement parts and technicians to install them.

The more advanced systems include MBTF (mean time between failure) calculations for each major module or component of each piece of equipment in the field to forecast requirements for spare parts and trained technicians to install those parts. For example, a manufacturer of robots that stuff electronic components onto circuit boards can track the number of their robots still in service, by year manufactured and

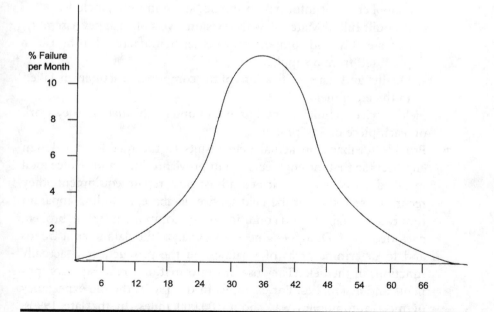

Figure 3.16 Life Span of Electric Motors

model number. They can track the number of new systems sold, old systems retired, and the number of replacement parts, such as electric motors and hydraulic pumps, used each year. They can forecast the number of replacement parts required for the future, both short-term and long-term, based on the MTBF of those items and projected number of robots in use, by model and year manufactured. These techniques can also project the numbers of field service technicians and their required training level, so that the manufacturer can fully support its customers. Relying on historical data and trend analysis can put the manufacturer in a very difficult position of inadequately trained service technicians and insufficient service parts. The day-to-day inventories for field service spares can be managed by the same kanban techniques as initial manufacturing.

5. Provide the actual "as-built" information on the equipment that the technicians are servicing. A field technician's nightmare (even worse than unavailability of parts) is not having any idea what components are actually in a machine that needs service. The initial information about the model numbers of the components *must* come from the manufacturer, including information from both the manufacturer and key suppliers. This information should, at a minimum, include:

    – As-built Bill of Material, with revision levels of each key assembly, subassembly, and component, whether manufactured in-house or procured from a supplier.
    – Quality and test specifications of the components actually installed in the equipment.

    Field service technicians maintain and update this data as they work on each piece of equipment.

6. Provide feedback on actual field results to the quality and design engineers so that the engineers can improve products and reduce total installed costs. As technicians adjust and repair equipment, they record these facts into the field service database, including apparent root cause of failure, and condition of the component (worn, broken, corroded, etc.). Design engineers can analyze the data to spot trends and to determine areas of weakness in the product, as it actually functions in the field. They use this information to redesign components and assemblies. For example, in the 1960s, the life expectancy of most automobiles was about 100,000 miles. In the late 1990s, automobiles were routinely lasting well past 150,000 miles, and a reasonable percentage were passing 200,000 miles and more. Finally, this information can be passed to suppliers as well.

7. Integrate with warranty tracking information on supplied components. If a supplied component fails under warranty, the supplier can be notified to provide replacement components. This information can have significant financial importance.
8. Integrate with customer maintenance contracts, so that the manufacturer can invoice the customer for repairs that are outside the maintenance agreement and/or manufacturer's warranty.
9. Integrate with accounting, for tracking the cost of maintaining each piece of equipment compared to the warranty reserve and maintenance contract revenues for that equipment.
10. Integrate with Human Resources (HR) with respect to projected staffing levels and training requirements for new and existing technicians. HR can also track the certifications of the technicians to ensure that they remain current.

"Field service" as a category also includes depot repair, and repair and refurbishment at a manufacturer's facility. The departments and functions that field service integrates with are shown in Figure 3.17.

Managing field service includes the following functions:

- Taking service calls at the call center, with the goal of returning the customer's equipment to full and productive service as quickly and inexpensively as possible. This involves:
  - Logging the calls into the call database
  - Determining the priority of the call
  - Asking the symptoms and diagnosing the possible or probable cause(s)
- Dispatching the correct technician(s). This can be a true balancing act, depending on the priority of the call and the availability of:
  - Technicians trained on the specific equipment and problem
  - Diagnostic equipment
  - Replacement parts
- Monitoring each piece of equipment being maintained, by serial number, with the initial as-built configuration, updated by each service call and other maintenance.
- Managing replacement parts inventories, including:
  - Forecasting future requirements for service parts
  - Monitoring the number of times a specific serial-numbered item (e.g., electric motor or circuit board) has been repaired or rebuilt. After a specific number of rebuilds, the item is scrapped

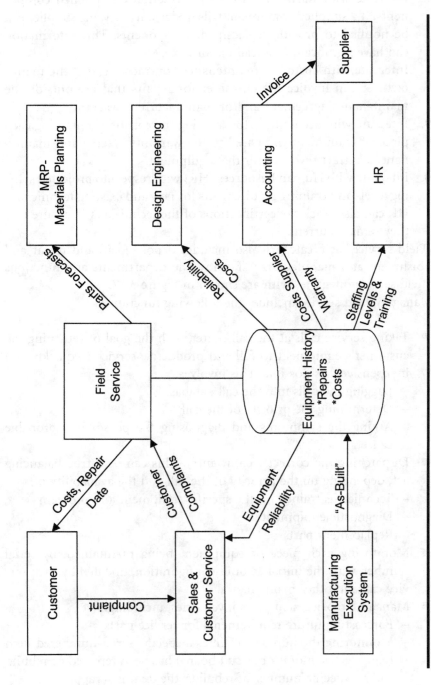

Figure 3.17 Field Service Integration

References

Alexander, Steve, "Printer Manufacturer Tracks Your Inventory," *Computerworld*, November 16, 1998.

Andel, Tom, "Manage Inventory, Own Information," *Transportation & Distribution*, May 1, 1996.

Association for Service Managers International (www.afsmi.org).

Bernstein, Ralph, "Premium Forecasting Cuts OJ Inventory," *Consumer Goods*, January/February 1999.

Bhote, Keki R., *Beyond Customer Satisfaction to Customer Loyalty*, 1996.

Carlberg, Ulf Casten, "Integrated Order Fulfillment as ECR's Enabling Application," *1998 International Conference Proceedings*, APICS, Falls Church, VA, 1998.

Chase, Charles W., "Selecting the Appropriate Forecasting Method," *Journal of Business Forecasting*, Fall 1997.

Copacino, William C., *Supply Chain Management: The Basics and Beyond*, St. Lucie Press, Boca Raton, FL, 1997.

Council of Logistics Management, Oak Brook, IL www.clm1.org.

Desirey, Stephen and Ozatalay, Savas, "Rough-Cut Value Management: Maximizing Business Value with Supply Capabilities," *1998 Conference Proceedings*, APICS, Falls Church, VA, 1998.

Eighmy, Scott and Wantuck, Ken, "Eight Weeks to Two Days: The ATP Story," *1996 Conference Proceedings*, APICS, Falls Church, VA, 1996.

Ford, Henry, *Today and Tomorrow*, Doubleday, 1926, Productivity Press special reprint edition, Cambridge, MA, 1988.

Fox, Mary Lou, "Integrating Vendor-Managed Inventory into Supply Chain Decision-Making," *1996 Conference Proceedings*, APICS, Falls Church, VA, 1996.

Fuss, Norman, "Voice of the Customer: Oxymoron or Competitive Edge?" *APICS Seminar I Proceedings, 1998*. (Available through BDO Siedman, New York, NY.)

Langenwalter, Gary A., "Why Use Repetitive? For the Results!" *1998 Conference Proceedings*, APICS, Falls Church, VA, 1998.

Margulis, Ron, "Reebok Runs On a New ERP Path," *Consumer Goods*, March/April 1999.

Martin, A. J., *Distribution Resources Planning*, Oliver Wight, Essex Junction, VT, 1990.

"Merge-In-Transit Yields Benefits," *Logistics Management & Distribution Report*, October 1998.

"New Accuracy Gains for Gerber," *Material Handling Engineering*, August 1997.

Parke, Shep, "Avoiding the Unseen Perils of Sales Technology," *Sales & Field Force Automation*, November 1998.

Schwind, Gene F., "A Systems Approach to Docks and Cross Docking," *Material Handling Engineering*, February 1, 1996.

Supply Chain Council, AMR Research, http://www.supply-chain.com.

Verwoerd, Wout, "Value Added Logistics: The Answer to Mass Customization," *1998 International Conference Proceedings*, APICS, Falls Church, VA, 1998.

"WMS: More Than an Accessory for Swank, Inc.," *Material Handling Engineering*, October 1997.

4 Engineering Integration

MRP II systems traditionally interfaced (meaning unintelligent data transfer) with engineering design systems to receive BOM and routing information. However, the interface was relatively crude and did not pass critical information back to the engineering design systems. A product's cost (90%) is determined during the design cycle; its quality characteristics are also fundamentally determined during product design and process design. A fully integrated TEI (Total Enterprise Integration) system includes:

- The design process
- Product phase-out
- Product Data Management
- Integrating with customers
- Integrating with suppliers
- Integrating with the rest of the company
- Project management

How the engineering disciplines integrate with the rest of a Total Enterprise Integration system is shown in Figure 4.1.

The differences between ERP and TEI systems, with respect to engineering, are illustrated in Figure 4.2. TEI encompasses all the functions in Figure 4.2; ERP systems typically include only those functions shaded in gray.

Design Process

Any product design is a compromise of many requirements that frequently conflict with each other. *All* facets of the product design process integrate to TEI.

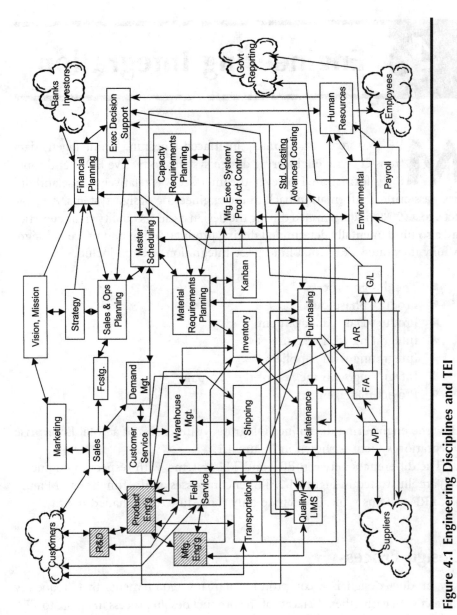

Figure 4.1 Engineering Disciplines and TEI

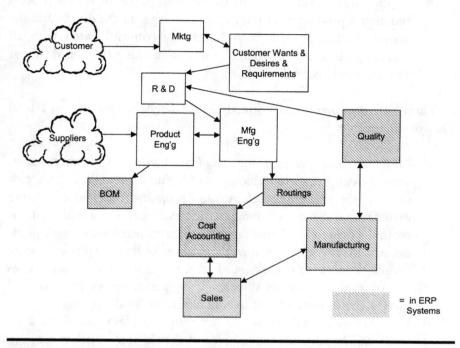

Figure 4.2 Engineering in TEI vs ERP

The product design process traditionally includes some activities that directly relate to ERP and some that do not. Those that are directly ERP-related include:

■ *Projected manufacturing cost* — This is determined by **cost account-ing,** based on the bill of materials, routings (or recipes), and cost estimates for purchased items and services. After adding SG&A (sales, general, and administrative) expenses and other costs, the total prod-uct cost, plus margin, must not exceed the projected sales price. If it does, the product is not economically viable as designed.

■ *Projected production volumes* — Planners can use **Rough-Cut Resource Planning** and/or **Capacity Requirements Planning** and/or **Advanced Planning and Scheduling** to determine the effect of the projected volumes on existing and projected capacities. If capacities will be exceeded, the projected manufacturing costs will probably increase due to the requirement to obtain additional capacity inter-nally and/or externally.

- *Engineering changes* — During the latter stages of the release process and after a product has been released, changes to the design and the manufacturing process must be clearly communicated with all affected parties, and the changes must be carefully controlled so that they are implemented correctly.

Those activities that are not directly ERP-related, but are part of a total TEI system, include:

- *Customer requirements (features and functions)* — Customers sometimes provide detailed specifications of requirements. Other times, customers provide only sketchy requirements information. Some manufacturers send their design engineers to spend time with customers in the field to learn how they actually use the manufacturer's product, and to observe the customer's processes so that the product can be revised to meet their true needs better. Frequently, the customer does not comprehend the possibilities of a manufacturer's product, and therefore does not even ask the manufacturer for the change.
- *Customer wants and desires* — Marketing provides most of this data. Some can be acquired using Voice of the Customer; other data can come from market research and surveys, such as focus groups. Engineers on site can also gather this information.
- *Technical functionality, based on engineering design* — This can include the types of engineering specific to a company, such as mechanical, chemical, electrical, electronics, biological, etc.
- *Manufacturing capabilities* — The Design for Manufacturability movement in the 1980s and 1990s was a reaction to product designs that could not be built on the shop floor or by suppliers. When this author visited the design engineering department of a manufacturer in the mid-1980s, one of the design engineers announced proudly that he had been with the company 15 years, and had "never once set foot on that filthy factory floor!" The author was not surprised, when touring the floor a bit later, to hear that the manufacturing workers had absolutely no respect for that particular engineer, because his designs were usually difficult or impossible to build.
- *Supplier capabilities* — The concept of Design for Manufacturability can be extended to the key suppliers in the supplier base. However, this extension requires partnering with suppliers, rather than the traditional arms-length, price-focused relationship that is still quite common.

Some manufacturers send their engineers to spend extensive time with their key suppliers. These visits are useful to both assess the capabilities of the supplier and also to exchange expertise that both the supplier and manufacturer possess. The supplier's expertise in its manufacturing process and capabilities may lead to better design decisions. The manufacturer's expertise with the customer's product requirements helps the supplier determine the best way to meet them. Not everything can be expressed easily on a drawing or written document. In order to make this work effectively, both parties must be willing to educate the other and learn from the other. Supplier capabilities include:

- Technical manufacturing capability — does the supplier have and know how to effectively use the technology to produce a product that meets all the needs and expectations? Is the supplier open to new technologies?
- Manufacturing capacity — can the supplier support the intended volumes? What if the required volume doubles or triples? What if it is only 50% of forecast — will the supplier's cost increase considerably?

- *Projected sales price* — This is determined by Marketing based on market research and existing products (both the manufacturer's and competitors').
- *The tradeoffs* between state-of-the art capabilities and features vs. affordability, reliability, and manufacturability. These tradeoffs reflect the vision and identity of the manufacturer, as well as the desires of the customer base.
- *Projected cost for support in the field,* or for warranty replacements — This ties to field service. Some manufacturers budget warranty repair costs into the design engineering department. If the product requires less than expected warranty service, design engineering keeps the unused warranty funds. However, if warranty expenses exceed expectations, the design engineering budget has to make up for the shortfall.
- *Projected time to manufacture/time to respond to a customer order* — This ties to product flow throughout the supply chain.
- *Projected future upgrade paths* (how to make this into the next model with minimal time and expense).
- *Projected cost of recycling* from customers, and re-using the recycled or returned products.

Concurrent Engineering

Concurrent Engineering involves all departments and functions in design sessions from the start, thereby dramatically reducing the elapsed design time and allowing a company to bring its product to market much more quickly. The radical and highly successful Ford Taurus was one of the first North American products that was designed using Concurrent Engineering.

In large companies, product design was traditionally a sequential exercise, with each department receiving information from the prior department, performing its function, then passing the information to the next department. This method has three serious drawbacks:

1. The total elapsed time is very long due to the sequential processing approach and the delays at the start of each process.
2. When a downstream department wants to suggest changes to the design, the time and cost of those changes is very high, creating economic incentives to avoid making changes, thereby causing total manufacturing costs to increase, and customer satisfaction to decrease.
3. None of the departments has real ownership of the process or the end result. They have no compelling reason to ensure that the entire information packet is error-free when it leaves their department. This environment fosters a "just doing my job" attitude.

Several studies have shown that time to market is much more important for long-term product profitability than staying on budget. For example, a McKinsey study found that a 6-month delay in entering a market (to avoid budget overruns) would result in a 33% reduction in after-tax profit over the lifetime of the product. The 6-month delay is five times more costly than a 50% development-cost overrun, and about 30% more costly than having production costs 10% over budget, as illustrated by Figure 4.3.*

Concurrent Engineering has another major advantage — it can substantially reduce the total manufacturing and procurement cost of a product. 85% of the total life-cycle costs of a product is determined in the design stage, and an additional 10% is determined before production ever commences.** The

---

* Blackburn, Joseph D., "Time-Based Competition," in *Strategic Manufacturing: Dynamic New Directions for the 1990s*, Patricia E. Moody, editor, Business One/Irwin, Homewood, IL, 1990, p. 196.
** Mather, Hal, "Strategic Logistics — A Total Company Focus," in *Strategic Manufacturing: Dynamic New Directions for the 1990s*, Patricia E. Moody, editor, Business One/Irwin, Homewood, IL, 1990.

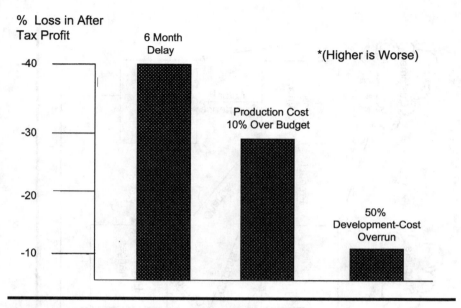

Figure 4.3 Effect on Profit of Delay vs. Cost Overrun

feedback from manufacturing professionals (and, hopefully, key suppliers), field service professionals, and others in a Concurrent Engineering environment can contribute to a significantly lower total life-cycle cost for a product.

Design Stages

The design process can be subdivided into seven stages, as illustrated in Figure 4.4. However, these stages should function concurrently or in parallel to minimize the total time to bring a product to market.

The stages are actually an infinite loop, because the initial design creates an initial product, which is bought and used by customers, who provide feedback for improvement, causing a revised product to start through the design process. For Figure 4.5 to illustrate this concept, the reader should copy it, cut the left and right margins off the copy, then form a cylinder by attaching the left and right edges of the diagram. One example is the Hewlett-Packard family of LaserJet printers. The initial LaserJet was superseded by a LaserJet II, then a LaserJet III, then an ever-increasing family of printers including slower (4 pages per minute), lower-cost "personal" printers, the standard 8 pages per minute midrange, and workhorse network printers of 17 pages per minute.

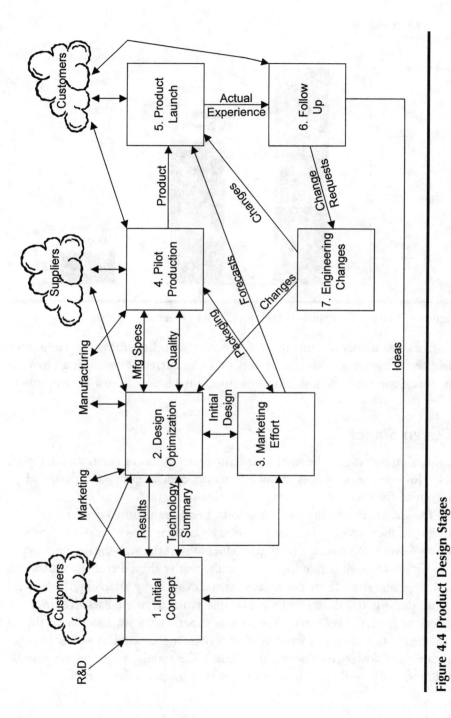

Figure 4.4 Product Design Stages

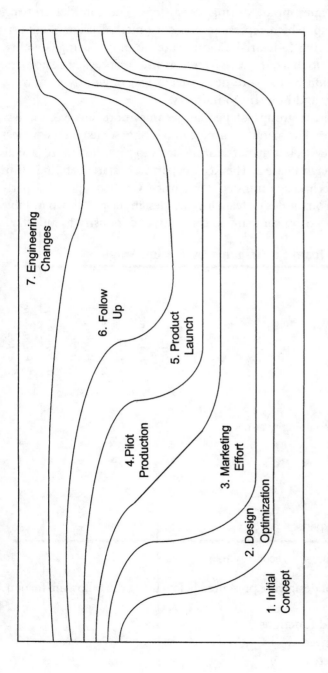

Figure 4.5 Product Design Continuum

7. Engineering Changes

6. Follow Up

5. Product Launch

4. Pilot Production

3. Marketing Effort

2. Design Optimization

1. Initial Concept

A core team performs the entire design process, supplemented by additional viewpoints as appropriate during some steps. The core design team can include Marketing, which represents the customers, Design Engineering/R&D, Manufacturing/Industrial Engineering, Manufacturing, Quality, Purchasing, and key suppliers; the core team can also include key customers. The actual composition of the core design team will obviously vary from company to company and industry to industry.

Additionally, different groups of people become more involved or less involved in these phases. The manufacturing group is represented on the project team throughout the cycle, but manufacturing starts to get much more heavily involved partway through Phase 2. The R&D department starts handing off in the pilot when the "technology transfer" takes place. One example of departmental representation on the design team for each design stage is shown in Table 4.1 (this again will vary from company to company, and industry to industry).

Table 4.1 Design Team Participants by Design Stage

	1. Initial Concept	2. Design Optimize	3. Marketing	4. Pilot Production	5. Product Launch	6. Follow Up	7. Engineering Changes
Marketing	x	x	x	+	x	x	+
Design Engineering	x	x	+	+	+	x	x
Manufacturing/Industrial Engineering	+	x		x	x	+	x
Manufacturing	+	+		x	x	+	+
Quality	+	+		x	+	x	+
Purchasing	+	+		+	+	+	
Key Customers	x	x	x	+	x	x	x
Key Suppliers	+	+		+	x	x	+
Outside Technical Experts	+	+			+		+

Notes: x = primary role; + = secondary role.

The seven stages of design are presented below using the following format:

- Objectives and functions
- Information needed
- Information created
- Participants

Stage 1: Initial Concept/Proof of Technology

Objectives and functions — In this stage the basic product functions are defined, and the technology issues are worked out. The organization with primary responsibility for defining product functions can be marketing, R&D or other product development engineering groups, or a combination of these groups.

Marketing integrates requests from customers and its market research to be used to define the basic functions of a new product, along with some rough cost parameters. Engineers and scientists design and integrate the chemistry, electronics, mechanical functions, etc., as a first attempt to fill the need. This can include computer-generated models and/or physical mockups. The information needed and created in this phase is illustrated in Figure 4.6.

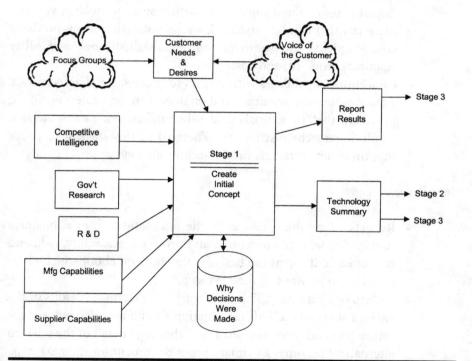

Figure 4.6 Stage 1 — Initial Concept

Information needed —

1. Desired features and functions. These can come from a variety of sources:
   - Focus groups
   - Voice of the Customer

– Customer visits by marketing and/or engineering
– Marketing awareness
– Competitive intelligence
– In-house research
– University and/or government research

Desired features and functions can ideally be stored in a product idea database. The ideas, cross-indexed by all kinds of attributes such as type of problem being solved, types of materials used, types of processes involved, are important. Equally important, however, is the data concerning how and why the ideas and specifications came into being.

2. The capabilities of manufacturing processes, both in-house and suppliers':
   – Actual demonstrated capabilities with respect to quality, volume, materials that can be processed, waste materials and by-products created, yields, environment required, skilled labor and other resources required, and cost.
   – Conceptual capabilities with respect to those same characteristics. This is where the scientists and engineers incorporate new ideas, processes that have worked in other industries, new materials, revolutionary chemistries, etc. The goal of this stage is to prove that these new concepts can be technically viable.

Information created —

■ Reports of results. This ranks the alternatives from a business standpoint, with the outcomes and projected scalability, risk, and cost of each. It forms the basis for the decision about which alternative(s) to forward to the next step.

■ Technology summary. This summarizes the technical results of the various alternatives. This information should be cross-indexed for future reference and analysis. The technology detail of the selected alternatives becomes a primary input document for the next step.

■ Why decisions were made. This database is maintained by engineering, because knowing "why" can sometimes be more critical than the decision itself. Six months after a decision has been made, remembering *why* a specific decision was made can be difficult, if not impossible.

Participants — The core design team, potentially supplemented by additional key customers, suppliers, and/or outside technical expertise.

Stage 2: Design optimization

Objectives and functions — Optimizing the compromise. The product is designed for its intended life cycle in the company's product line. The goal in this stage is to create a product design that optimizes the compromises between competing elements. The design, as it leaves this stage, must meet several basic criteria:

- Customer needs — the product will help customers do their jobs better, faster, easier. There is a clear reason why customers will want the product, and they will pay the projected selling price because of those benefits.
- Technical viability — The various functions that comprise the final product can coexist and/or work together, and these technologies will survive in the field as the product will actually be used by customers. For example, a screwdriver is used by customers not only to drive screws, but to pry (e.g., remove paint can lids), to punch holes, to score surfaces, as a hammer (using the handle) and as a shim, including the handle.
- Volume — the technology will support projected manufacturing volumes, and is sufficiently scalable that it can support dramatic changes to sales forecasts, both up and down.
- Manufacturability — preferably using existing manufacturing processes. It can also be a member of an existing product family, using some common modules, subassemblies, or components.
- Cost-effectiveness — the total manufacturing cost, including purchased components, meets the budget expectations.
- Environment:
  - Internal — using environmentally friendly processes and materials
  - External — designed to be reusable, refillable, returnable, or recyclable
- Life cycle — The product will have sufficient features and functions to be attractive to customers for its intended life cycle, and is setting the stage for the next generation of products that will follow.

This stage of the design concept requires information from Stage 1 and other sources, and provides information for Stages 3 and beyond, as shown in Figure 4.7.

Information needed — The information that is needed for the design team to create the most effective design comes from a variety of sources, including:

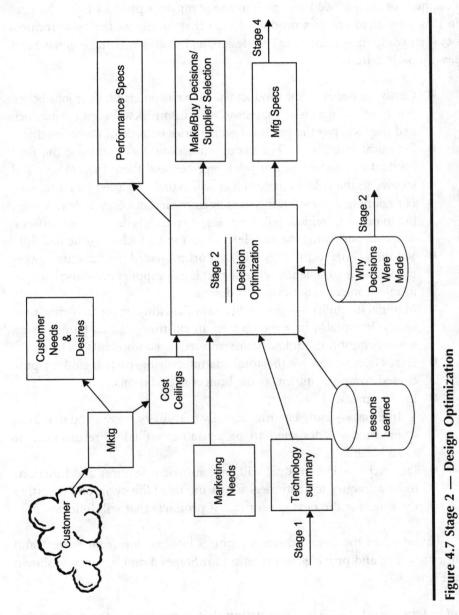

Figure 4.7 Stage 2 — Design Optimization

- Technology summary — the main output from Stage 1. During the design optimization stage, the team might discover critical drawbacks or additional issues with the technology that was originally chosen in the initial concept stage. Then the scientists and engineers would review their findings to propose other alternatives.
- Customer needs — these were also initially addressed in the design optimization stage, but can be refined during this stage by talking with customers directly and/or by using focus groups. One of the more difficult questions is what different kinds of applications customers might eventually use the product for. The screwdriver is again a superb example. For totally new products, customer perceptions may carry less weight. For example, the *New York Times* announcement of the invention of the transistor, buried in a small article in the middle of the paper, said that it might be useful in hearing aids.
- Marketing needs — not only must the product meet customer needs, it must also be able to be sold to the customers. Marketing and sales can each define features, functions, specifications, etc., that will help them market and sell the product.
- Cost ceilings — how much are customers willing to pay for the product? What are they paying for similar products? If the product, as proposed, appears to require a selling price higher than customer research anticipated, marketing can reassess the elasticity of the market.
- Lessons learned — this database contains lessons learned from designing and launching previous new products. As the database grows, it becomes invaluable, because it encapsulates the wisdom of the company's experience.

Information created — Stage 2 creates information that is much more detailed than Stage 1.

- High-level product performance specifications, including the performance specifications themselves and the intended (and potential) uses for the product.
  1. Critical performance specifications can include the following:
     - Expected life in use
     - Shelf life
     - Size
     - Look and feel

-   Projected cost and selling price
2. Intended and potential uses:
    -   How will the customer use the product? How will the customer *abuse* the product (for example, a screwdriver)?
    -   What is included with the product? Batteries? Spare parts?
    -   Where will the product be used (outside vs. inside, industrial vs. consumer)? What environments (temperature, light, vapors, vibration, etc.) will be detrimental to the product? For example, home stereos are usually used in nonhostile environments. In contrast, car stereos are built into automobiles, which have vibration and much wider fluctuations in temperature and humidity.
    -   How skillful and knowledgeable will the average user be?

■ Make/buy decisions. Which manufacturing functions will be performed in-house, at other plants of our same company, and outside at suppliers? Do these facilities have the skills, equipment, and capacity required?

■ Manufacturing specifications (both in-house or outside). These are the initial specifications, including both engineering drawings (blueprints) and process control information. These specifications define attributes, target or goal measurement for each attribute, and acceptable tolerances.

■ Supplier choice. As suppliers are selected, the manufacturer starts preparing the supplier to succeed by providing:
    – Preliminary drawings, so that the supplier can start procuring needed raw materials and any other long lead time resource.
    – Process control information.
    – Tooling — whether it is financed and supplied by the manufacturer or the supplier, tooling is frequently a long lead time resource that might require immediate procurement. Alternatively, the process could start with "temporary" tooling, to be replaced by more permanent tooling after a few months.

■ Why decisions were made. This database, coupled with the product request database, enables the decisions based on assumptions or specific technology to be reviewed. Engineering maintains this database.

Participants — The core design team, with marketing, design engineering/R&D, and manufacturing/industrial engineering having primary roles. The team can be supplemented by sales, key customers, and outside technical experts.

Stage 3: Marketing effort (in parallel with Step 2, design optimization)

Objectives and function — Marketing defines the product iteratively by showing samples, mock-ups, etc., to bellwether sources (such as selected customers, focus groups) to learn their reaction and get ideas for improvement. Marketing's focus includes the following:

- Look and feel of the product, including the ergonomics that affect the user. One example of a more ergonomic version of a very common device is a "natural" keyboard for a computer, which reduces wrist strain, although it looks unconventional.
- Packaging. The packaging can be more important in selling the product than the product itself, especially for consumer packaged goods. The packaging needs to protect the product, attract the customer's attention, and be informative and persuasive enough for the customer to purchase. Packaging is capable of delaying product launch due to long lead times.
- Marketplace positioning:
  - How will this product be positioned in comparison with other company products? If it replaces existing products, what should the upgrade path for the customers be? If it supplements existing products, will it cannibalize their sales?
  - How will it be positioned with respect to existing and projected competitive products?

The information required and provided by this stage is illustrated in Figure 4.8.

Information needed —

- Technology summary from Stage 1.
- Report of results from Stage 1.
- Information about current and future competitive products, from marketing.

Information created —

- Additional specifications for the product, which are used in pilot production.

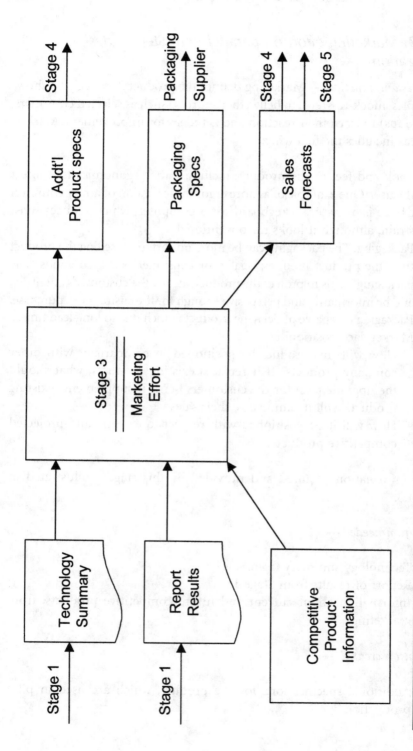

Figure 4.8 Stage 3 — Marketing Effort

- Additional specifications for packaging, which are given to the packaging supplier.
- Revised sales forecasts.

Participants — The primary participants are marketing and key customers, supplemented by sales and design engineers/R&D.

Stage 4: Pilot production

Objectives and functions — This stage proves the product, the manufacturing process, and the technical capabilities of the product. In some companies, the R&D group hands off the design to Manufacturing via a "**technology transfer**" process when the pilot proves itself:

- Proving the product itself. Marketing takes early versions to customers for field testing and suggestions. Marketing and/or Engineering watch the customers use the product, listen as customers compare the product to other products, and ask questions to help understand additional features and functions or changes to existing features and functions that would make this product more attractive to customers.
- Proving the manufacturing process. The plant and suppliers learn how to make the product cost effectively and so that it meets specifications. They work the kinks out of the raw material supply systems, the quality management systems, the material handling systems, and the equipment itself. They propose changes to the product, the materials, and the manufacturing processes. They focus on creating the infrastructure that can ramp up volume to meet projected customer demand.
- Proving the technical capabilities of the product. Engineering watches how the product reacts to actual field use (and some abuse), to verify their assumptions about usage, environment, and skill level of customers. Engineering also observes how well the technology functions in a "real-world" environment.

The information required and provided by this stage is illustrated in Figure 4.9.

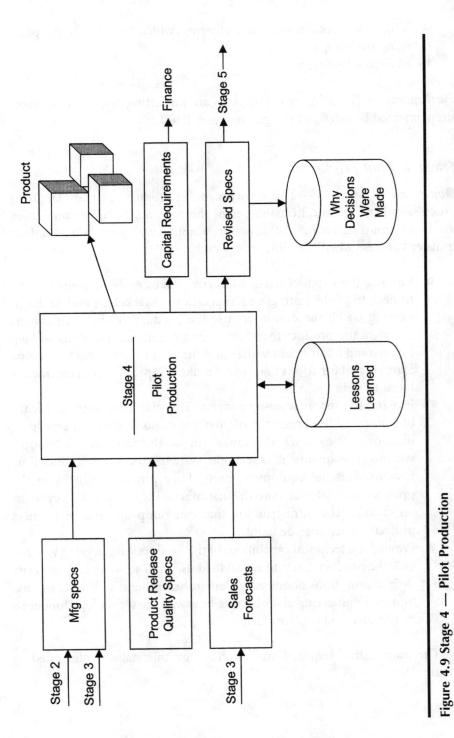

Figure 4.9 Stage 4 — Pilot Production

Information needed — Includes the following:

- Manufacturing specifications from industrial/manufacturing engineering, such as setup procedures, tools, and run rates.
- Product release/quality criteria from design engineering, quality, and manufacturing engineering, such as:
  - Tolerances and acceptability criteria for each critical attribute
  - Control charts
  - Sampling plans
- Sales forecasts, including dates and quantities at assumed pricing levels, from marketing.

Information created — Includes the following:

- Product itself — The pilot process creates initial versions of the product for trial use by customers and field testing by engineers.
- Lessons learned during manufacturing — As the plant and suppliers actually make the product and its components, they learn how to build it and test it more efficiently.
- Capital requirements — for financing full-scale production.

Participants — The core team with manufacturing, manufacturing/industrial engineering, and quality having primary roles, supplemented by additional representatives from manufacturing, plus key customers.

Stage 5: Product Launch

Objectives and functions — This stage manufactures product to be sold to customers. The product can be launched using a limited-release phase-in approach, or a full-scale approach.

1. Limited release. The product is available to a smaller market, or with otherwise limited sales. The advantages to this approach are that it defers the requirement for investing in additional capacity, and it allows the feedback from the field to change the product design and/or manufacturing methodologies before major investments have to be committed. The disadvantage is that it provides time for competitors to copy, and even to improve on, the product.

2. Full-scale release. This strategy provides product throughout the entire distribution area on the first day. The advantages to this approach are that it can overwhelm the competition and make advertising efforts much more effective. The obvious disadvantages are the increased initial resources (financial and time) and coordination required, thereby increasing the risk, and the loss of ability to fine-tune the product.

The information required and provided by this stage is illustrated in Figure 4.10.

Information needed — The information needed is that of full-scale production of a product. This includes:

- Revised forecasts for product sales, from marketing.
- Capacity constraints at bottleneck processes in-house plants and at suppliers, (and alternatives, with cost and quality considerations) from manufacturing and purchasing.
- Material constraints, from materials planning and purchasing.
- Other resource constraints (e.g., packaging in the volumes required), from materials planning and master scheduling.
- Capital constraints, limiting investment in plant and equipment and advertising.
- Revised designs and specifications, from design engineering.
- Regulatory clearance, if necessary.

Information created —

- Production plans, which feed the TEI systems so that it can plan requirements and schedules for materials, capacity, and other resources.
- Product launch plans, including advertising, trade shows, and promotions.

Participants —

- The core team, with Marketing, Manufacturing/Industrial Engineering, and Manufacturing assuming the primary roles.
- Other essential contributors include key customers, key suppliers, and outside technical experts.

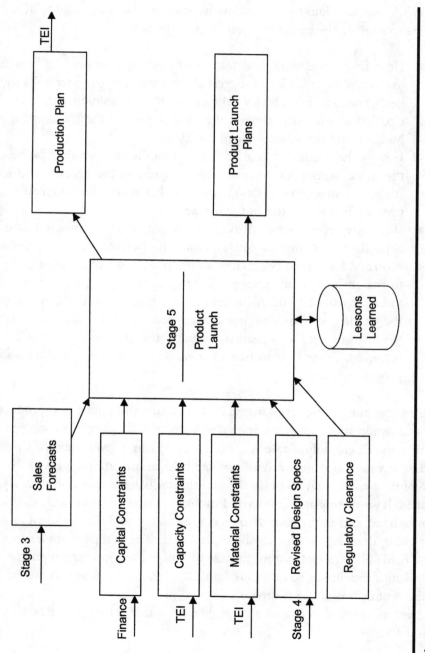

Figure 4.10 Stage 5 — Product Launch

Stage 6: Follow-up

Objectives and functions — The follow-up stage analyzes the results of the process to provide the basis for future improvements:

- How did process work? The team meets shortly after product launch to discuss the process and suggest changes and improvements for the next time. The team reviews the entire process, including the participation of each department, the effectiveness of the meetings, the budgets, and the schedules and due dates.
- How is the product doing? In 3 to 6 months after product launch, the team meets again to review the progress of the product and to suggest changes to the design process that would have helped the product perform better in the market.
- Warranty returns and customer complaints. The ultimate test of a product is customer satisfaction. The percentage of products returned for warranty service can be tracked, by underlying cause, to determine which components or manufacturing processes need to be improved to decrease field failure rates. This ties directly to the quality system and the design process. Likewise, customer suggestions and complaints, even if the product itself is not returned, are a rich source of ideas for continued product and process improvement.

One computer peripherals manufacturer started shipping a new product line at a rapidly increasing rate. Several months later, they became concerned because their field failure rate was exceeding 5% in a given month. Upon further investigation, they realized that the field failure rate was greater than 20% of the product shipments in the month in which the failed product was shipped! It was taking approximately 1 month to install the product, a second month to fail, and a third month to report the failure, and the shipment rates kept rising dramatically during those 3 months. The company understood that a field failure rate of that magnitude would quickly ruin their reputation for technical excellence, so they took immediate and direct action to find and fix the root causes of the failures.

The information required and provided by this stage is illustrated in Figure 4.11.

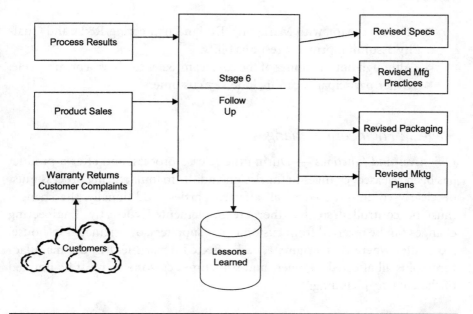

Figure 4.11 Stage 6 — Product Follow-up

Information needed —

- Results of the design process
- Actual product sales, from marketing
- Warranty returns, from the marketing, with reasons for failure from quality
- Customer complaints and suggestions, from marketing and sales

Information created —

- Revised product specifications
- Revised manufacturing practices
- Revised packaging
- Revised marketing plans
- Lessons learned

Participants —

- The core team, with Marketing, Design Engineering/R&D, and Quality assuming primary responsibility.
- Although not a member of the core team, Sales can have a primary role.
- Other participants can include key customers.

Stage 7: Engineering changes

Objectives and functions — During the release process, and after a product has been released, changes to the design and the manufacturing process must be clearly communicated to all affected parties. Additionally, the changes must be controlled so that they are implemented correctly. Engineering changes can be received from customers or suppliers, or originated in-house. No matter where they originate, each affected department in the manufacturer, plus all affected suppliers and sometimes customers, must be notified of the change, including:

- Type of change (for example, new material, new or revised process, changes in tolerances, etc.)
- Effective date of change, or other type of phase-in (e.g., lot number)
- Urgency and seriousness of change, and whether retrofit of existing products is required

Even in the early stages of product development a modest level of engineering control is appropriate so people are not making changes at will and so the company can learn from the changes. As the product solidifies, the level of formality increases.

Most companies have an engineering change committee comprised of the same departments that are on product design teams, including Design Engineering, Manufacturing Engineering, Manufacturing, Purchasing, Sales, Marketing, Quality Management, and Cost Accounting. The process is controlled and communicated by **engineering change orders** (ECOs), or **engineering change notices** (ECNs).

The information required and provided by this stage is illustrated in Figure 4.12.

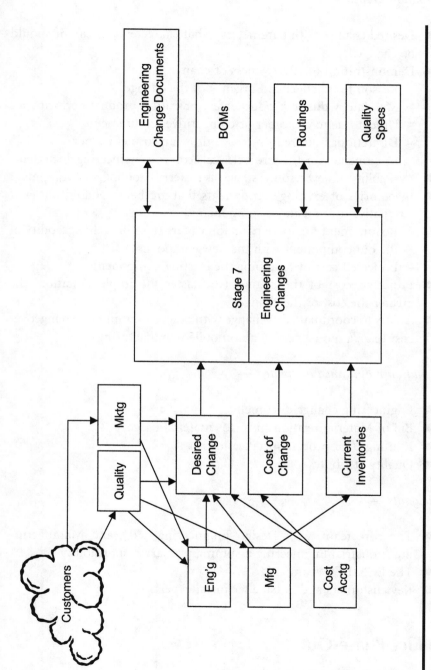

Figure 4.12 Stage 7 — Engineering Changes

Information needed —

- Desired change, with parameters (what characteristics can or should be changed?)
- Demonstration of effectiveness of change
  - Reason for change, and urgency of the change:
  - Mandatory due to product safety or critical product performance
  - Urgent due to customer or competitive requirements
  - Discretionary, to reduce cost and/or improve efficiency
  - Documentation, to correct clerical errors on engineering documents
- Availability of new resources, such as materials, tooling, and equipment
- Inventories of existing components that are being phased out, and alternative uses for those components:
  - Requirement for spare parts for x years (and interchangeability of the old component with the new component)
  - Projected cost of scrapping the existing components
- Projected cost of the change (the faster the implementation, the greater the cost of the change)
- Ability to coordinate this change with others, to minimize changeover cost (e.g., a model year in automobile manufacturing)

Information maintained or created —

- Engineering change documents
- Bill of Material relationships (for material usage)
- Routings (for process specifications)
- Quality attributes

Participants —

- The core team, with Design Engineering/R&D, and Manufacturing/Industrial Engineering assuming primary responsibility
- The ECN/ECO team
- Key customers and outside technical experts

Product Phase-Out

Product phase-out has several objectives:

- Retain customer loyalty
- Minimize expense; maximize revenues (for old product and new product)
- Minimize disruptions in the supply chain, both with customers and with suppliers
- Minimize disruptions in the manufacturing process

Engineers coordinate phasing a product out of the product line by changing effective dates (or serial numbers) in the BOM, and/or turning on the "obsolete" flag for the end item. However, product phase-out is a decision which requires input and discussion from the departments below. Most of the data is either already in the TEI system, or needs to be added (e.g., the forecasts for service parts usage).

Marketing and Sales —

- Inventories in the distribution channel (e.g., at customers, warehouses, etc.)
- When the market will accept the replacement product
- Forecasts for the old product as its sales drop to 0
- Alternatives for selling or disposing of any excess quantities of the old product (e.g., selling to an off-price closeout store, if a consumer good; selling to international markets that are still interested in that product)
- How long to support the old product from a service standpoint — forecasts for service parts and spares

Production —

- Timing of availability of machinery and tooling for the new (replacement) product
- Alternatives for machinery and tooling for the old product
- Alternative manufacturing processes for lower volumes

Materials and Purchasing —

- Availability of materials to support production of the new product
- Current and projected inventories of the old product and any components that will also become obsolete
- One-time buys of purchased parts for service spares

- One-time production of manufactured parts and assemblies for service spares
- Possible outsourcing of continued low-volume production of old product

Human Resources —

- Retraining workers
- Hiring workers for the new product

Engineering —

- Forward and backward compatibility of components

Accounting —

- Costs of phasing the old product out
- Costs of alternative production methods and suppliers for lower volumes

Product Data Management (PDM)

Product data management (PDM) originated in engineering departments concurrently with MRP II's growth in the materials and manufacturing functions. PDM and TEI overlap in product and process definitions and in controlling engineering changes. Field Service also uses PDM data when it maintains equipment.

PDM software manages and controls the product information necessary to specify, analyze, and ultimately build a product. It also coordinates the processes used to create, review, release, and change product information. A PDM system sits on top of other application software and data files, including CAD/CAM (Computer-Aided Design/Computer-Aided Manufacturing) systems. However, PDM systems can also access TEI, purchasing-department databases and other sources of product information.

A PDM system plays a number of roles. It serves as a librarian, keeping track of the myriad of versions and thousands of ancillary files pertaining to a single product. Implicit here is that the data is well structured; thanks to PDM-provided product structures, a user can jump easily from one type of information pertaining to a product to another type, for instance, from geometric data to tolerances, materials, test results, and the like.

A PDM system also acts as traffic cop, ensuring that various parties all operate on the same master records in a secure manner. Additionally, PDM software functions as a project manager by forwarding tasks automatically to the appropriate individuals when certain events occur (this is an example of workflow, which is discussed at the beginning of Chapter 7). For instance, the PDM system could request a sign-off from manufacturing when an engineering change is proposed:*

PDMs provide the technology for engineers to integrate with:

- Customers (linking with their systems, so that the manufacturer's engineers can easily exchange drawings, specifications, etc.)
- Suppliers (the same as customers)
- Field service (so that field service technicians can access the detailed engineering drawings and specifications while they are servicing equipment in the field)

PDM and TEI overlap, and therefore must link, in the following areas:

- BOM (Bill of Materials) — (Both PDM and TEI require and use the fundamental data. Product structures in PDM are oriented toward product capabilities, and how the products are defined. Product structures in TEI systems are oriented toward material planning and manufacturing use. There are five potential ways to interface or integrate the two systems:
  1. No electronic interaction — all interchange of data is manual, with manual controls for keeping the two systems synchronized.
  2. PDM is the master; TEI is the slave — PDM views TEI as a static recipient. All file updating occurs in the PDM system, which downloads data at specified intervals to the TEI system.
  3. PDM and TEI are equal — PDM and TEI share information bidirectionally.
  4. PDM is the engineering design workspace, but TEI maintains "real" master data — Engineering uses PDM for its creative work, but maintains the corporate master data in the TEI system.
  5. TEI functionality includes PDM — some TEI software suppliers include full PDM functionality in their software, with full integration.

---

* Piszczalski, Martin, "The Importance of PDM," *Automotive Manufacturing & Production,* September 1998.

- Routings — Like BOMs, both TEI and PDM can define how a product is actually assembled on the floor, with specifications and standards. The alternatives for integration are the same as BOMs, above.
- Engineering change control — Since PDM systems originated in the engineering department, they frequently have more robust change control capabilities (such as viewing/markup and graphics), than TEI systems. Thus, the PDM system is probably the better choice for managing and maintaining engineering control information, downloading that information to the TEI system. However, the PDM systems generally lack the ability to analyze the costs and economies of proposed changes, which the TEI system provides.

Integrating with Customers

If customers have design engineers, integrating the design process with customers' engineers can reduce design errors, tighten the relationship between the two companies, reduce costs, reduce the manufacturer's time to respond to the customer, increase the manufacturer's visibility, and improve performance and market acceptance of the final product. Integrating the design process with customers can include direct answers from the customer with respect to their true needs. Because customers sometimes are not aware of alternatives that could be truly beneficial, visits by design engineers as well as marketing professionals are absolutely essential for industrial products, and highly beneficial for consumer products. An engineer will watch the customer use the product, looking for opportunities to help the customer do their job better (more easily, more quickly, less costly, etc.). An engineer might see some additional opportunities in the way the product interfaces with other products in the customer's manufacturing cycle.

For consumer products, an engineer can still accompany the product to see how it is handled, used, and stored, so that the manufacturer can help the customer save money and time.

One consumer packaged goods manufacturer had traditionally packed its products 6 to a box, because 6 products would fit on a single peg on the retailer's display. But even though the retailer did not have additional storage space in the back room, they would generally fail to reorder until the last item was sold from the peg. This caused the peg to be empty for about a week, although the manufacturer would ship within 24 hours of receipt of order. The manufacturer proposed changing the shipping carton quantity to 4 products, so the retailer could reorder when there were 2 left on the peg, thereby minimizing stockouts. The retailer accepted the idea, because it meant fewer stockouts; sales increased about 10% as a result.

Many consumer packaged goods manufacturers work very closely with the large retailers to refine their packaging (the color, the size, the appearance, the wording, etc.) to maximize sales.

At the very minimum for industrial products manufacturers, the customers must supply specifications that are sufficiently detailed that the manufacturer can design and make a product that fits the customer's needs. This same process holds true for engineering changes to existing products as well as new products. Many manufacturers prefer the customer to specify the desired functionality or result from the product, plus other critical environmental attributes (size, electrical constraints, vibration, etc.), and let the manufacturer be somewhat creative in designing the specific product.

Manufacturers can also integrate the design process with customers by providing ideas directly to the customer during their design cycle. One of the major benefits to both customer and manufacturer is including the manufacturer's design and manufacturing expertise as an integral part of the product design team. The customer gains additional insights and ideas, which result in lower total cost and a superior product. The manufacturer gains the assurance of the business. Some tightly integrated supply chains includes the manufacturer's key suppliers in the design process as well.

Industrial products manufacturers usually crave more detail from process and product engineers at their customers. This can be provided in at least two ways:

- The manufacturer's engineers can visit the customer at relatively frequent intervals. The cost of these visits to both customer and manufacturer can be relatively high, thereby effectively encouraging the customer to move toward single sourcing. The benefit to the customer is the fruit of an intense partnership – continuous improvement, resulting in lower total costs. It should be a two way exchange.
- The manufacturer can be invited to join the design team for new products, and for redesigning existing products. This practice almost requires single sourcing, because the design team would have great difficulty working with two engineers from two competing suppliers.

Integrating with Suppliers

Likewise, if suppliers have design engineers, integrating the design process with suppliers' engineers can reduce design errors, tighten the relationship between the two companies, reduce costs, reduce the suppliers' time to respond to the the manufacturer, and improve performance and market acceptance of the final product. Integrating the design process with suppliers can include the following:

- Investing engineer time in suppliers to build a solid relationship. Some ways to accomplish this are as follows:
    - Visiting suppliers frequently and routinely (even to the extent that they start commenting about the engineer "living there").
    - Certifying suppliers with respect to their processes, and insisting that they certify the technical skills of the people who manufacture the product.
    - Educating suppliers on techniques, such as process control and process improvement, so that they have the technical capabilities to perform the required work.
- Single sourcing as a matter of policy, because each supplier requires an extensive investment of time to insure the optimum communication and understanding.
- Inviting the suppliers to participate in designing new products and redesigning existing products. This essentially requires single sourcing.
- Working collaboratively with suppliers to jointly develop the best alternatives to delight the customer. Sometimes this involves using a supplier's data to prove to them that something can actually be done, even if they think it can't.
- Providing specifications in a format that the supplier can readily use.
- Communicating and controlling engineering changes, including dates, specifications, and tolerances.
- Receiving, hearing, and acting upon communications from the suppliers, such as:
    - Actual tolerances and yields from processes (which are forwarded to Quality and to the engineering group to be filed for future analysis), and
    - Ideas for improvement.

Joseph Rogers, a Product Development Manager at i-STAT Corporation, observed, "The manufacturing people at the supplier often get too tolerant of problems that they are having. The problems do not get raised to the customer quickly enough to take some corrective action. The best corrective action needs to be determined between the supplier and customer since there is often more than one option.*"

Integrating with the Rest of the Company

Jody Tirinato, Director of Systems Engineering at i-STAT Corporation, states, "The communication of information is frequently more important than the information itself. You need to decide whether a single individual or the team will manage the communication process, because it will not manage itself."**

The philosophy of the engineering department directly affects the amount of data it gathers and the circumstances under which it gathers the data. Engineering can be:

- Reactive or Proactive:
  - Reactive — Engineering waits for a problem to surface, then starts gathering data to try to determine how to correct the problem. This minimizes the amount of data, communication, and integration within the company; it also delays responses to opportunities.
  - Proactive — Engineering tries to anticipate problems, gathers data to predict when a problem might occur, and attempts to avoid or eliminate problems before they occur. This can substantially increase the amount of data, communication, and integration within the company, thereby increasing the company's investment. However, it substantially improves responsiveness to opportunities and product quality.
- Service or Supplier to the shop floor or other internal customers:
  - Service — Engineering will listen to the problem or idea then go help gather data.
  - Supplier — Engineering expects the internal customer to provide data with the complaint or idea.

---

* Joseph Rogers, personal interview, January 14, 1999.
** Jody Tirinato, personal interview, January 14, 1999.

The coordination of engineering changes throughout a company is discussed in subsection 7, Engineering Changes, of the Design section of this chapter.

Project Management

For growing manufacturers, managing construction projects is as important as managing the flow of materials through the plant. In fact, in such companies more than half the purchase orders issued can be for new buildings and equipment. As illustrated in Figure 4.13, the project management module of an integrated system connects with:

- Engineering, for designing the new processes, including buildings and equipment.
- Purchasing, for sending RFQ's and issuing purchase orders. Purchasing, in turn, communicates with:
  - Suppliers of materials (issuing RFQ's, receiving quotations, issuing purchase orders, and tracking deliveries to schedule)
  - Contractors (same information as material suppliers), and
  - Inspectors and government agencies, for filings and approvals.
- Maintenance and internal engineering, for installing the equipment and recording the "birth record" of equipment and warranty information on the equipment and its components.
- Accounting, for budgeting, payroll and fixed assets.
- Master Scheduling, for the availability of the new equipment for production. Master Scheduling, in turn, communicates with sales and marketing, and with customers.

Project management techniques can also be applied to the product development process itself. Companies that have done so have reduced their average product development times by 30 to 50%, because:[*]

- Projects get done faster if the organization takes on fewer at a time.
- Investments to relieve bottlenecks yield disproportionately large time-to-market benefits.

---

[*] Adler, Paul S., Avi Mandelbaum, Vien Nguyen, Elizabeth Schwerer, "Getting the Most Out of Your Product Development Process," *Harvard Business Review,* March 1996.

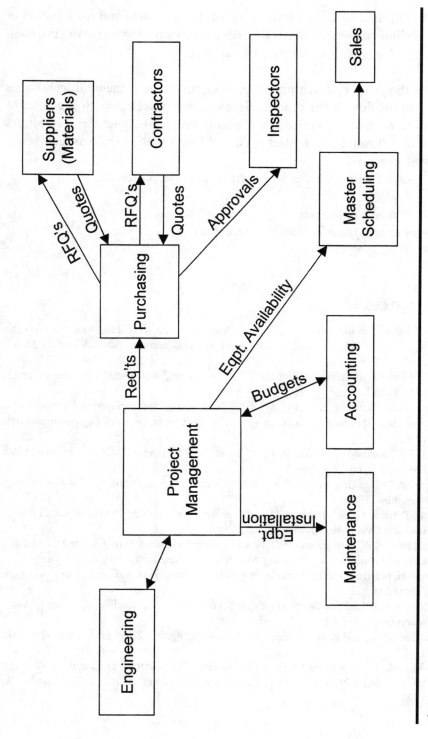

Figure 4.13 Project Management Integration

- Eliminating unnecessary variation in workloads and work processes eliminates distractions and delays, thereby freeing up the organization to focus on the creative parts of the task.

For the product development process, project management techniques focus on the flow of the product development process, which is similar to the flow of materials through a plant. Project management monitors capacities, throughput, bottlenecks, and lead times in the product development process.

Other activities that can be managed as projects include:

- Product phase-out
- Product modification/reformulation
- Packaging change.

References

Adler, Paul S., Mandelbaum, Avi, Nguyen, Vien, and Schwerer, Elizabeth, "Getting the Most Out of Your Product Development Process," *Harvard Business Review*, March 1996.

"Design for Manufacturing Under the CE Environment," *Machine Design*, December 11, 1997, p. 112.

Kempfer, Lisa, "Linking PDM to ERP," *CAE: Computer-Aided Engineering*, October 1998.

Kempfer, Lisa, "Speeding Products to Market," *CAE: Computer-Aided Engineering*, March 1998.

Miller, Ed, "Focused Solutions Bring PDM to the Mainstream," *CAE: Computer-Aided Engineering*, January 1999.

Miller, Ed, "Managing the Design Supply Chain," *CAE: Computer-Aided Engineering*, November 1998.

Moody, Patricia E., ed., *Strategic Manufacturing: Dynamic New Directions for the 1990s*, Business One/Irwin, Homewood, IL, 1990.

Oden, Howard W., Langenwalter, Gary, and Lucier, Raymond, *Handbook of Material and Capacity Requirements Planning*, McGraw-Hill, New York, 1993, pp. 91–94.

Piszczalski, Martin, "The Importance of PDM," *Automotive Manufacturing & Production*, September 1998.

Piszczalksi, Martin, "The Necessary Expansion of ERP Functionality," *Automotive Manufacturing & Production*, December 1998.

Stalk, George, Jr. and Hout, Thomas M., *Competing Against Time*, Free Press, New York, 1990.

Thomas, Merle, Jr. and Sadat-Hossieny, Moteza, "Concurrent Engineering: Winning Worldwide," *1995 International Conference Proceedings*, APICS, Falls Church, VA, 1995.

Tirinato, Jody and Rogers, Joseph, engineers at i-STAT corporation, East Windsor, NJ; Interview on January 14, 1999.

Wallace, Bob, "Ford Suppliers Get Call to Design," *Computerworld*, March 8, 1999.

5 | Manufacturing Integration

Manufacturing integration includes planning and execution of the materials and manufacturing functions, plus the supply network that feeds those activities. It also includes quality and maintenance, because they are integral to the manufacturing and materials process.

Although this area is the design center and traditional strength of MRP II, ERP, and TEI systems, complete integration across the entire area was virtually nonexistent in 1999. We discuss the following functions:

- Material and Capacity Planning
- Manufacturing Execution Systems (Enterprise Production Systems)
- Just-In-Time (JIT)
- Advanced Planning and Scheduling
- Supplier Integration
- Quality Management Systems
- Maintenance

The relationships between each of these functions and the rest of a Total Enterprise Integration system are shown in Figure 5.1.

Material and Capacity Planning

Background

Material and capacity planning includes the following functions, which in older MRP II and ERP systems are separate modules:

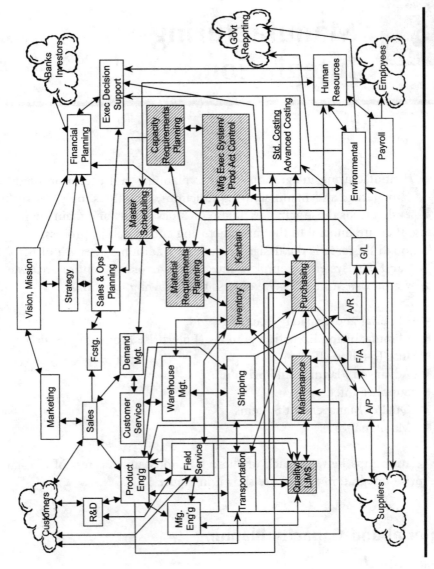

Figure 5.1 TEI and Manufacturing

- Master Production Scheduling (MPS)
- Rough-Cut Planning, the capacity side of master production scheduling
- Material Requirements Planning (MRP), the original foundation of MRP II systems
- Capacity Requirements Planning (CRP), the capacity reporting system that corresponds to MRP
- The perpetual inventory system

However, the hierarchical model of running MPS, then Rough-Cut, then MRP, then CRP, was created when computers were slow and expensive, and reacting in a week was considered to be world-class. The basic interfaces between these functions is illustrated in Figure 5.2. The entire material and capacity planning suite is now starting to be replaced by Advanced Planning and Scheduling systems, discussed later in this section.

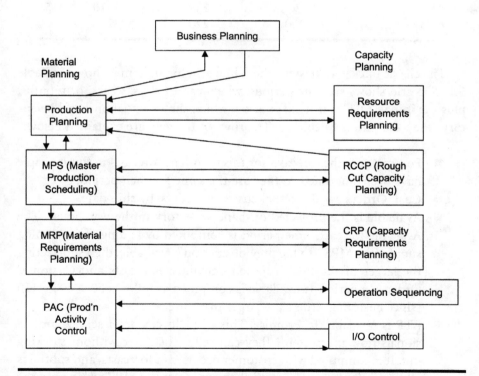

Figure 5.2 Traditional Material and Capacity Planning Hierarchy

Master Production Schedule (MPS)

A Master Production Scheduler, or Master Scheduler, continually balances demand and production by monitoring fluctuations in actual customer demand and/or forecasts, actual production and supply, and adjusting the production schedule, using inventory as a buffer. The Master Scheduler has the final answer to the question, "When can we ship an order to Customer X?"

Table 5.1 Master Scheduling Grid

	OH	1	2	3	4	5	6
Forecasts		100	100	100	100	100	100
Cust. Orders		110	120	75	40	10	0
Available	50	140	20	140	40	140	40
ATP		20	20	125	125	315	315
MPS		200		220		200	

The classic bucketed Master Scheduling grid for an item is shown in Table 5.1. The grid shows six time periods, which can be days, weeks, or months, plus the initial "OH" (on-hand) bucket, which shows actual on-hand inventory when the grid is calculated. The rows in the grid are explained below:

- **Forecasts** are the forecasts for this item. The forecasts in this example have been smoothed so they are the same for each period.
- **Cust. Orders** are the actual customer orders, by ship date.
- **Available** is the projected on-hand inventory in the warehouse. The Available for each time period is computed by adding the incoming supply (the MPS), to the previous period's Available, then subtracting the larger of the two projected demands: Forecasts and Customer Orders. In period 1, Available is computed as follows: 50 + 200 − 110 (since customer orders are larger than forecasts).
- **ATP** is Available To Promise. This line tells customer service professionals how many items they can sell a customer without stocking out. It is computed with customer orders, not forecasts, and subtracts all the customer orders until the next incoming MPS order from the MPS in the period in question. In period 1, the ATP is computed as follows: 50 + 200 − 110 − 120. Thus, even though 200 items are

arriving in period 1, all but 20 are already sold. If a customer wants more than 20 before period 3, there are several alternatives:
- The customer can receive 20 now, and the rest in period 3.
- The Master Scheduler can try to increase the MPS order in period 1, which might take capacity or materials from another product.
- Some other customer's order can be rescheduled into period 3.

- **MPS** is the Master Production Schedule, showing how many of this item will be manufactured (completed) each period. The company makes at least 200 items at a time, because of lot sizes of incoming raw materials.

Virtually all manufacturers run their Master Production Scheduling programs at least weekly; many run them daily, and some even run them continuously (so that a Master Scheduler can make changes that are immediately reflected throughout the company and its direct suppliers).

The ATP line in the Master Scheduling grid is very useful if customers place orders for future delivery. However, industry after industry has dramatically reduced future orders and current stock on hand, instead using *kanbans* or Vendor-Managed Inventories.

Integration

The Master Schedule must be integrated with the following systems to receive accurate input:

1. Demand
   - The Sales and Operations Plan
   - Forecasts (automated or manual)
   - Actual customer orders
   - Logistics and transportation
   - Outlying warehouses controlled by the company (potentially through DRP)
   - Customer distribution centers (to support Vendor-Managed Inventories)
2. Material Supply
   - Perpetual inventory system (for actual on-hand quantities)
   - Work orders already placed
   - Purchase orders already placed

3. Capacity Supply
   - Rough Cut Resource Planning
   - Maintenance schedules

This is illustrated in Figure 5.3.

When the Master Schedule changes, it can directly affect the following functions:

- Customer shipments (which customer order will be ready to ship when)
- Sales and Marketing departments, which must call customers to let them know of changes
- Transportation schedules (adjusted for the changes in finished goods due dates)
- Manufacturing schedules, including
  - Staffing levels for the plant
  - Work order priorities
  - Material requirements
- Supplier schedules
- Cash requirements, which are tied to manufacturing and supplier schedules
- Inventory levels and investments (the changed schedule can buffer the plant and its suppliers from changes in demand by planning to increase or decrease the inventories of specific items)

This is illustrated in Figure 5.4.

Rough Cut Planning

A good Master Scheduler knows the capacity limits of the people and equipment. However, reviewing the requirements on all critical resources can be very time-consuming, even impossible, when performed manually. And some companies also have additional resource constraints outside of the people and equipment, such as capital, or storage space, or shelf life of critical items. Rough-Cut Resource Planning explodes the master schedule, using rough-cut routings, to determine the approximate load on each critical resource during each user-specified time period. Any resource loads that exceed capacity, or maximum, are flagged for review by the Master Scheduler. A Rough-

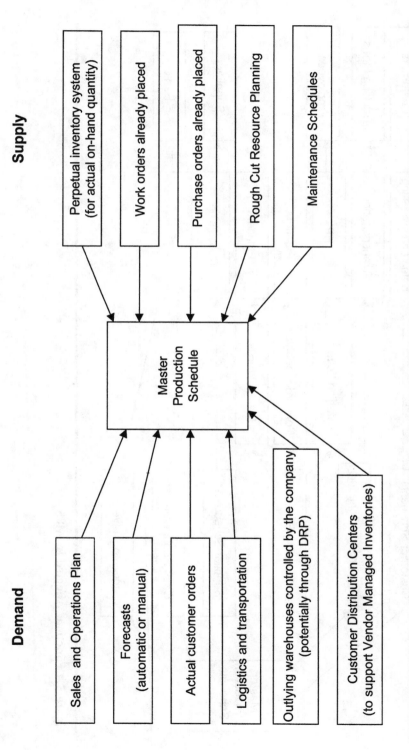

Figure 5.3 Systems Which Feed MPS

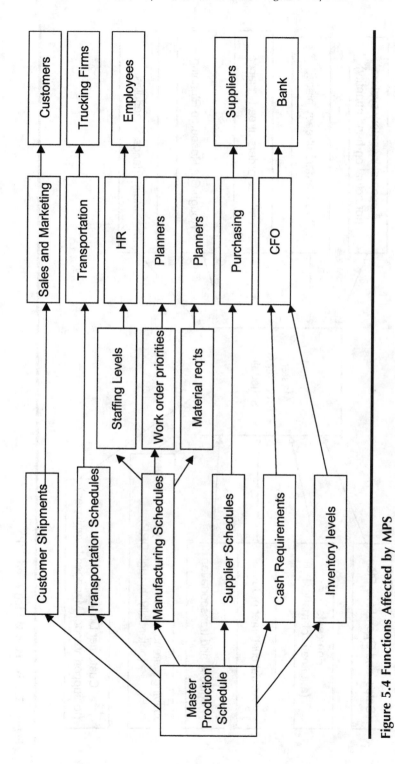

Figure 5.4 Functions Affected by MPS

Table 5.2 Rough-Cut Resource Planning Grid Report

	Assembly & Test					
	3/5	*3/12*	*3/19*	*3/26*	*4/2*	*4/9*
Max. Capacity	60	60	60	60	60	60
Requirements	70	60	75	40	35	20
Available	−10	0	−15	20	25	40

Cut Resource Plan can be viewed as a grid, as illustrated in Table 5.2, or a bar chart, illustrated by Figure 5.5.

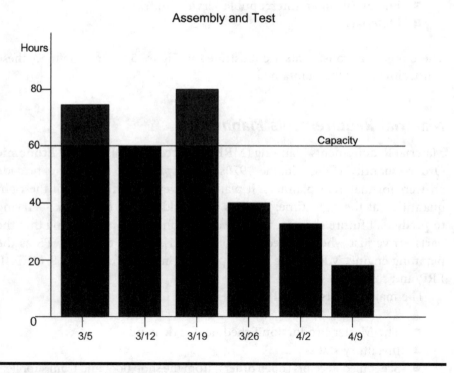

Figure 5.5 Rough-Cut Resources Bar Chart

Integration

From a technical standpoint, Rough-Cut Planning (RCP) directly integrates only with the Master Production Schedule. However, the purpose of the module is to tell management which resource constraints will be exceeded. Thus, management should define *all* business constraints that it wants RCP to check, including:

- Capacity, internal
- Capacity at suppliers
- Transportation
- Cash
- Labor
  - Skilled setup
  - Machine operators
- Warehouse space
- Energy (if on an interruptible service contract)
- Materials

These potential constraints are illustrated in Figure 5.6. Once defined, these constraints must be maintained.

Material Requirements Planning

Material Requirements Planning (MRP) replaced Order Point and **Economic Order Quantity (EOQ)** in the 1970s as the preferred method to provide answers for materials planners. It plans to have the right items, in the right quantities, at the right time. It views the world like an expeditor — trying to predict all future shortages, then work around them by ensuring that the parts arrive just when needed. Except for TEI systems that use APS as the planning engine, MRP is the central planning module for all MRP, MRP II, ERP, and some TEI systems.

The major inputs to MRP are:

- The Master Production Schedule, for demand
- Inventory status
- Scheduled Receipts (open orders) from the shop floor and from suppliers
- Planned Orders from the shop floor and from suppliers
- The Bill of Materials

Using that information, MRP plans to cover all projected demand on the required dates. It first uses all available inventories, then scheduled receipts. When both those sources are completely consumed, it creates new planned

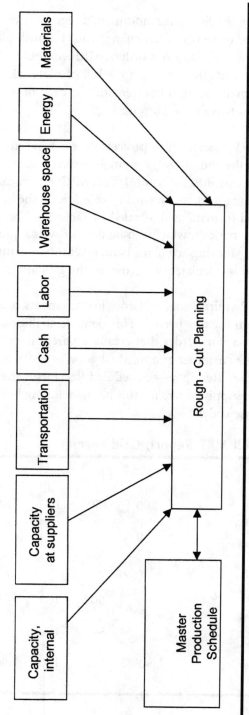

Figure 5.6 Rough-Cut Planning Constraints

orders for precisely the right amount (in a regenerative run), or reschedules existing planned orders (in a net change run) to finish filling all the demand. As it creates new planned work orders, MRP computes the demand for each of their components by exploding the bill of materials for the parent item. It adds this demand to all other demand for each of the components.

MRP creates two major outputs:

1. Full MRP report, which projects the on-hand inventory status of each item to the end of the planning horizon (at least 6 months, and sometimes a year into the future). This MRP report can be condensed into a planning grid, as shown in Table 5.3, or shown in more detail in a "vertical format," as illustrated in Table 5.4. The planning grid shows six time periods, which can be days or weeks, plus an on-hand (OH) column showing actual on-hand inventory quantity for this item when the grid is calculated. The rows in the grid are explained below:

- **Gross Requirements** — Gross Requirements is the total demand for this item for this period. This demand includes both internal (to be used in a work order that creates a parent item), and external (to be sold to a customer as a finished good or replacement part) demand.
- **Scheduled Receipts** — Scheduled Receipts is the total open, or committed, supply orders for this item, including both manufactured and purchase orders.

Table 5.3 Full MRP Report, Grid Format

	OH	1	2	3	4	5	6
Gross Requirements		100	150	100	120	90	130
Scheduled Receipts		110					0
Projected Available	50	60	0	0	0	0	0
Net Requirements			90	100	120	90	130
Planned Order Receipts			90	100	120	90	130
Planned Order Releases		90	100	120	90	130	

Table 5.4 MRP Vertical Report

Item:35129 - Bicycle Wheels, 27"; LT: 3 days; OQ: LFL; SS: 0

Date	Reference	Parent	Start	Recpt Qty	Req't	Avail Qty
6/15						50
6/16	WO 3519	32197			50	0
6/18	WO 3476		6/16	110		110
6/18	WO 3535	21857			50	60
6/22	WO 3548		6/18	90		150
6/22	WO 3597	30853			150	0
6/26	WO 3645	32197			60	–60
6/28	WO 3631		6/26	60		0
6/29	WO 3689		6/27	40		40
6/29	WO 3694	30853			40	0
7/3	WO 3739		7/1	60		60
7/3	WO 3740	32197			60	0
7/6	WO 3787		7/3	60		60
7/6	WO 3801	21857			60	0

■ **Projected Available** — This shows projected on-hand inventory for this item at the end of each period. MRP calculates this by starting with the projected available at the end of the previous period, then subtracting the gross requirements for the period being planned and adding the scheduled receipts for the period being planned. If the resulting projected available is greater than the specified safety stock level (which is zero in this example), the calculation for this period is complete. If the resulting Projected Available Quantity is less than safety stock, that shortage becomes the positive Net Requirements in the row below. Once MRP has calculated the Planned Order Release Quantity and the Planned Order Receipt Quantity, it adds the Planned Order Receipt Quantity to the initial Projected Available, to bring the final Projected Available above the Safety Stock Level.

■ **Net Requirements** — Net Requirements is the projected shortage, after subtracting gross requirements and adding scheduled receipts for a period. It forms the basic quantity for Planned Order Receipts. MRP plans to fill all Net Requirements, to eliminate all potential shortages.

- **Planned Order Receipts** — MRP plans replenishment orders (either manufactured or purchased, depending on how this item is defined) to fill the shortage defined by Net Requirements. Planned Order Receipts are the quantity that is expected to be received into the stockroom during the period, that is the Planned Order Release quantity less any yield or shrinkage.

- **Planned Order Release** — MRP calculates the Planned Order Release quantity by increasing the Net Requirements to compensate for yield losses, then comparing that quantity to the minimum order quantity for this item (using the minimum order quantity if it is greater than the net requirements), then increasing the quantity again to be a multiple of the Order Multiple quantity for this item. It puts the Planned Order Release quantity not in the current time period, but in the time period which it computes by subtracting the item's lead time from the current planning period. For example, if the time period being planned is 3, and the lead time is one period, the Planned Order Release will be in period 2, while the Planned Order Receipt will be in period 3. While this may initially sound confusing, it reflects the real world, because most manufactured and purchase orders require 1 or more days to finish after they are released.

Both these MRP reports (as shown in Tables 5.3 and 5.4) are available on computer screens as well as in printed format.

2. MRP Action Report, which contains the exceptions that materials planners must take action on, including rescheduling existing orders (both manufactured and purchased) and releasing new orders (both manufactured and purchased.) An example is shown in Table 5.5.

Table 5.5 MRP Action Report

Item	Description	Action	Order	Qty.	Date From	Date To
35129	Bicycle Wheels 27"	Rel/Exp	WO 3631	60	6/28	6/26
22193	Seat – Touring	Release	PO 3899	100	6/24	
21857	Mountain Bike Spec	Resched Out	WO 3613	50	6/16	7/2
14925	Frame 27"	Cancel	WO 3548	60	6/14	

All systems have a full "regenerative" mode, which replans the entire material plan. Some MRP II, ERP, and TEI systems also have the ability to run MRP in a "net change" mode, which only lists the items which have been affected by the latest run.

Integration

MRP is still the detailed planning heart of most ERP and many TEI systems. It uses information from MPS and many of the same areas as MPS, including the following (see Figure 5.7):

- Demand:
  - From MPS
  - Customer orders
  - Forecasts
- Supply:
  - Perpetual inventory system (for actual on-hand quantities)
  - Work orders/repetitive schedules already placed
  - Purchase orders/repetitive schedules already placed
- Reference:
  - Bill of Materials
  - Routing (in some systems)

When MRP runs, it reschedules planned work orders, repetitive schedules, and purchase orders, thereby affecting many of the same areas that MPS affects. Additionally, management can set a parameter in some ERP and TEI systems that allows MRP to automatically reschedule scheduled receipts (released work orders and released purchase orders). If the MRP system is allowed to automatically reschedule scheduled receipts, analytical time required by the planner each week is theoretically reduced. However, a person must still be accountable for the schedules, or the ERP or TEI system will eventually lose credibility and be ignored.

MRP affects the following functions (see Figure 5.8):

- Manufacturing schedules, including:
  - Staffing levels for the plant
  - Work order priorities
  - Material requirements

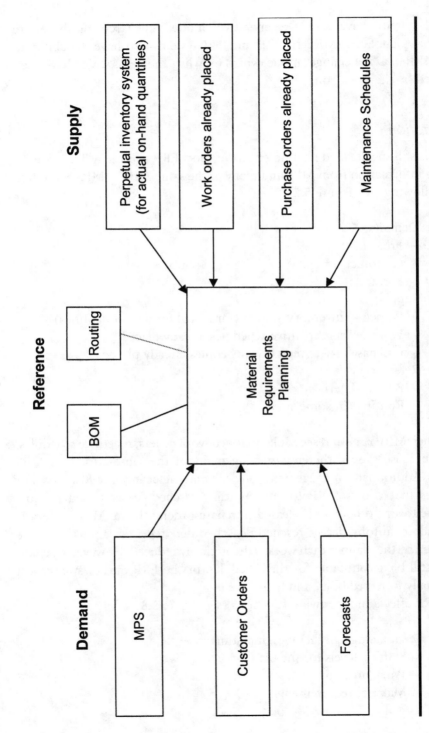

Figure 5.7 Systems Which Feed MRP

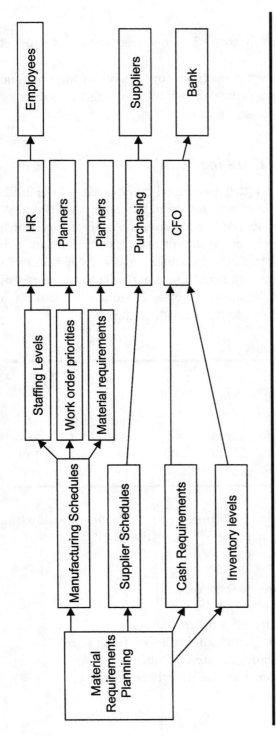

Figure 5.8 Functions Affected by MRP

- Supplier schedules
- Cash requirements, which are tied to manufacturing and supplier schedules
- Inventory levels and investments (inventory can buffer the plant and its suppliers from changes in demand by planning to increase or decrease the inventory levels of specific items)

Capacity Requirements Planning (CRP)

One of MRP's major weaknesses is that it assumes infinite capacity, both inside the company and at suppliers. In companies where the assumption is unrealistic, the CRP report is critical to successful operation, because it predicts which resources will have capacity problems so that planners can take action. Two examples of CRP reports are shown below: a tabular report (Table 5.6), and a bar chart graphic report (Figure 5.9). Both reports are available on screen, as well as in paper form. When CRP shows a problem, planners can also run a cumulative CRP report, shown in graphic format in Figure 5.10.

Table 5.6 CRP Tabular Report

	Past Due	*1*	*2*	*3*	*4*	*5*	*6*
			Workstation: Final Assembly				
Capacity	0	120	135	96	96	120	135
Req'd Capacity	60	110	120	100	90	120	140
Over/Under		−50	15	−4	6	0	−5

When CRP predicts capacity problems, materials planners and/or the master scheduler must take corrective action. If the problem is too little capacity, the corrective options include:

- Using alternate machines or work centers
- Using substitute parts or assemblies
- Outsourcing one or more work orders
- Working overtime (short term); adding a shift (long term)
- Acquiring (buying or leasing) more equipment
- Delaying the final customer shipment or back ordering

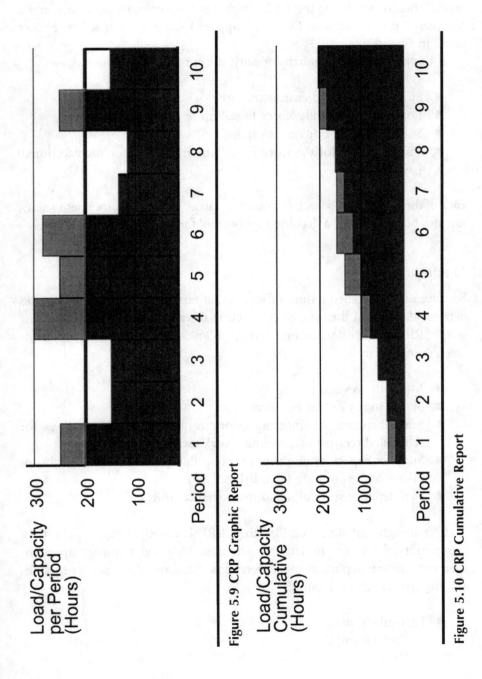

Figure 5.9 CRP Graphic Report

Figure 5.10 CRP Cumulative Report

Before the advent of executive decision support tools, decision-makers had great difficulty predicting the actual impact of their capacity decisions on the company's profit and loss. Decision support tools are discussed in greater detail in Chapter 2.

If the problem is too much capacity, the corrective options include:

- Shipping orders to customers early
- Encouraging the sales force to sell more
- Subcontracting our excess capacity
- Cutting hours for the work force, temporarily (enforcing vacations)
- Layoffs

Each of these actions impacts other plans and areas of the company. These actions can also be reviewed by a decision support tool for their impact on the P&L.

Integration

Because of the detailed nature of its calculations and reports, CRP requires detailed data about the state of completion of each scheduled receipt in the shop. CRP receives information from the following systems and departments (see Figure 5.11):

- MRP (the revised plan)
- Shop Floor Control/Feedback
- Manufacturing Engineering (work center capacities, routings for scheduled receipts and planned work orders)
- Supplier capacities and supplier shop floor feedback (if critical supplier work centers are included in CRP)
- Maintenance schedules and maintenance orders

Like Rough-Cut Resource Planning, CRP is merely a report. The CRP program itself does not update any schedules. However, planners and management use this report to make decisions that can affect many functions and departments, (see Figure 5.12):

- Part substitution:
  - Costing and P&L
  - Quality

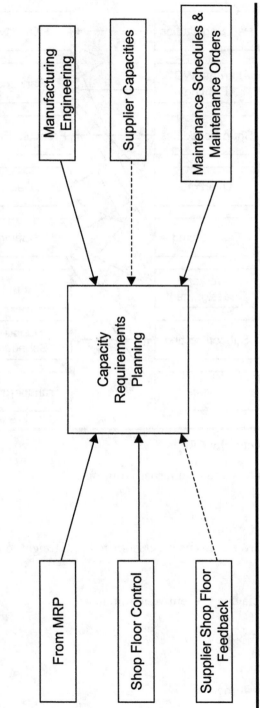

Figure 5.11 CRP Inputs

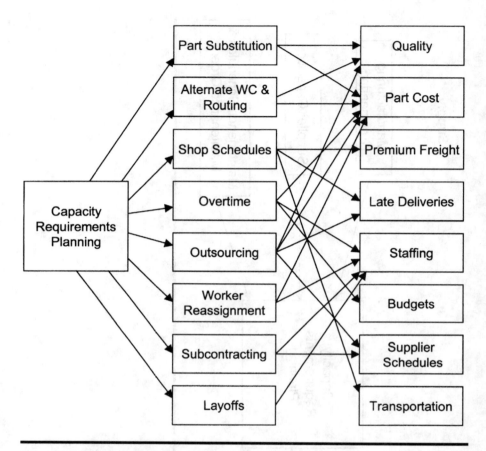

Figure 5.12 Functions Affected by CRP

- Alternate work centers and/or alternate routings:
  - Costing and P&L
  - Quality
- Shop schedules and priorities:
  - Potential late deliveries to customers, or premium freight to deliver on time
- Maintenance:
  - Expediting or delaying preventive maintenance
- Overtime:
  - Staffing (Human Resources)
  - Budgets and P&L
- Outsourcing:
  - Lead times to customers

- − Supplier schedules and relationships
- − Quality
- − Costing and P&L impacts
- − Transportation
- ■ Reassignment of workers to other departments (Human Resources):
  - − Training for the new assignments
- ■ Subcontracting our capabilities to other companies:
  - − Training workers how to run new products (Human Resources)
- ■ Temporary layoffs of workers (Human Resources)

Inventory

Whenever material moves between the stockroom and the plant floor, or through a critical work center, cell, or line, the TEI system needs to be informed so that it can accurately report the current location of each item. This requirement for information can easily create a heavy transaction reporting load with its inherently high operating cost. A perpetual inventory system needs to have the ability to be adjusted, by cycle counting (using the APICS two-step process), and by an annual physical inventory.

While relatively straightforward, inventory is not always simple. Many TEI systems can track material usage by lot, or serial number, of one of more components into a lot-numbered or serial-numbered parent. They can then report precisely which serial-numbered or lot-numbered end items contain a serial-numbered or lot-numbered component. They can also track lots by expiration date, insuring that the oldest lots are pulled first. The inventory module can be part of an MES system.

Integration

Inventory receives its data from the physical transactions in the MES or TEI system that track the movement of each item. In many TEI systems, the system itself creates the material usage transactions using a technique known as "backflushing." In this technique, the TEI system computes how much of each direct component should have been consumed for a quantity of parent items that is being reported on the floor or is entering the stockroom. For example, if the stockroom is receiving 100 computer mice, the TEI system will create the "issue" transactions and deduct the components from inventory, including 100 cases, 100 mouse cords, 100 rubber balls, etc. The quantity of each component to be deducted is automatically increased to allow for predicted scrap and other losses, based on the data in the Bill of Materials. As manufacturers put more materials at the point of use on the shop floor and reduce the quantity manufactured in each lot, backflushing becomes a necessity from an operational standpoint. However, backflushing usually does not support lot or serial control. The inputs to inventory are shown in Figure 5.13.

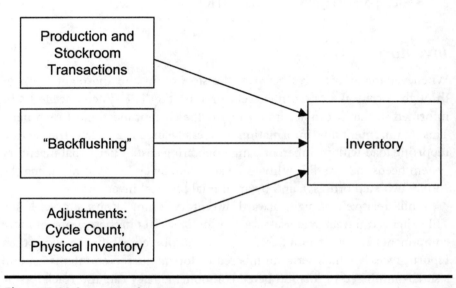

Figure 5.13 Inventory Inputs

Since on-hand inventory balances are the starting point for MPS and MRP planning and for customer order promising, they must be absolutely accurate. Therefore, most inventory systems support cycle counting.

Inventory directly affects the functions listed below (see Figure 5.14):

- MPS — inventory provides the starting balance for the MPS calculations for each item.
- MRP — inventory provides the starting balance for the MRP calculations for each item.
- Customer Order Promising — some manufacturers promise shipment based on on-hand inventories of finished goods; in the future, customer computer systems might be directly tied to the manufacturer's system to obtain this number.

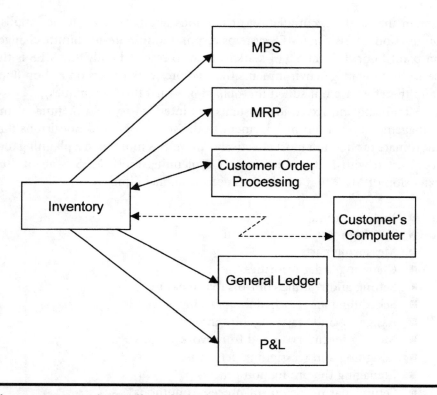

Figure 5.14 Functions Affected by Inventory

- General Ledger — inventory provides the on-hand balance and standard cost for general ledger to calculate inventory asset value.
- P&L (from inventory adjustments) — inventory provides the standard cost for the items being adjusted.

Manufacturing Execution Systems (Enterprise Production Systems)

Shop floor systems were communicating MRP's detailed requirements to the shop floor in the 1970s, with dispatch lists and priority lists. However, there was a significant gap between the planning systems and actual execution, because the planning data was frequently late and was rarely current or sufficiently accurate. Many systems evolved to integrate execution to planning, including data collection, work-order tracking, and SPC. A Manufacturing Execution System (MES) is an on-line, integrated, computerized system that is the accumulation of methods and tools used to accomplish production.* Real-time MES systems respond to minute-to-minute changes on plant floor; ERP and TEI systems tend to respond daily. An MES is the best way to manage environments that require work orders on a shop floor (and therefore are not suited for *kanban* or visual flow techniques).

Manufacturing Execution Systems are intended to help manufacturing management, from top management to the shop floor, make decisions that coordinate production most effectively. An MES is more than a planning tool (contrasted with MRP, which is only a planning tool). MES is an on-line extension of MRP that emphasizes execution, including:

- Making products
- Turning machines on and off
- Measuring parts
- Changing order priorities
- Setting and reading controls that measure
- Scheduling and rescheduling machines
- Assigning and reassigning inventory
- Moving inventory to and from workstations
- Assigning and reassigning personnel
- Managing the production process
- Setting alarms for out-of-process conditions**

MES Functionality

MES functionality can be organized into two categories: core functions and support functions. *Core functions* include the following:

1. Planning system interface, which provides MES integration with:
   - MRP — MES receives information on new work orders and reschedules for existing work orders from MRP, and returns data to MRP concerning actual execution status for each work order.
   - CRP — MES provides the status of each work order and machine/work center, for CRP to use each time it calculates required capacities.

---

* McClellan, Michael, *Applying Manufacturing Execution Systems*, St. Lucie Press, Boca Raton, FL, 1997, p. 6.
** McClellan, Michael, *Applying Manufacturing Execution Systems*, St. Lucie Press, Boca Raton, FL, 1997, p. xi.

- Cost Accounting — MES provides actual time spent and actual material used at each manufacturing step to the cost accounting system.
- Inventory Control — MES reports material actually used (both for good items and for items that have been scrapped).
- Product Data Management — MES reports the quantities of each component actually used during manufacture, which can be used to verify and maintain Bills of Materials. MES also provides information about tools actually used, setup time actually required, and quality actually achieved, which can each be used to verify and maintain their respective data sources, and to monitor the effectiveness of the manufacturing process.

2. Work order and PLC management, which manages and schedules work throughout the plant using a real-time view, including the following functions:
   - Accepting work order information from the planning system (MRP), and allowing unscheduled work orders to be created.
   - Managing changes to work orders, such as due dates, quantities, actual steps to be accomplished (e.g., alternate work centers and/or alternate routings), and splitting or combining work orders.
   - Prioritizing and sequencing work orders to achieve the company's objectives; this can integrate with an Advanced Planning and Scheduling system.
   - Managing PLCs to direct actual production on a real-time basis.

3. Workstation (work center and machine) management, which implements the work order plan at the work station, and plans and schedules each operational work station, including the following functions:
   - Requesting and managing the delivery of all required resources (such as inventory, tooling, engineering drawings, and quality specifications) to the workstation prior to the operation start time.
   - Directly connecting with and controlling the workstation (such as CNC equipment, automatic insertion equipment, paint booths, and automatic valves), so that human intervention is unnecessary for setup and/or routine operation. This requires retrieving and downloading programs to the plant floor devices, and maintaining a current map of workstation status and availability.

4. Inventory tracking and management, which develops, stores, and maintains the details of each lot or unit of inventory. For the purposes of MES, "inventory" means anything that is needed for production, such as tooling, fixtures, raw materials, WIP, engineering drawings,

and any other item that could be included in a bill of materials. Inventory tracking accomplishes the following:

- Manages, directs, and controls all raw material and WIP inventory, by lot number and physical location.
- Locates and retrieves all supporting material and information, including electronic information (such as CAD data), tooling and fixtures, and quality specifications.
- Maintains and provides access to detailed information for each item, such as ID number, location, and quantity.

5. Material movement management, which determines and causes materials to be moved from their current location to their needed location at the right time. Material movement is inherently a non-value-added activity, and must be continually monitored and minimized. The materials movement function in an MES:

- Issues move tickets to a fork truck operator.
- Advises the AS/RS (automated storage and retrieval system)control system to deliver a specific pallet of material.
- Instructs the PLC (programmable logic controller) of a conveyor system to deliver materials to a specified workstation or location.
- Instructs an AGV (automated guided vehicle) system to pick up at a specific location and deliver to another location.
- Opens a valve and turns on a pump to deliver liquids.

6. Data collection acts as a clearinghouse and translator for *all* information that is generated within the plant, thereby allowing the MES to remain current. The different kinds of physical sources that an MES can accept data from include:

- Bar code scanners
- PLCs (programmable logic controllers)
- Time and attendance systems
- Machine and process monitoring systems
- Quality management systems
- RF (radio frequency) devices

7. Exception management, which is the ability of an MES to respond to unanticipated events, such as machine breakdowns, excess scrap, and material shortages. An MES should be able to respond to such events by:

- Rescheduling production or using alternate routings or workstations to respond to unavailable productive capacity.
- Adjusting machines and processes to conform to specifications, as a result of monitoring quality management information.

- Informing management of exceptions that are outside the capabilities of the MES to remedy.

A graphical representation of an MES is shown as Figure 5.15.*

There is a three-tier level of systems applicable to manufacturing: the TEI, the MES, and the controls level systems such as PLCs. The primary difference between these systems has been the division of functions into decision support systems (such as TEI) and on-line-transaction-processing systems (MES and controls). Once systems are viewed on this basis, it is easier to understand what functionality is likely to exist where, not in the sense of ownership, but in the sense of integrated functionality. The result is tighter integration within each layer, a direction that is leading toward combining the execution and controls layers.

Enterprise Production Systems

Following the lead of ERP systems, the current focus in MES systems is on integrating this array of functional systems into a more holistic, inclusive, synergistic system. Eliminating the lines between silos of information and providing a seamless on-line combination of controls and plant floor functions is the equivalent of the integration progress in TEI systems. This new combination of plant floor systems is called the **Enterprise Production System (EPS)**. Enterprise Production Systems are the integration of MES, plant floor applications, and controls. Integrating all real-time activities into one system can result in much simpler hardware configurations, and real-time information availability that is more responsive to plant events as they occur.

What does this increased integration mean to the people on the plant floor? A few examples might include:

- A much easier method to connect operator input through the local human–machine interface to the advanced planning and scheduling system providing real time information for rescheduling as needed.
- Automatic inclusion of incoming raw material data into the supervisory order tracking to determine the optimum inventory transaction event.

---

* McClellan, Michael, *Applying Manufacturing Execution Systems,* St. Lucie Press, Boca Raton, FL, 1997, p. 15.

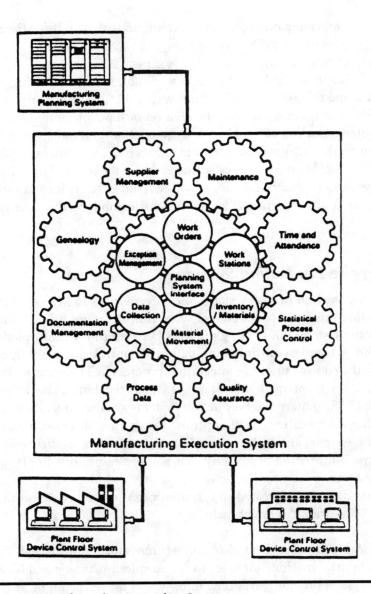

Figure 5.15 Manufacturing Execution System

- A simple interface to the document management system to include the latest available information with a work order at a particular workstation.
- An easier interface between the maintenance management system equipment status and the current process recipe.

- A more effective way to collect and analyze SPC data to effect current production lots.
- Direct information input to and from supplier company production functions.
- The ability to connect the warehouse management system to the production scheduling and work-in-process tracking system.
- An easy way to include laboratory information system current information into rescheduling methodologies.
- A method of system development that easily includes existing legacy systems or any other third-party software products, all implemented essentially on a plug and play basis.

Just-In-Time (JIT)

JIT and TEI systems have inherent difficulty coexisting. From a scheduling standpoint, JIT is a "pull" system, meaning that no materials move and no work is done until a downstream customer consumes a product. Then the vacuum left by the product's departure very rapidly "pulls" a replacement product through the production system. TEI's central planning systems are "push" systems, which anticipate customer requirements and push materials through the production system to be ready for the customer.

However, JIT is much more than a scheduling system; it is also a philosophy that focuses on identifying and eliminating *all* waste, and on continuous improvement. JIT identifies seven wastes:

1. Overproduction
2. Waiting
3. Transportation
4. Processing
5. Stock (inventory)
6. Motion
7. Making defective products*

Demand Flow Manufacturing, Lean Manufacturing, and Repetitive Manufacturing are newer offshoots of JIT. Repetitive Manufacturing methodologies integrate TEI and JIT.

---

* Hall, Robert W., *Attaining Manufacturing Excellence*, Irwin, 1987.

Classic MRP and MRP II systems were originally designed to support the job shop/work order paradigm (see Figure 5.16), which is based on several assumptions:

- Each job will be unique.
- Like machines must be grouped together for maximum efficiency and flexibility. This way, a supervisor or lead worker can train new workers on what to do and how to do it, and the supervisor can oversee work from a position of technical know-how.
- Machines are expensive, and inventory investment is cheap. Machines must be kept busy to justify our investment in them. It is better to have inventory waiting for machines to be available, instead of machines waiting for work.
- The company earns money by running machines to make components and subassemblies (even if there is no demand for the components, and they must eventually be scrapped).
- Inventory is an asset.
- Workers must be controlled in detail.
- Large lots are necessary to cover setup costs.*

In a company that makes the same products repeatedly, these assumptions are not necessarily true. If we are willing to challenge these assumptions, we can create an entirely different operating model, with the objectives of:

- Maximum profitability
- Maximum flexibility
- Superior customer service
- Minimum inventories
- Minimum lead times

This new model assumes the following:

- We make the same items or item families many times. (These items or families do *not* have to be made continuously!)
- Products and parts can be grouped with other products or parts that are made with similar processes.

---

* Langenwalter, Gary A., *White Paper on Repetitive Methodologies for Manufacturing*, APICS, Alexandria, VA, 1999.

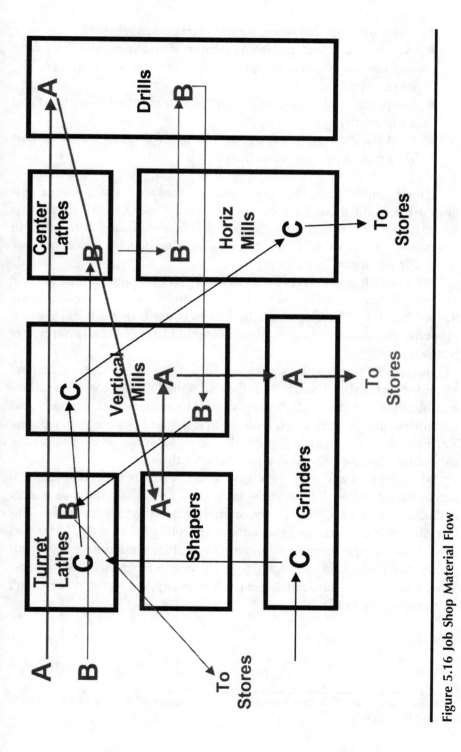

Figure 5.16 Job Shop Material Flow

- When we slash lead times, we will increase market share.
- When we slash lead times and inventory correctly, we will slash waste and inefficiency, but increase on-time shipments and dramatically increase profits.
- Setups can (and should) be eliminated or minimized (done faster and more effectively).
- Workers are capable of making intelligent decisions, adding value with their brains as well as their hands.*

In their simplest form, Repetitive methodologies are basically production-line oriented. All items flow down "production lines," in which the raw material starts at one end and is converted to finished goods at the other, in a very short time period. Since items are flowing down a line, setups are essentially eliminated (see Figure 5.17).

TEI and ERP systems do not intentionally seek out and eliminate waste, as does JIT/Repetitive/Flow/Lean. In the 1980s, many U.S. manufacturers learned that JIT reduces costs and lead times better than MRP II. However, properly combining JIT-based approaches and TEI can create an even greater competitive edge.

The best TEI and ERP systems support JIT/Repetitive scheduling and execution on the shop floor, and use the rest of the TEI/ERP communications and planning systems (including electronic connections with suppliers and customers, fully integrated data, and constraint-based planning). Integrating TEI/ERP and JIT/Repetitive requires that TEI/ERP systems have the specific capabilities that are detailed in Appendix A of this book.

When features and options can be added at the final assembly stage, a manufacturer can use JIT/Repetitive techniques throughout the subassembly and other feeder lines, and quickly assemble to specific customer order. This assemble-to-order strategy (also known as "configure to order") provides rapid response to customers, minimum inventories, maximum configurability, and minimum cost (see Figure 5.18). Assemble-to-order and ship-from-stock strategies are particularly well suited to support e-commerce-based, customer-entered orders.

---

* Langenwalter, Gary A., *White Paper on Repetitive Manufacturing Methodologies,* APICS, Alexandria, VA, 1999.

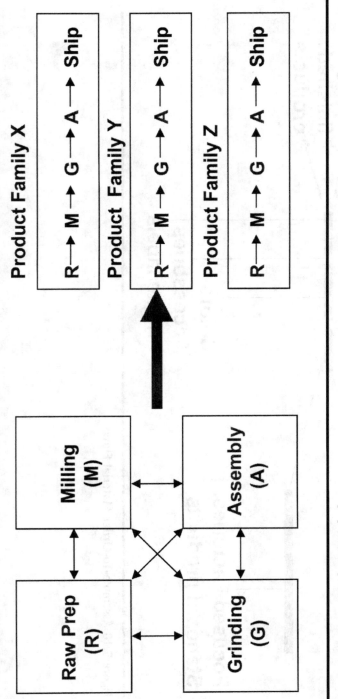

Figure 5.17 Line-Based Material Flow

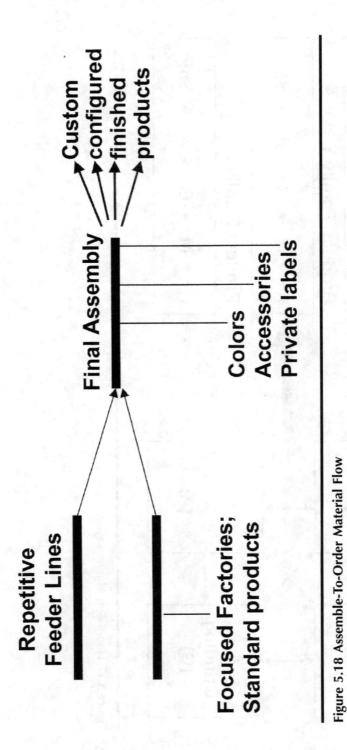

Figure 5.18 Assemble-To-Order Material Flow

Advanced Planning and Scheduling

Capitalizing on the availability of very powerful and very inexpensive computer technology, APS (Advanced Planning and Scheduling) systems use linear programming and other advanced mathematics to optimize schedules at varying levels in an organization. The simplest level is the local plant, in which the APS maximizes management's choice of one or more metrics, including on-time customer deliveries, profits, and labor force stability. Such a system becomes the heart of the customer support and material planning systems, replacing the old MPS, Rough-Cut Planning, MRP, and CRP systems. An APS integrates with forecasting, customer order promising, purchasing, costing, shipping, and the shop floor.

A more advanced type of APS system, called a "**Supply Chain Execution**" system, integrates several plants and warehouses, determining which plant should make which products to maximize customer service and profitability. It integrates fully with the logistics and distribution systems (and possibly directly with selected carriers). Even more advanced APS systems integrate not only the manufacturer's plants, but also integrate suppliers and customers directly.

APS technology can help in the following types of decisions:

- Strategic, with horizons from 1 year to 5+ years. This focuses on capital investment, infrastructure, customer and supplier partnerships, and new product development.
- Tactical, with horizons from 1 week to 1 year. This focuses on demand allocation, resource planning, and customer and supplier capacities, capabilities, and information exchange.
- Operational, with horizons from minutes to 1 to 2 months. This focuses on resource scheduling and execution monitoring.

APS technologies are designed to help manufacturers determine, then actually execute, optimal decisions. "Optimal" can be defined from a performance-oriented standpoint:

- Meeting customer requirements (delivery quantity, time, place configuration, price, and quality), *and*
- Respecting all real constraints (capacity, materials, workforce, financial, and political), *and*
- Maximizing company objectives (profit, market share, and/or return on investment) *simultaneously!*

Synchronizing Plans

Making optimal decisions requires synchronizing strategic, tactical, and operational plans. Each type of planning has special needs and uses different kinds of APS technologies, as shown in Table 5.7.*

Table 5.7 APS Technologies by Problem Level

Problem	Special Needs	Technology
Strategic	Whole number results	Mixed Integer Programming
	Discontinuous costs	
	Optimal results	
	Sensitivity analysis	
Tactical	Whole/variable results	Mixed Integer Programming
	Fixed/variable costs	Linear Programming
	Optimal results	Stochastic Methods
	Sensitivity analysis	
Operational	Computational speed	Heuristics, rules-based
	Near optimal results	Genetic Algorithms
	Models detailed reality	Theory of Constraints ("TOC")

At the strategic planning level, mixed-integer programming is the most appropriate optimization technology. It considers constraints and costs to determine a lowest-cost solution. It can generate 10% to 20% savings throughout an entire supply chain. Because mixed-integer solutions require time to run, they are ideal for periodic planning cycles. One example of strategic planning is deciding the number and location of distribution centers or warehouses.

A tactical plan is constrained by the strategic plan that it implements. For example, a tactical plan can optimize inventory levels at specific warehouses; if the strategic plan is flawed and has located the wrong number of warehouses at the wrong locations, the tactical plan can only correct that strategic error to a limited degree. In this example, tactical planning generates the maximum inventory turns and throughput through the distribution chain. Tactical planning can use tools based on mixed-integer programming and/or linear programming.

---

* Gumaer, Robert, "New Rules, New Tools: Attaining Optimal Financial Performance," *APS Magazine*, November 1998.

At the operational planning level, managers need to continually adjust the current schedules based on the plans and priorities determined by the tactical plan. In the warehouse example above, an operational plan understands that a truck for Customer "X" will be leaving the dock at 2:00 p.m. The daily production schedule should reflect the truck's departure time. The items for the truck should be pulled efficiently from finished goods or the production line. The operational planning systems integrate directly with MES systems.

Tools at all three levels should be able to optimize for multiple selected objectives in each of three main performance areas:

1. Customer satisfaction (including prioritizing between customers), such as on-time shipment
2. Financial performance, such as minimal total cost (including transportation), maximum profit margin, and/or maximum sales or market share
3. Competitive advantage, such as mass customization

For example, if a workstation goes down, or material proves defective, the operational planning system will suggest a plan that compromises between additional cost and customer satisfaction by including the appropriate selection of any combination of the following alternatives:

- Substituting a higher-cost raw material for defective raw materials
- Expediting more of the normal raw material
- Paying for air freight to deliver the original configuration items
- Using alternate routings
- Using alternate workstations or production facilities
- Working overtime
- Outsourcing components
- Outsourcing production
- Shipping the original configuration items from other distribution centers
- Delivering a smaller quantity than the customer requested
- And so on ...

APS Models

An APS system is based on one of three fundamental models*:

---

* Layden, John, "The Reality of APS Systems," *APICS — The Performance Advantage*, September 1998.

1. Network
   - Approach — Works from the top down. Starting from a customer order, the system builds, then resolves a deterministic network of real-world paths that the order must travel through production, totally synchronizing the facility for each component and part required for production. Models first appeared in the mid-1990s.
   - Advantages — Ability to resolve global priority issues, anticipate bottlenecks, and synchronize customer orders without relying on queueing, which means that the manufacturer is not forced to release all the materials when the job is started. Almost no inventories are required because there is no queuing. Adapts quickly to changes in the current reality.
   - Limitations — Most early systems operated in batch mode. Some systems require multiple passes through the schedule. Not all networking systems offer good sequencing options.
   - Application — Batch-mode processors, assembly operations, and industries where job sequencing is a secondary concern. Configure-to-order manufacturers concerned with order-level execution may find that the newer single-pass systems work best for them.
2. Finite Capacity Schedulers (FCS)
   - Approach — Works from the bottom up. Assumes that MRP will create the work order. Starting with individual workstations, FCS systems build a factory-wide plan using rule-based sequencing and queueing theories. FCS systems emphasize local workstation efficiency, rather than global synchronization or customer-based priorities. Used since the late 1980s.
   - Advantages — Maximizes workstation efficiencies and utilizations. Good analytical tools.
   - Limitations — Requires queues to function effectively. May suboptimize global decisions. Cannot adjust for future collisions; can only approximate global synchronization. Runs in batch mode; limited capability to adjust to rapidly changing customer demands or factory status.
   - Applications — Capital-intensive industries, as well as manufacturers whose equipment is fully loaded.
3. Optimizers
   - Approach — Uses advanced mathematical techniques to develop a "perfect" schedule, based on a snapshot of a fixed state. Mathematical approaches include neural networks, genetic algorithms,

linear programming, evolutionary operations, heuristic iteration, and artificial intelligence. First available in crude form in the 1960s.

- Advantages — Helps manufacturers achieve optimal balance between productive yield and timely delivery, machine utilization, and inventory requirements. Some optimizers "learn" from repetitive processes.
- Limitations — Batch mode is not synchronized, and there is no collision detection feature. Since optimizers cannot support a dynamic environment, they limit a manufacturer's ability to respond to changing customer needs.
- Applications — Continuous process and some batch process industries where environments are stable. Not well suited for environments with dynamic customer requirements.

As illustrated in Figure 5.19, APS systems replace traditional MPS, MRP, and CRP. APS systems integrate with:

- Demand Management — for customer demand
- Forecasting — for projected future demand
- Customer order systems — for actual demand
- MES — for actual status of the shop floor
- Supply chain systems — to communicate with customers and suppliers
- Inventory management systems — for on-hand inventory balances
- Transportation management systems — for transportation costs and schedules
- Warehouse management systems — for inventory balances

Supplier Integration

Purchasing is integral to achieving on-time shipments at profitable margins. In many manufacturers, purchased items account for more than 50% of the cost of goods sold; in those companies, a 5% saving in purchased items results in a 2.5% increase in profit before taxes. Purchasing integrates with the rest of a TEI system, as shown in Figure 5.20.

If a TEI system is working properly, it frees Purchasing professionals to spend much of their time finding new suppliers and coordinating with existing suppliers. If not, Purchasing professionals spend the bulk of their time calling suppliers with rush orders, changing due dates, and trying to find out where a supplier's invoice went and when it will be paid.

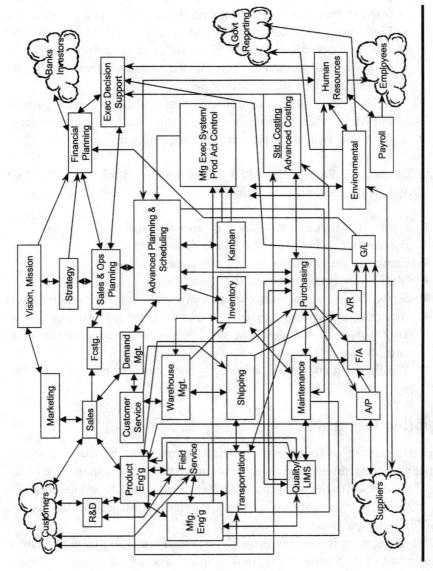

Figure 5.19 APS Integration

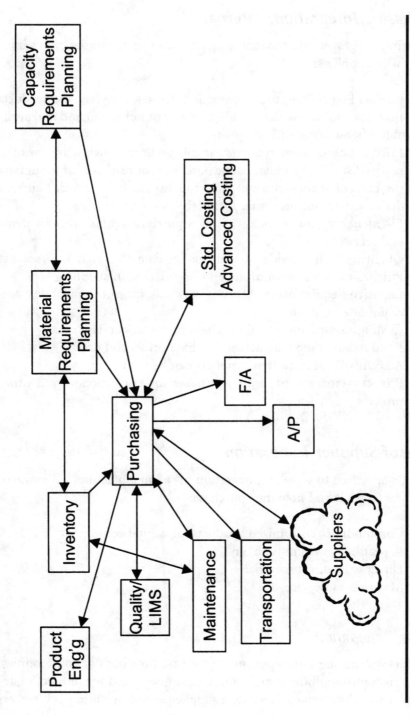

Figure 5.20 Purchasing Integration

Purchasing Integration, Internal

Purchasing integrates with the following functions in a manufacturer's integration with suppliers:

- Product Engineering, to source requests for new materials and products
- Inventory, to review the actual quantities of items on hand and available when talking with suppliers
- MRP (Material Requirements Planning), from which it receives the revised list of items that must be purchased or rescheduled to support the current manufacturing plan, and to which it provides current delivery dates for incoming materials
- Maintenance, from which it receives purchase requisitions for items and services
- Quality, which provides actual quality data to Purchasing so that Purchasing can communicate and negotiate with suppliers
- Capacity Requirements Planning, to track capacity availability and requirements at suppliers
- Costing, comparing actual purchase prices to standard costs
- Fixed Assets, supplying actual purchase prices and dates
- Accounts Payable, so that suppliers can be paid
- Project Management, with purchases for construction and other projects

Types of Supplier Integration

No single approach to supplier integration fits all manufacturers, because of differences in what and how they purchase:

- Commodities, customized products, or capital equipment
- Repeat buys vs. one-time buys
- Direct vs. indirect material
- Materials vs. services

Manual Integration

"Manual" systems are most appropriate for first-time buys of commodities, and for customized products and capital equipment, and for indirect materials. A "manual" system can include a supplier as one or more work centers in the manufacturer's TEI system, with long transportation times to and from those work centers, as illustrated in Figure 5.21. This form of integration assumes that the supplier can and will deliver products up to a specified level, within a specified lead time. This approach works relatively well as long as the supplier can meet their throughput commitments. It does not check actual available capacity or materials at the suppliers each time a planning run is performed at the manufacturer's site. This form of integration can operate with e-commerce, EDI, *kanbans,* or even fax and phone.

For capital equipment, partnering with suppliers implies that the customer specify the function that the equipment is supposed to perform, with detailed interface specifications. Additionally, the customer's engineers, the manufacturing professionals who will use the equipment, and the supplier's engineers can exchange ideas and data to develop the optimum design.

Electronic

Typical electronic integration with supplier systems includes using EDI (electronic data interchange), which transmits material release notices directly to the supplier's computer to eliminate the time and expense of printing out the requirements from the manufacturer's computer, mailing or faxing, and keying the data into the supplier's computer. The Internet is becoming an alternative to EDI, providing similar business functionality.

Fully Integrated

Fully integrated systems are most appropriate for repeat deliveries of predefined products. A fully integrated system does not assume that supplier capacity or materials are infinite, but instead verifies that information with each supplier's computer before computing its own optimum schedule. This type of system is the most advanced APS, called Supply Chain Execution (SCE). An SCE system requires electronic links between manufacturer's and supplier's computers, probably using some form of e-commerce. Because these systems require extremely high reliability of the data in the computers at each location, and of the data communications system between the companies, systems of this type were just starting to be deployed in 1999. Figure 5.24 illustrates the theoretical ultimate example of such a system, which would be able to go "x" suppliers deep in the chain, all the way back to the basic industries that remove

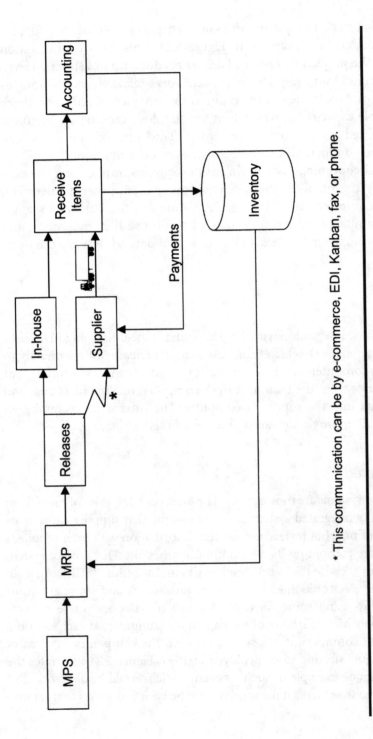

* This communication can be by e-commerce, EDI, Kanban, fax, or phone.

Figure 5.21 *"Manual" Supplier Integration*

minerals and ores from the earth for their initial processing. This type of system will have great difficulty in actual operation, because of the many potential points of failure throughout the information chain.

In late 1998, Dell Computer created customized Web pages for its top 30 suppliers, so that employees at those suppliers could view detailed demand forecasts and other sensitive Dell customer data, so that suppliers in turn could match their own production to Dell's needs. Dell is also passing on data about defect rates, engineering changes, and product enhancements to these same suppliers. In turn, suppliers are required to provide sensitive information, such as quality problems, to Dell. The much higher rate of communication between Dell and its suppliers has reduced response cycle times, inventories, and the margin of error.[*]

Another example of supplier integration is the relationship between Rayonier, Inc., a supplier, and its largest customer, Eastman Chemical Co. Eastman forecasts based on sales data, including seasonal and general trends by product, customer, and the entire company. It has created an Intranet so that its salespeople access the supply chain data from the road and update the forecasts with new information. Eastman currently uses EDI to communicate with its suppliers. It is intending to use Internet connections to let some of its suppliers look at its production schedules and replenish according to production plan, and to go to those suppliers' Web sites to track logistics movements. Eastman is involving suppliers in developing the company's supply chain, sharing final product data, schedules, forecasts, and production campaigns — all information that they once jealously guarded. Charlie Spell, Rayonier's director of marketing, says, "accurate forecasting from customers such as Eastman is really key to the smooth performance of our production schedule." [*]

The tight connections described in the case of Dell and Eastman can be implemented only when the customer has a very tight, long-term relationship with suppliers. The easiest way to implement such relationships is to use a single source of supply for families of items, rather than spreading the purchases between two or more suppliers.

Other Methods

There are two other methods of integrating with suppliers:

---

[*] Stein, Tom and Sweat, Jeff, "Killer Supply Chains," *Information Week*, November 9, 1998.

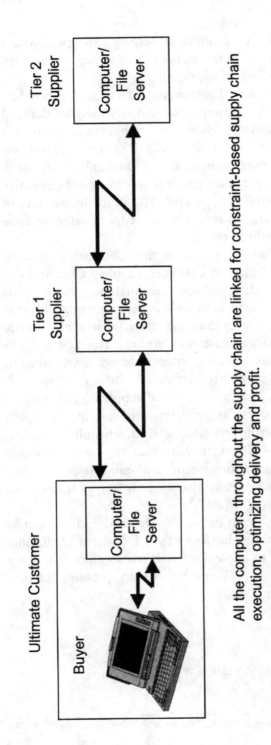

All the computers throughout the supply chain are linked for constraint-based supply chain execution, optimizing delivery and profit.

Figure 5.22 Supply Chain Execution System

1. *Kanban*, in which the supplier rapidly replenishes products whenever those products are used, with prespecified buffers (of "x" days or weeks of inventory) at the manufacturer and/or the supplier. For more information, see Robert Hall, *Attaining Manufacturing Excellence*.
2. Vendor-Managed Inventory relationships with suppliers, letting suppliers manage and replenish inventory at the manufacturer's site.

Supplier integration also impacts the invoice/payment cycle. Rather than requiring a supplier invoice to trigger payment by the manufacturer, the manufacturer can pay either upon receipt of the supplier's shipment into the plant, or automatically, when the supplier's components are used in the production process (based on the components called out by the bill of materials for subassemblies or finished goods). This topic is explored in more detail in the Accounts Payable subsection of the Accounting Integration section, Chapter 6.

Optimum Performance

To attain optimum performance for the manufacturer, Purchasing needs to become a commercial liaison between the manufacturer and its suppliers. Its primary mission should become supplier relations, helping the manufacturer to be the best customer for its suppliers. This includes:

- Providing all the information the supplier needs as quickly as it needs it
- Working with the suppliers to define and use the most appropriate technology
- Paying suppliers promptly (the ultimate mode: no invoices; automatically pay electronically based on receipt of products)
- Rewarding flexibility
- Helping suppliers minimize lead times, to keep their lead times less than the manufacturer's lead time
- Cultivating and maintaining trust — keeping commitments
- Working directly with the customer base to gain straight information — no sifting, coloring, or delay
- Passing signals, rewards, and pain through the supply chain

However, purchasing itself cannot effectively partner with suppliers. Such partnering must be done strategically at the CEO or VP level, on a corporate to corporate basis, so that the partnership will transcend the turnover of individuals in specific positions, and will have sufficient commitment of both organizations to withstand stress caused by changing business conditions.

Purchasing is being charged with managing the supply base. But Purchasing can't *manage* the supply base, because it is not a fixed entity. Instead, Purchasing needs to maintain a flexible, fluid relationship with suppliers, supported by the TEI system. The keys to partnering with suppliers include:*

- Corporate to corporate relationship, which may almost look like a buy-out in some cases.
- Having the manufacturer be the best possible customer for its suppliers.
- Appropriate information that flows freely in both directions.
- Using time as the most important measure, with quality the second most important measure.
  - The right product at the wrong time is the wrong product; being first to market is more important than costs,
  - Driving toward costs may hurt quality or time.
- Recognizing all products have life cycles, and always looking for the replacement product.

Just as a manufacturer's own plants must be continually rescheduled to accommodate changes in customer demand, material availability, equipment availability, and worker availability, suppliers must also receive continually updated schedules so that they can meet the changed needs. However, virtually all MRP II systems, most ERP systems, and even some TEI systems assume that suppliers can meet all demands, sometimes in extremely unrealistic lead times.

Quality Management Systems

MRP II systems generally ignored the role of quality assurance and quality control. ERP and TEI brought a newer business model that provides the possibility of integrating, rather than segregating, internal and external

---

* Michael Harding, conversation, January 3, 1999.

sources for improved customer satisfaction. Quality Management Systems (QMS) evolved from the initial concept of "inspecting in quality" to a realization that "all factors contributing to quality product and service must be addressed" in order to achieve true customer satisfaction.

QMS is a system in which "all activities of the overall management function that determine the quality policy, objectives, and responsibilities, and implement them by means such as quality planning, quality control, quality assurance, and quality improvement …" are effectively developed, implemented, and monitored (Figure 5.23).*

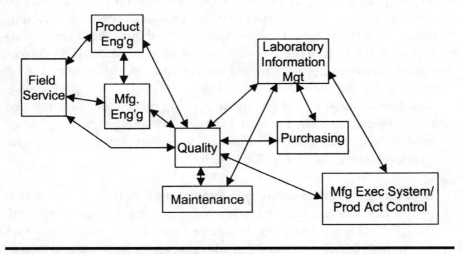

Figure 5.23 Quality Management System Integration

Driven by global economics and the need for a common baseline from which all quality-related factors can be measured, current Quality Management Systems have taken on an international flavor. The ISO 9000 Series has become the accepted standard upon which industry-specific requirements can be developed. Originally released in 1984, the ISO 9000 Series have evolved from a 20-element approach to a 4-process approach. Regardless of the format for the ISO Standard, the concept has remained the same: "active integration of executive-level management involvement, corrective/preventive action, and internal monitoring of the documented

* ANSI/ISO/ASQC A8402, *Quality Management and Quality Assurance – Vocabulary*, 1994.

processes versus actual practice"* will lead to continuous improvement and customer satisfaction.

The ISO Series model provides the framework around which an effective system for achieving customer satisfaction can be developed and implemented. One fundamental concept that is frequently ignored is that "customer" means both internal (i.e., employees) and external (the purchaser of the product and/or service) customers. A company can use the model to first develop documented practices and then implement them through trained personnel. This allows routine practices to become standardized, freeing people to "focus their energy on the new rather than re-correcting the existing". By drawing upon the cross section of a company, the internal monitoring process (quality system audits) provides people from various departments with an opportunity to learn more about other departments by assessing the effectiveness of the documented practices. The corrective/preventive action process provides a common mechanism for implementing change into the QMS.

The data acquired by the quality monitoring process can be integrated into the TEI database. Quality then becomes "just another resource" to be planned and then managed. The following are some examples of quality data being integrated throughout an TEI system:

- **Laboratory information management system (LIMS)** integration provides the raw data for quality analysis later. A fully integrated link is critical to manufacturers who must verify the specifications of a lot of material before it ships, but who choose, for handling and storage space reasons, to place the lot in a trailer waiting for approval from the lab. When the lot has been approved, the trailer is released. On those rare occasions when the lot is rejected, an integrated system will not print the shipping paperwork, thus preventing a bad lot from being sent to a customer. The laboratory system is, in turn, integrated with the following functions:
  - The manufacturing execution system and/or the production activity control system, to receive the actual data from the production areas
  - Purchasing, to receive data from suppliers and feed LIMS analysis data back to suppliers.

---

* ANSI/ISO/ASQC A8402, *Quality Management and Quality Assurance – Vocabulary*, 1994.

- Quality systems should also be integrated with field service to receive actual data on field failures (comparing that data to projected MTBF (mean time between failures), flagging anomalies) and returning failure data to the field, so that field technicians can make better decisions when repairing equipment. Quality systems can also track the number of times a specific serial-numbered unit has been repaired, notifying the repair facility when the unit reaches the maximum allowable, so that it is scrapped or removed from circulation.
- Tight integration with Manufacturing Engineering and Product Engineering allows the engineering disciplines to review actual quality data on existing products when they are revising existing products or designing new products and processes, to continually improve quality.
- Quality systems and LIMS must also integrate with Maintenance, so that a machine can be adjusted before the parts that it is producing fall outside specified quality tolerances.

Maintenance

Virtually all maintenance systems include both preventive and reactive capabilities, tracking actual labor and material against predetermined standards. They also include stock and tool controls.

In "reactive" mode, they provide a repair order to fix a broken piece of equipment. The repair order can be predefined, or can be created by the maintenance professional during the repair. If predefined, it can be modified during the repair based on that particular situation. Repairs can be categorized by activity type (remove and replace motor), severity, type of equipment, and/or reason code (the reason for the failure). Repair history is then available for future analysis to determine the major reasons for equipment failures, and the total cost of ownership for each piece of equipment.

In "predictive" and "preventive" modes, the equipment is scheduled in advance to be down, and all necessary materials and personnel are scheduled to be available. Preventive maintenance is common; it is like the 3000-mile oil and filter change on a car, or replacing all the fluorescent lightbulbs on a set schedule. Predictive maintenance requires data that can predict an upcoming failure (such as the line on an SPC chart moving toward a control limit, or vibration setting off a vibration sensor).

More advanced maintenance packages are event-based and are integrated with a knowledge base that includes failure analysis, maintenance procedures, and feedback from previous maintenance activities (see Figure 5.24).

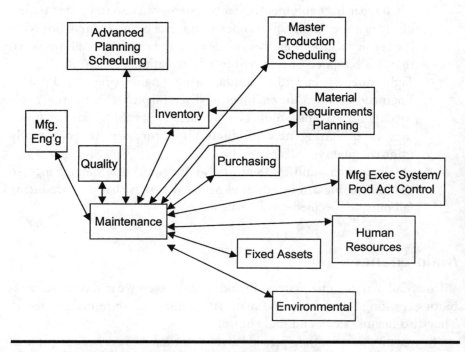

Figure 5.24 Maintenance Management System Integration

Maintenance has historically been excluded from MRP II systems. However, in TEI systems it is integrated with the following functions:

- Material and capacity planning — When maintenance professionals start to rebuild a machine or repair a facility, they often need a standard, predictable set of parts, plus other parts that depend on the status of the unit being repaired. When predictive and preventive maintenance is scheduled, the material planning system should automatically insure the availability of all required parts.
- Inventory — Rather than Maintenance maintaining its own inventory planning system, it can use the material planning capabilities of the TEI system. This provides automatic links to Purchasing, Receiving, and Accounting.

- Equipment and facility scheduling — When maintenance professionals are going to work on a piece of equipment, that equipment is no longer available for production. In many facilities, the workers who normally staff the equipment are then available for other jobs in other work centers. The plant scheduling system needs to include these facts in its schedules.

- Purchasing — Maintenance acquires both goods and services. Its purchases should go through the purchasing system easily, efficiently, and effectively. This is an ideal application for work flow, because many Maintenance purchases are for nonstandard items and services. Contracts for outside maintenance services should also be routed through Purchasing for ease of tracking and payment.

- Engineering — Maintenance needs access to engineering drawings and specifications for piping, wiring, heating, and other building characteristics, plus similar attributes for machines that have been installed by the plant's own engineers.

- Equipment history — Maintenance and Fixed Assets should share information on capital equipment. The equipment master record (which is part of Fixed Assets) should also carry the complete maintenance history for the equipment, as well as depreciation data.

- Quality — If a machine's output is starting to fall outside SPC tolerance, Maintenance should be automatically notified and given the SPC data.

- Human Resources — Certifications of maintenance professionals should be tracked by the Human Resources system, so that the certifications can be maintained. Some TEI systems can also track exposure, by person and incident, to hazardous and suspected hazardous materials.

- Environmental — From time to time, maintenance personnel must handle or use or dispose of hazardous materials. The environmental module must be notified of all these activities. Additionally, the MSDS (Material Safety Data Sheets) that are maintained by the Environmental module must be accurate, informative, and available to maintenance personnel wherever and whenever they need them.

References

ANSI/ISO/ASQC A8402, *Quality Management and Quality Assurance — Vocabulary*, 1994.
APS Magazine, MFG Publishing, Beverly, MA; www.apsmagazine.com.
Banker, Steve, "Supply Chain Execution Systems," *APS Magazine*, November 1998.

Greengard, Samuel, "Get Lean," *IW Growing Companies,* March, 1999.

Gumaer, Robert, "New Rules, New Tools: Attaining Optimum Financial Performance with APS Technology," *APS Magazine,* November 1998.

Hall, Robert W., *Attaining Manufacturing Excellence,* Irwin Publishing, Toronto, 1987.

Hirano, *JIT Factory Revolution* Productivity Press, Cambridge, MA, 1989.

Jackson, Thomas L. and Jones, Karen R., *Implementing A Lean Management System,* Productivity Press, Portland, OR, 1996.

Langenwalter, Gary A., *White Paper on Repetitive Methodologies for Manufacturing,* APICS, Alexandria, VA, 1999.

Langenwalter, Gary A., "Why Use Repetitive? For the Results!" *1998 Conference Proceedings,* APICS, Falls Church, VA, 1998.

Layden, John, "The Reality of APS Systems," *APICS — The Performance Advantage,* September 1998.

Lewis, Raymond S., *Integrating Kanban With MRPII,* Productivity Press, 1997.

Liker, Jeffrey, ed., *Becoming Lean: Inside Stories of U.S. Manufacturers,* Productivity Press, Portland, OR, 1997.

Mattson, Stig-Arne, "APS and ERP: A Powerful Synergy," *Midrange ERP,* January 1999.

McClellan, Michael, *Applying Manufacturing Execution Systems,* St. Lucie Press, Boca Raton, FL, 1997.

MESA International, *MIS Functionalities and MRP to MES Data Flow Possibilities,* MESA International, Pittsburgh, PA, 1994.

Oden, Howard W., Langenwalter, Gary A., and Lucier, Raymond A., *Handbook of Material and Capacity Requirements Planning,* McGraw-Hill, 1993.

Peach, Robert W., *The ISO 9000 Handbook,* Irwin Publishing, Toronto, 1997.

Pine, B. Joseph, and Davis, Stan, *Mass Customization: The New Frontier in Business Competition,* Harvard Business School Press, Cambridge, MA, 1999.

Repetitive Manufacturing Specific Industry Group, APICS, Falls Church, VA – call (800) 444-APIC, or visit the Web site at www.apics.org for more information about this organization.

Stein, Tom and Sweat, Jeff, "Killer Supply Chains," *Information Week,* November 9, 1998.

6 | Support Services Integration

S upport services are those functions that do not directly touch manufactured items or meet with customers, but are required for a company
to operate, such as:

- Accounting
- Costing (standard and advanced)
- Human Resources
- Environmental Management.

Accounting Integration

The traditional objective of accounting systems is to communicate the financial situation of the company, in terms that enable people to understand
what is happening, why it is happening, and how to improve it. Accounting
systems and theory view the world in terms of control; they ensure that all
information is accurate, and that all activities are properly recorded. The
challenge to accountants as they implement TEI systems is to think of new
and creative ways to achieve the necessary level of controls, while eliminating
or minimizing the paperwork and human effort. Accountants, like all other
functions in a company, are learning how to ask the question, "How does
this activity add value to the customer?" and to respond to the answer. Thus,
accounting and information systems need to be designed and implemented
to differentiate between value-adding and non-value-adding activities and

expenditures. Additionally, these systems must be designed to mirror changes in the marketplace and supplier communities; a product or feature or service that added value to a customer in the past might be viewed as non-value-added in the present, and as negatively value-added in the future.

A second, nontraditional objective is to maintain superb relationships with employees, suppliers, and customers, enabling the company to attract the best employees and suppliers, and to be the supplier of choice for customers.

In virtually all TEI systems, accounts payable, accounts receivable, and the general ledger are fully integrated into the system. Additionally, most TEI systems have the ability to feed third-party payroll; some have their own payroll module. Most have a fixed assets module. Accounting's integration with the rest of a TEI system is illustrated in Figure 6.1.

Accounts Payable

The goals of accounts payable are to:

- Maintain superb relationships with suppliers
- Ensure timely and accurate payment of moneys owed to outside organizations
- Ensure accurate, complete, and timely financial statements and data inside the company.

The ways that accounts payable integrates with the rest of a TEI system are illustrated in Figure 6.2. Accounts payable integrates directly with purchasing and receiving, paying the supplier after the ordered items and services are received. In more traditional companies, payment to a supplier requires a match of the following documents (performed by the computer system):

- Purchase order or release (already in the system)
- Invoice from supplier (entered as a voucher into the manufacturer's TEI system)
- Receiving report (for materials — services such as air conditioning repair, rent payments, etc., do not appear on the Receiving report).

Once the documents have been matched, the invoice is scheduled for payment. The system should allow a person to put a particular payment, or part of a payment, on hold pending the resolution of a disagreement.

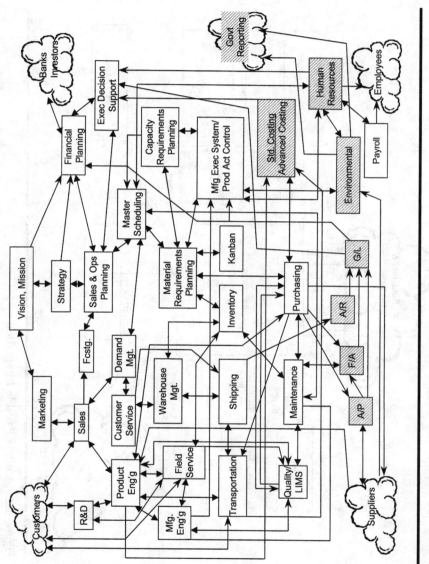

Figure 6.1 Accounting Functionality in a TEI System

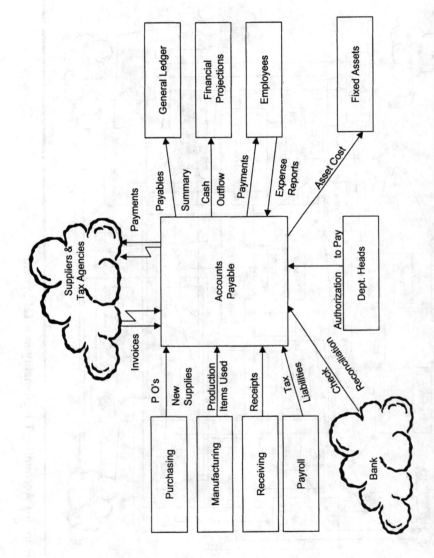

Figure 6.2 Accounts Payable Integration

More advanced versions of accounts payable allow manufacturers to:

- Bypass physical check writing, instead transferring funds electronically to the supplier's bank account.
- Bypass traditional paper invoices, receiving invoices instead via EDI or the Internet.
- Use work flow to route and track the status of approvals for invoice payment inside the company.

Accounts payable systems can help the company manage cash flow very closely, calculating whether to take a discount or not for each invoice received. (Many systems permit a company to take a discount even after the discount date.)

Accounts payable systems can have other potential interfaces, including the following:

- Paying expense reports to employees (one other way to accomplish this is to add the employees as "suppliers").
- Check reconciliation capabilities, some of which integrate directly with the bank's computer.
- Sending actual asset cost data (for asset purchases, installation costs, and ongoing maintenance costs) to the fixed assets system.
- Paying the local and national tax agencies at appropriate intervals, based on tax liability data from the Payroll and sales tax systems.

A few leading manufacturers are completely eliminating the three-way match requirement. Instead, they pay their suppliers of their production materials for the materials that were used on the production line, "x" days after the material has been used. For example, let's assume that Ford Motor Co. has a contract with Michelin Tires to supply all tires for light pickup trucks and that Ford will pay Michelin weekly under this arrangement. If Ford assembles 1000 pickup trucks during a week, Ford will transfer the money for 4000 regular tires and 1000 spare tires directly to Michelin's bank account. When this concept was originally presented to auditors at some of the large accounting firms, they reacted very strongly because they were extremely concerned about the potential loss of control.

"How does Ford know that Michelin delivered the tires?" they asked.

We answered, "Have you ever tried to drive a car without tires?"

"But what if Michelin ships too few tires?"

"The workers will stop the final assembly line because they won't be able to drive the cars off the end. Stopping an automotive assembly line will attract a lot more attention than a shortage notation on a receiving report."

"But what if the tires were defective?"

(Same answer.)

"But what if Michelin ships too many tires?"

"Ford only pays for what they use; so there is no financial risk to Ford."

"But there's no receiving report."

"A receiving report is a piece of paper which represents a person's word that something was physically received. I can drive a car without a receiving report. I cannot drive a car without tires. Maybe we don't need the receiving report any more; all we really want is tires. The fact that the car can be driven off the line proves that it has at least four tires; the assembler who puts the spares in the trunk can vouch for the spare tires. The customer wants a car with tires, not a receiving report, and an invoice, and a purchase order, and a check. If we can prove that we got the tires, all the other paperwork is waste, because it does not add value to the consumer."

(Silence.)

This practice requires:

- Full integration between accounts payable and Manufacturing
- Accurate Bills of Materials
- One single supplier for each item used
- Excellent relationships between manufacturer and supplier.

In some companies, many of the phone calls and faxes that accounts payable personnel receive (from suppliers, and from purchasing on the suppliers' behalf) are asking, "When will we be paid?" Maintaining superb supplier relationships requires that suppliers be paid on the promised date. Some manufacturers are investigating making accounts payable data directly accessible to the suppliers (with appropriate security).

EDI is an accepted means of data transmission between companies, including invoices and payments. The Internet is just starting to be accepted for these functions.

Accounts Receivable

The purposes of accounts receivable are as follows:

- Maintain superb relationships with customers.
- Ensure timely and accurate receipt of moneys from outside organizations.
- Insure accurate, complete, and timely financial statements and data inside the company.
- Provide credit decisions that maximize profits and minimize risk.

Integration of accounts receivable is illustrated in Figure 6.3.

Accounts receivable sends invoices, which are usually triggered by shipments, to customers. Invoices can also be generated for services other than the sale of the manufactured items, including rent on land and buildings that the company owns, patent and royalty payments, engineering services, and product maintenance services. A manufacturer can also invoice customers for freight, separate from invoices for merchandise. Freight bills have traditionally been relatively slow in arriving at the manufacturer — frequently weeks after the transportation actually occurred.

Customers can pay the company directly, using checks, or the company can have customers pay a bank lockbox directly using checks or EDI (thus getting the cash to the bank more quickly). If the company receives a check, the company ensures that the check is deposited in the bank as quickly as possible. In either case, the amount of the payment must be accurately applied to the customer's account. When customers deduct for chargebacks, allowances, disputed items, or other reasons, accounts receivable forwards that information to sales for a decision on whether to agree with the customer's position.

Accounts receivable provides account balance and payment history data to the credit department, and to outside credit reporting agencies. The credit department uses the customer history and balance information from inside

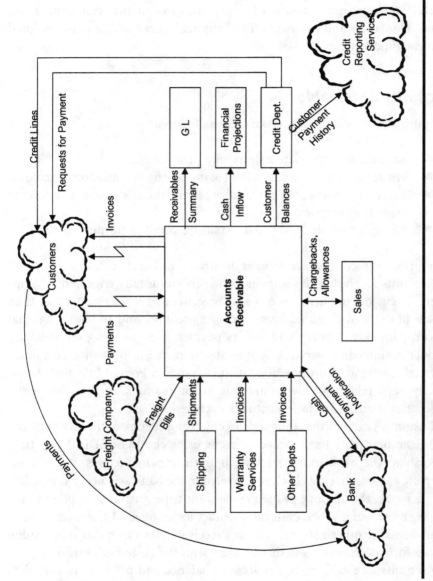

Figure 6.3 Accounts Receivable Integration

the company and information from the credit reporting agencies to review and determine the level of credit that will be extended to each customer. The system provides aged receivables reports so that the credit department can encourage customers to pay their invoices.

Accounts receivable also provides outstanding invoice data to financial projection software, which can project company-wide cash flow, and summarized invoice data to the general ledger for its reporting.

A manufacturer can ask its customers to automatically pay directly into its bank account, based on product usage rather than invoices (this is the reverse of the scenario presented in the Accounts Payable section, above). While this sounds attractive in theory, it requires:

- Excellent relationships between the manufacturer and the customer
- A very straightforward system of ensuring payment (e.g., the manufacturer should be the single supplier of that item to the customer)
- The ability for the manufacturer to audit the customer's actual usage of the manufacturer's items, compared to the payments made

Credit departments monitor the creditworthiness of customers. This requires noticing changes in payment patterns, receiving credit reports from credit agencies, and reporting customer payment patterns to credit agencies. Integrated ERP and TEI systems are designed to automatically check credit during order entry. Some systems also allow credit to be checked before a customer order is assembled, and/or before it is picked from the finished goods warehouse, and/or before it is loaded on a truck. Some TEI systems may integrate directly with credit reporting agencies, periodically uploading data about the payments they have received from customers, and automatically downloading changes in credit status of selected customers.

General Ledger

Since the goal of a company is to make a profit, the profit and loss (P&L) statements are probably the most important documents that a TEI system produces. The purposes of the general ledger system are to:

- Ensure accurate, complete, and timely financial statements and data for analysis inside the company.

- Report the company's financial status to outside agencies, including owners, securities exchange authorities, and lending institutions.
- Provide budgeting capabilities.

Figure 6.4 illustrates the information that flows through a plant or single company-level general ledger. The general ledger prints a range of financial statements at periodic intervals, based on information from the payables, receivables, payroll, fixed assets, and inventory systems. The primary financial statements include:

- Balance sheet (annually, quarterly, and monthly)
- Profit and Loss (annually, quarterly, and monthly)
- Cash flow (annually, quarterly, and monthly)
- Budgets (annually, quarterly, and monthly)

Most general ledger packages include an ad-hoc financial report writer, so that executives can see the financial results presented in ways to help answer specific questions.

If a company is using flex budgeting, the basis for the budgets (e.g., sales) must be supplied to the budgeting program before budgets are run.

General ledger packages can also consolidate subsidiary companies and divisions, both domestic and international, as illustrated in Figure 6.5. The corporate general ledger receives payables, receivables, payroll, fixed asset, and inventory data from the subsidiaries for consolidation. At the corporate level, intercompany transfers must be appropriately identified.

The chart of accounts, which defines the organization of the general ledger reports, provides the backbone for the financial reporting structure of the company. The chart groups similar accounts together for ease in reporting. Ad-hoc financial report writers support creation of reports and inquiries that ignore the inherent account numbering structure.

Payroll

The purposes of the payroll system are to:

- Ensure accurate, complete, and timely payments to employees,
- Report the company's payroll data to outside agencies, including taxing authorities.

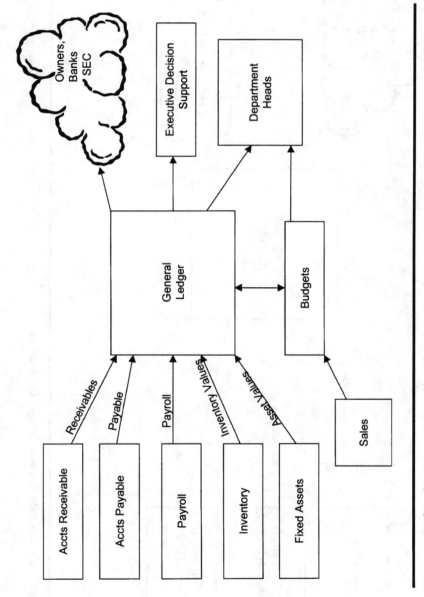

Figure 6.4 Plant/Company General Ledger Integration

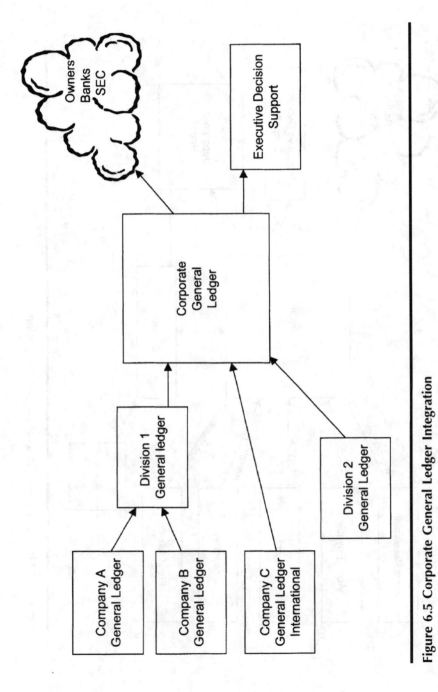

Figure 6.5 Corporate General Ledger Integration

The payroll system computes payroll periodically (weekly, every 2 weeks, twice per month, and/or monthly), based on data that it receives from:

- Time reporting systems (possibly time and attendance systems, and/or shop floor reporting, and/or other time reporting systems for factory, warehouse, and office employees)
- Human resources (employee data, including pay rates)
- Sales (commissions for salespeople)
- Taxing authorities (tax table updates).

The payroll system can provide the checks directly to employees, or make direct deposit into a bank for transfer to employees' accounts.

It also reports payroll amounts to taxing agencies at appropriate intervals (weekly, monthly, quarterly), and to the general ledger. It provides tax liability data to the accounts payable system, which can pay the tax agencies at the appropriate intervals.

Because of the complexity and constant state of flux of state and local income and withholding taxes, some manufacturers choose to outsource the payroll function to a third-party service provider. The manufacturer reports the gross pay for each employee for a pay period, and the payroll service computes the withholding and net pay. The payroll service also computes the tax payments that the manufacturer must remit to each taxing authority at each locality. ERP/TEI systems that offer payroll packages must maintain the tax tables and data for all localities that their customers need. Integration of payroll is illustrated in Figure 6.6.

Fixed Assets

The purposes of the fixed assets system are to:

- Compute the financial value of each of the company's capital assets
- Compute the depreciation for each of the company's capital assets
- Provide reports and analytical data to decision-makers.

Many companies still keep fixed assets data on spreadsheets rather than integrating that data with the rest of the TEI system. For companies with considerable capital equipment, full integration can include on-line integration with:

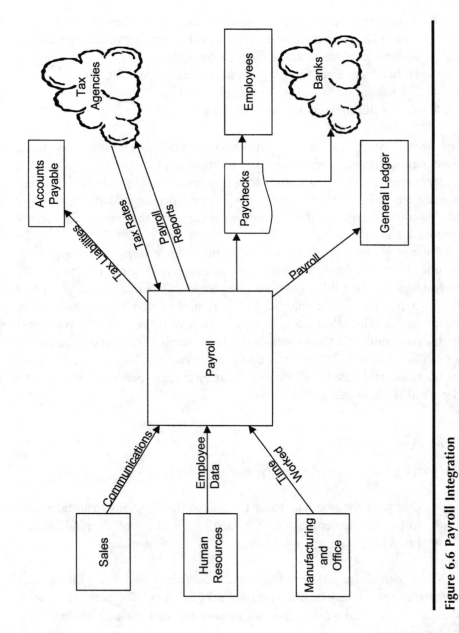

Figure 6.6 Payroll Integration

- Maintenance management system, sharing the same equipment master record, so that ongoing maintenance costs are readily available for analysis
- General ledger and executive decision support modules, with "what-if" depreciation scenarios for P&L impact
- Purchasing and accounts payable, for actual expenditures for each piece of capital equipment (initial purchase, installation, warranty, maintenance, and modification)
- Engineering, for specifications for the capital equipment
- Capital budgeting, which creates the original justification for the asset

Integration of fixed assets is illustrated in Figure 6.7.

Costing (Standard and Advanced) Integration

If a company makes only one product in a plant, the total cost for a period of time can be divided by the total number of products made for that period to determine the total cost for each unit of product. Unfortunately, most companies make multiple products, in varying quantities, at different times, in their plants. The purpose of the costing system is to help management understand the actual costs of each product, so they can ensure sufficient profitability when they determine the selling price. A product's cost is composed of several factors:

- Direct materials (the materials that become the product)
- Direct labor (the people who actually build the product)
- Indirect materials (the materials that assist in production, such as lubricants and tool bits)
- Indirect labor (the people who directly assist the direct labor, such as factory supervision, hands-on quality and manufacturing engineers)
- Selling labor (the salespeople who sell the product)
- Selling indirect expense (advertising expenses, marketing people)
- Design (engineering)
- Quality (manufacturing scrap, warranty returns)
- Other administrative and general (engineering, accounting, human resources, information technology, executive management)
- Technical support costs (help desk, customer hot line)
- Training costs

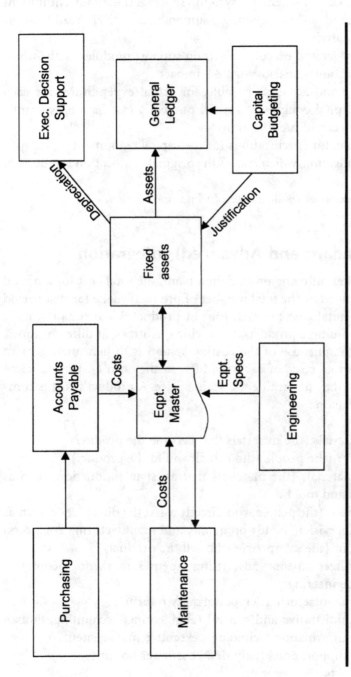

Figure 6.7 Fixed Assets Integration

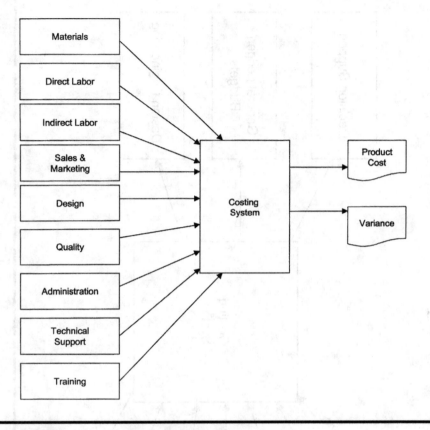

Figure 6.8 Elements of Product Cost

These cost elements are illustrated in Figure 6.8. Figure 6.9 shows how these cost elements integrate with the rest of a TEI system.

Standard Costing

The most common approach to determining product cost is **standard costing,** which calculates a "standard cost" for a product for a year by determining direct materials and direct labor costs, then adding an **overhead** or **burden** factor for all other costs. A standard costing system traditionally allocates the overhead as a percentage of direct labor hours or dollars. For example, if a compact disk manufacturing plant has a direct labor payroll of $1,000,000

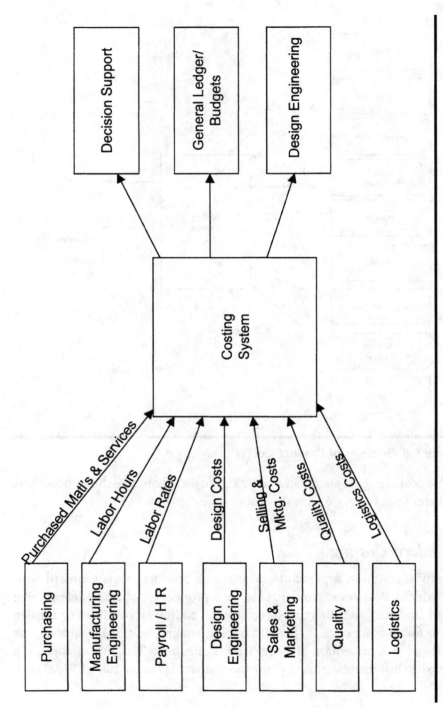

Figure 6.9 Costing Integration

per year, and the total overhead costs are $5,500,000 per year, the overhead factor would be 550%. A standard cost (Table 6.1) of a compact disc might be:

Table 6.1 Standard Cost Example

Cost Category	Cost
Direct Material	$0.75
Direct Labor	$1.00
Overhead	$5.50
Total	$7.25

If a particular work order for CDs had a scrap rate that was higher than anticipated, and used less experienced labor (at a lower cost, but requiring more hours), the cost for that work order (Table 6.2) might be:

Table 6.2 Work Order Variance Example

Cost Category	Std. Cost	WO Cost	Variance
Direct Material	$0.75	$0.80	$0.05
Direct Labor	$1.00	$1.10	$0.10
Overhead	$5.50	$6.05	$0.55
Total	$7.25	$7.95	$0.70

Standard costing systems can report **variances** from standard, such as the following:

- Material usage variance:
  - Quantity of materials (e.g., using more or less of the standard component)
  - Cost of materials (e.g., substituting a higher or lower cost component)
- Labor usage variance:
  - Quantity of labor (e.g., more or less direct labor hours)
  - Cost of labor (e.g., different labor grade)
- Quality variance:
  - Scrap rate (higher or lower than planned)
  - Warranty costs (higher or lower than planned)

These variances attempt to help management understand why costs were different than planned, so it can take corrective action.

In a standard costing system, items are received into the stockroom at standard cost, and the variances between the computed cost of the work order or purchase order and the standard cost for that work order or purchase order are distributed in the accounting system. Items are then carried in the inventory at standard cost. Standard costing is a standard feature of MRP II, ERP, and TEI systems.

Some systems also support **FIFO** (First In, First Out) and **LIFO** (Last In, First Out) costing. FIFO and LIFO costing approaches do not affect physical inventory movement. They affect the cost of goods sold calculation in the P&L, and are especially important in times of rapidly changing prices (e.g., inflation or deflation). During inflation, LIFO increases the calculated cost of materials, because it uses the price of the last materials into the company as the cost of the usage (until that quantity has been used up). This decreases the gross profits for that time period, thereby reducing the income tax burden.

Integration

Standard costing systems integrate data from:

- Budgets, as the standards to compare costs against
- Purchasing or accounts payable, for the actual prices paid for materials and services
- MES/shop floor reporting, for each work order, for:
  - Planned time that should be spent
  - Planned labor grade of each person who will be working on the work order, for both setup and run
  - Planned material
  - Actual time spent, by each individual
  - Actual material used, and quantity
- Payroll, for the actual pay rate of each person who performed the work
- Inventory or work orders, for the materials actually used for each work order
- Scrap reporting, for the total quantity of scrap

Advanced Costing

TEI systems support the more advanced product costing techniques, such as **activity-based costing (ABC)**, **life-cycle costing**, and **target costing**. Most ERP systems still lack those capabilities.

Activity-Based Costing

ABC recognizes that direct labor is usually less than 10% of the total cost of a product, and that allocating overhead on that small base is not conducive to making superb decisions. To support ABC, an TEI system needs to be able to support multiple "**cost drivers**," and to allocate various costs to those drivers. A cost driver is an activity or event that causes cost to be incurred. For example, issuing a purchase order can cost more than $100, because of the efforts required to obtain quotes and negotiate price, delivery, and quantity, receive the items, receive the invoice, and pay the supplier. The manufacturer's actual costs are driven by the number of purchase orders created, not by direct labor hours or dollars. ABC would allocate the cost of purchasing (and accounts payable) to the activities that caused the purchase orders to be created, such as specific products, or maintenance.

Engineering is normally included in overhead allocated to all manufacturing activities. However, a manufacturer might have one engineer who works full time on one or two product lines. In ABC, that person's full salary expense (direct payroll plus fringes, plus their percentage of the cost of the engineering department's management and support staff) would be allocated to those product lines. Likewise, if one product line absorbed significant quality management resources, ABC would allocate those costs to that product line.

Is ABC useful? The author consulted with a high-tech company in the late 1980s that was slowly going out of business; it had already laid off half its work force and had lost its competitive edge. It had two basic product lines: an old, low-tech, high-labor product that was viewed as a commodity by its customers, and a new, high-tech, low-labor, high-engineering, cutting-edge product. Its standard costing system allocated the engineering expenses on the basis of direct labor dollars. Therefore, the management priced the low-tech products higher than their actual cost to the company, and had lost most of that business (resulting in continuing layoffs). Management priced the new products too low, resulting in contracts that looked as if they were profitable, but that in reality did not cover the total cost of the product. Once the company had entered into the cost/price spiral, the factors caused the spiral to accelerate. Every time that management cut back on the direct labor force, overhead percentages increased, causing an increase in the standard cost of the low-tech product, and thus causing management to bid even higher on future contracts, which they would lose because their price was even more out of line with the competitors, so they would lay off more of the direct labor force.

Life-Cycle Costing

Life-cycle costing recognizes that products have life cycles, and that the entire cost of supporting the life cycle (from product inception to abandonment by manufacturer and the consumer) should be allocated to each product. These costs include product development, manufacturing, marketing, and support. This approach is particularly appropriate for companies whose products have short life cycles. Current costing systems focus on assigning costs to the correct time periods. Life cycle costing requires that major non-production activities (such as engineering, initial marketing, etc.) should be viewed as capital investments and ultimately charged to products that benefit from those investments. Life-cycle costs are illustrated in Figure 6.10.

Target Costing

Target costing uses competitive intelligence and market research to determine the prices that will command market share, then determines the target cost of the product based on the selling price. Some firms used target costing approaches to dominate the hand-held calculator market in the 1980s. They assumed a high volume of production and a learning curve, which assumes increased efficiencies and production as volumes increase, then priced their calculators at the low price which reflected high volume when they initially introduced them.

Human Resources Integration

Human Resources systems are much more than just an adjunct to payroll so that the company can track the date of a person's last performance review.

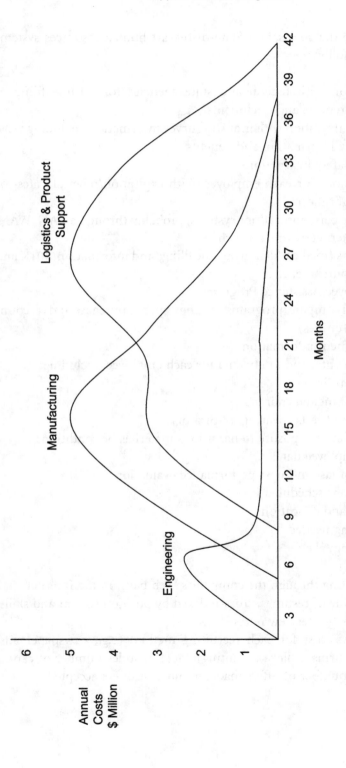

Figure 6.10 Life Cycle Costing Example

This section also includes safety. State-of-the-art human resources systems can include the following:

- Integration with federal and state agencies for on-line filing of required reports and documents
- On-line integration with industry survey information, including wage and salary information and benefits
- On-line safety instructions
- Certifications for each employee, with expiration/renewal dates for each certification
- Employee communications systems, probably through a LAN, WAN, or the Internet, with data such as:
    - Benefits (medical/dental on-line filings and information, 401K and stock purchase, etc.)
    - Employee Assistance Programs
    - Special company programs (outings, special purchase and discount opportunities)
    - Retirement information
- Environmental and safety data for each employee, including:
    - Safety training
    - Environmental training
    - Results of tests (hearing, respirator)
    - Cumulative exposure to hazardous materials or conditions
- Other employee data:
    - Date of last and next performance evaluations
    - Vacations scheduled
- Training and education:
    - Training needed
    - Training taken
- Recruiting:
    - Recruiting through the company's Web page on the Internet
    - Open file of resumes, cross-indexed by position sought and skills, including interview notes
    - Yield vs. cost for each recruiting method (e.g., newspaper ads, search firms, college recruiting); yield includes number of candidates, number of offers made, number of offers accepted

Integration

ERP systems can integrate in varying degrees with human resources programs and functions. TEI systems offer full, advanced integration, as shown earlier in Figure 5.1. Human resources (HR) system integration (Figure 6.11) can include the following:

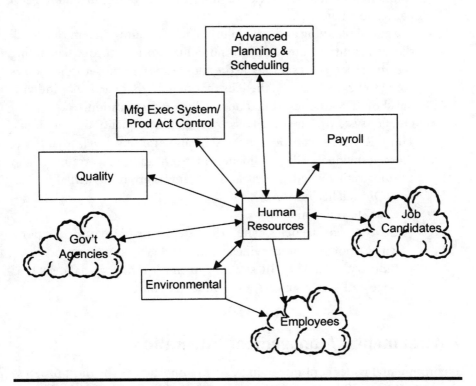

Figure 6.11 Human Resources Integration

- Payroll. Payroll and HR use common employee data as their main foundation. Many HR systems are, in fact, sold by payroll software suppliers. When a new employee joins the company, they should be added to the HR system as an employee, then to the payroll system to be paid.
- Job tracking system. This can track which employees perform which jobs, for future information about environmental exposure (e.g., hazardous materials, heavy lifting, or noise levels). HR systems can also flag instances of employees performing tasks that they are not trained or

suited for (e.g., a person with asthma in an environment with irritating vapors, or a trainee welder performing critical welding tasks alone).

- Security system. The HR system can define which employees have permission for access to certain areas, functions, or materials.
- Environmental system. The HR system can integrate with the Environmental system to track training, by employee, on handling of hazardous materials.
- Advanced planning and scheduling. The scheduling system can check the availability of the qualified individual workers before scheduling specific tasks. For example, if the most experienced setup person is going to be on vacation, the jobs that require that particular individual should not be scheduled during his or her vacation.
- Quality systems. The quality system can track quality by individual. The HR system can document skill and training level, identifying those individuals who could benefit from additional training, and demonstrating whether the training that was given was actually effective (Did quality improve?).
- External to the company —
  - Government agencies. The HR system can file required reports with national, state/provincial, and local government agencies.
  - Industry data. The HR system can import current data, such as wage and salary surveys, from industry sources.

Environmental Management Integration

Environmental issues continue to increase in importance. The most progressive companies wish to be model corporate citizens, leading their industries in improving workplace and neighborhood safety. As they have changed processes to minimize or eliminate the use of hazardous materials, they have frequently reaped financial benefits as well (the environmental version of "quality is free").

Environmental health, safety, and transportation (EHS&T) regulations require that all hazardous or environmentally dangerous substances be closely tracked and accounted for. Documentation is required to clearly identify each such substance included in a product and transported in a shipment, with full descriptions, warnings and instructions, and to meet employee "right to know" requirements, which mandate that complete documentation be available to any employee exposed to any designated substance. Integration with TEI offers the opportunity to substantially reduce manual efforts and insure full compliance.

EHS&T systems help companies track, manage, and comply with country-specific regulations that govern hazardous materials. At a minimum, EHS&T systems:

- Maintain current **MSDS (Material Safety Data Sheets)** materials readily accessible to their employees. Many factory employees speak languages other than English. An excellent EHS&T system will ensure that:
  - The most current MSDS information is available, by downloading the information whenever a supplier updates it,
  - The information is available in the languages that are appropriate for the workforce.
- Report storage and usage of any hazardous materials through mass balance computations. An excellent EHS&T system will:
  - Track all hazardous and EPA-listed materials through all functions, integrating fully with the TEI inventory management module:
    - Track location by lot number, supplier, and expiration date
    - Track all acquisition and disposal, including shipment in finished goods, recycling, and venting to the air
  - Monitor the total amount of each substance and group of substances, and automatically trigger warnings when a threshold is neared and when a threshold is exceeded.
  - Interface to Chemical Abstract list of chemicals to allow tracking by generic chemical name/number.
- Print reports for state and federal agencies.

More advanced EHS&T systems functions include the following:

- Automatically analyzing a product's physical and chemical properties, then applying up-to-date hazardous materials regulations to generate master compliance documents.
- Creating and printing COSHH (Control of Substances Hazardous to Health) documents whenever the manufacturer receives raw materials that contain hazardous chemicals.
- Monitoring exposure, by employee, to hazardous materials.
- Monitoring the conditions of the monitoring instrumentation, including calibration schedules.
- Automated environmental incident reporting.

- Integrating with Human Resources to monitor employee training on hazardous materials.
- Reviewing and recommending product formulations for reducing compliance costs associated with production, distribution, and transportation.

Integration

Environmental systems can integrate with the following systems, departments, and organizations, as illustrated in Figure 6.12:

- Inventory. The inventory system actually tracks inventory by lot and location. If that material is hazardous, the EHS&T system uses the inventory system data.
- Human Resources. The Human Resources system can track training by employee on handling hazardous materials. It can also track potential exposure, by employee, to hazardous materials by integrating with the Manufacturing Execution System, or Production Activity Control database.
- Engineering:
  - The EHS&T system monitors BOM and formula changes for any changes in usage of hazardous materials.
  - The EHS&T system can identify the major reasons for usage of hazardous materials. Engineering can then start searching for processes that use nonhazardous materials. One common example is replacing TCE-based cleaning processes with water-based cleaning processes.
- Manufacturing and Warehousing. The EHS&T system can generate all required documentation, including warning labels.
- Purchasing. If Purchasing tries to purchase a new chemical without prior approval by the Environmental department, that purchase can be flagged or blocked.
- Maintenance. The EHS&T system can be integrated with sensors at strategic locations throughout a company, including air monitors and water quality testing devices. If the EHS&T system detects the presence of hazardous chemicals that exceed expected values, whether in the air, water, or other waste stream, it can automatically notify Maintenance of its findings.

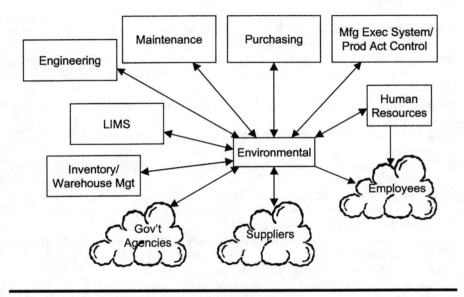

Figure 6.12 Environmental Integration

- Laboratory information management system (LIMS). If the LIMS detects hazardous materials in products that exceed the company's specifications or tolerances, it can notify the EHS&T system of its findings.
- Suppliers. The EHS&T system can download MSDS sheets from suppliers. It can also check supplier databases, or a master hazardous materials database, to ensure that MSDS sheets are current.
- Governmental Agencies. The EHS&T system can automatically create and submit the required reports, including:
  - Mass balance
  - Hazardous materials being stored
  - Any incidents involving hazardous materials (spills, venting).
- Industry Hazardous Materials Database. The EHS&T system can interface to chemical databases to determine:
  - Generic chemical name and number (replacing manufacturer's name)
  - All the regulations that a given chemical falls under.

References

Ansari, S. L., J. Bell, and the Target Cost Core Group, *Target Costing: The Next Frontier in Strategic Cost Management*, Irwin, Chicago, IL, 1997.

Berliner, Callie and James A. Brimson, eds., *Cost Management for Today's Advanced Manufacturing: The CAM-I Conceptual Design*, Harvard Business School Press, Cambridge, MA, 1988.

Bower, Patrick, "Delivering Enterprise-Wide EHS&T Compliance," *Midrange ERP*, January 1999.

CAM-I, the Consortium for Advanced Manufacturing — International, Bedford, TX; www.cam-i.org.

CAM-I, *Proceedings of the Second International Congress on Target Costing*, CAM-I, Bedford, TX, 1998.

CAM-I Target Cost Core Group & Profs. Ansari & Bell, *Target Costing: The Next Frontier in Strategic Cost Management – a CAM-I/CMS Model for Profit Planning and Cost Management*, CAM-I, Bedford, TX, 1996.

Cooper, Robin and Slagmulder, Regine, *Target Costing and Value Engineering*, Productivity Press, Portland, OR, 1997.

Johnson, H. Thomas and Kaplan, Robert S., *Relevance Lost: The Rise and Fall of Management Accounting*, Harvard Business School Press, Cambridge, MA, 1987.

Society of Management Accountants of Canada, the Institute of Management Accountants, and CAM-I, *Implementing Target Costing: Management Accounting Guideline #28*, 1996.

Society of Management Accountants of Canada, Institute of Management Accountants, American Institute of Certified Public Accountants, and CAM-I, *Redesigning the Finance Function: Management Accounting Guideline #43*, 1997.

White, Timothy, *The 60 Minute ABC Book For Operations Management*, CAM-I, Bedford, TX, 1997.

7 Technical Considerations (in Nontechnical Language)

The people that are particularly concerned with the technology that underlies an TEI system are the IT (information technology) professionals. However, there are eight technical topics that warrant attention by executives and others outside the IT organization:

1. Work flow
2. Object orientation
3. Client/server
4. E-commerce/Internet commerce
5. Data warehousing
6. Internet
7. Outsourcing
8. Security

Work Flow

"Work flow" in a TEI system operforms the same function for information as a routing does for a work order on the shop floor — it tells the person who has a task (such as reviewing or approving a document) what to do; when the person finishes with the document, work flow automatically routes it to the next person to whom it is intended. With work flow, the person can be at any level in the company, including the president. Work flow can be rules-based, or "intelligent" — it can determine where to send a document based on rules defined when it is implemented. In other words, a company can define its internal policies and procedures in work flow, and the TEI system will automatically carry them out.

For example, a maintenance requisition for less than $100 for common items might only require the requisitioner's signature (electronically, in the system), and be faxed or E-mailed directly to the supplier. Requisitions between $100 and $1000 might require the Maintenance Supervisor's approval, so they would appear in the supervisor's electronic in-basket on the computer; the supervisor can sign them (electronically), and then work flow would send them directly to the supplier. Requisitions between $1000 and $10,000 might require the signature of the Vice President of Manufacturing; they would appear automatically in the VP Manufacturing's electronic "in-basket" after approval by the Maintenance Supervisor. If the VP Manufacturing approves, work flow automatically forwards the requisition to the supplier. At any stage, the person who is supposed to approve the requisition can instead disapprove it, causing it to be returned to the previous person. Or they can put it "on hold" to ask some questions. In this example, no paper has been touched; the maintenance person selected the items using the computer, and all signatures are on the computer. This example is illustrated in Figure 7.1.

> *Advantages:* Because work flow has the inherent ability to eliminate paper-based documents and save time, manufacturers who use it effectively will gain a competitive advantage over those who ignore it or use it ineffectively. Work flow automatically enforces company policies and procedures.
>
> *Disadvantages:* Using work flow effectively requires changing the culture and formalizing the control systems of companies. Some ERP systems were designed before work flow became popular, and have tried to retrofit work flow into their system. With those systems, work flow does not function as well. TEI systems have been designed using work flow as a design center from the ground up.

Object Orientation

Object-oriented software design and programming were developed to enhance software maintainability and to simplify creation of advanced

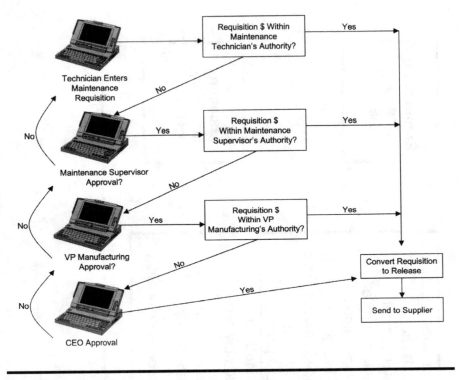

Figure 7.1 Work Flow Example

graphical user interfaces. Object orientation means that design, linkages, etc., use *objects* as their basic building blocks, which is a radical departure from traditional "procedural" design and coding methodologies.

An **object class** is a combination of data and processing logic, as illustrated in Figure 7.2. The data for a class may correspond to a relational database table, but this is not necessarily the case. The processing logic comes in methods, which are similar to subroutines or procedures. By maintaining processing logic with the data it works with, programmers have an easier time finding reusable pieces. Thus, object-oriented systems can be significantly smaller and easier to maintain than classical procedural code in which procedures and data are separated.

Two main principles of object-oriented software are:

1. **Encapsulation** — Processing logic and details of data management are known only to the object class's programmer. Other objects use them by calling the object's methods with published protocols.

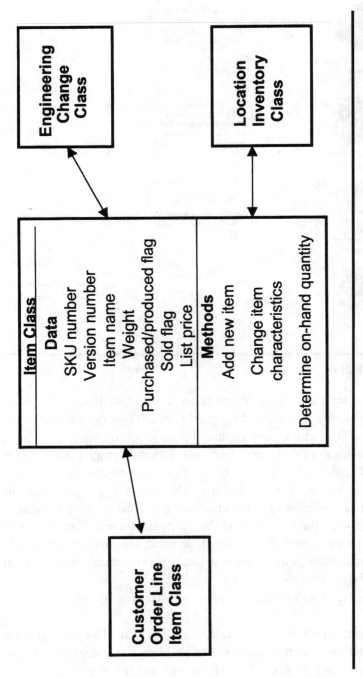

Figure 7.2 Object Classes Example

2. **Inheritance** — An object class may be a special case of another object class, inheriting properties already defined for the parent object. For example, inheritance can be used to provide consistent appearance and behavior of data entry and reporting screen displays.

The primary object-oriented language used by ERP and TEI systems at the turn of the century is C++ (an extension of the "C" programming language, which is the foundation of UNIX). A new language, Java, is rapidly gaining favor as companies move from client/server to Internet/Intranet technology. Java "applets" (application code) download to the user's PC, Macintosh, or UNIX workstation where they are rapidly compiled for execution.

Advantages:

- A well-designed object-oriented application is smaller, easier to debug, and faster to add additional capabilities than a procedural language such as COBOL or C.
- Object-oriented languages provide "natural" ways to control widgets (the graphic and text elements) of a screen window.
- Inheritance helps object-oriented developers achieve consistency in the behavior of each type of window.

Disadvantages:

- Designing object-oriented applications is notoriously difficult. Most groups require several attempts and a couple of years to get the basic design right.
- Java tools are new and unproven.
- Performance issues abound in current Java applications.

Client/Server

"Client/server" means that the processing of work is divided between two computers. The "client" is the computer on the desktop, which performs display functions (e.g., the Windows interface) and often computations as well. The "server" is the more central computer that contains the database and the TEI programs.

Prior to the PC and engineering workstations, the only device with any intelligence for business logic was a mainframe or minicomputer. Terminals had essentially no processing power; they could only display what the computer sent and send to the computer what a person entered. The graphic user interface of Macintosh and PC/Windows machines gained popularity with office applications, including word processing and presentation software. Users then clamored for the same graphic user interfaces with their enterprise applications. Unfortunately, graphic processing is highly CPU intensive and is impractical to perform at a central computer. Hence, it became necessary to offload that processing to PCs.

The primary strategies for implementing client/server are two-tier, three-tier, and Internet/Intranet. Figure 7.3 illustrates the difference between two-tier and three-tier. In a two-tier approach, the client machine connects to a single server machine. Usually the server controls the central database and the client controls the user interface. The designer decides how much of the processing logic should be implemented at the client and how much at the server. If most of the work is done at the client PC, it is called a "fat client" application. A "thin client" application means that most of the work is done at the server.

In a three-tier approach, the client machine controls the user interface and some processing logic, an **application server** manages the enterprise business application processing, and one or more **enterprise servers** manage the corporate database. This approach aids management of version releases and the enterprise business rules.

Client/server technology relies on robust communications between the machines that are involved. Local Area Networks, Metropolitan (or Campus) Networks, and Wide Area Networks become an expense and a management headache for most companies. Moreover, updating software versions, particularly on the numerous distributed PCs becomes an almost unsolvable problem. Many IT departments are moving toward Internet/Intranet technology as a solution.

In the Internet/Intranet approach, communications utilities provide the wide area communications backbone. PCs merely communicate to the Uniform Resource Locators (URLs, like www.Exxon.com) to reach the servers they need help from. Software coded in Java that runs on the PC clients is downloaded when needed, so it is always the latest version.

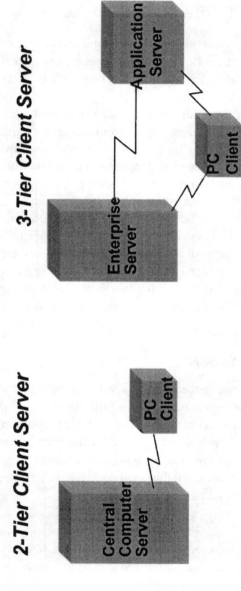

2-Tier Client Server

3-Tier Client Server

Central Computer Server

PC Client

Enterprise Server

Application Server

PC Client

Figure 7.3 2-tier and 3 tier Client/Server Approaches

Advantages: Some form of client/server technology is required to maintain control of the enterprise data asset while offering users the ease of a graphic user interface.

Disadvantages: The main issues as work is spread among many PCs are performance and system integrity.

- Performance: Unless a client/server system is implemented carefully, it can experience bottlenecks (causing long response times) in the network as data passes from server to client and back or between servers.
- System integrity: When all programs ran on one single computer, recovery from system crashes was relatively easy and straightforward. If a company experiences a power outage while various programs are running on multiple PCs, recovery is far more complex. Likewise, if a single PC "hangs up" while running an application, locking part of the shared database at this client, recovery can be difficult.
- Applications management: It can be virtually impossible to upgrade every employee's PC with the latest version of client software applications. For this reason, many organizations are moving toward "thin clients" and applications managed by applications servers. Java gives the option of having the logic run on the PC, after being refreshed with the latest version at the start of the user's session.

E-Commerce/Internet Commerce

"E-commerce" means "electronic commerce," which involves moving data between companies electronically rather than by paper or phone. Compared to communications inside a single plant, communications between customer and manufacturer have traditionally been much less efficient, and even primitive. Through the 1970s, communication was by phone with paper copy following by mail. Then the paper copies started being faxed. Either way, the process involved many steps, as outlined below:

1. The customer printed their requirements on a piece of paper.
2. The customer called the manufacturer and repeated all the requirements.
3. The manufacturer manually entered all the requirements into their computer system, attempting to be error-free.
4. The customer usually followed the phone call with a fax (sometimes virtually unreadable) or a mailed copy.

5. The manufacturer reviewed the fax or paper copy against the data they entered, to catch and correct as many mistakes as possible.
6. The manufacturer frequently sent an acknowledgment by fax or mail.
7. If there were time, the customer might compare the acknowledgment to their original order to try to reduce errors.

EDI

In the 1990s, EDI (electronic data interchange) became the norm as the means for communicating between customer and manufacturer in several major industries, notably retail and automotive. However, EDI was sufficiently expensive that smaller manufacturers ignored it when they could, using fax machines or phone calls instead. Most EDI transactions went through a third-party EDI service, which would group the EDI transactions, then download them to a given company when the company requested, in a manner similar to e-mail providers in PC networks.

The format for each EDI transaction is frequently specified by an industry group (such as AIAG, for automotive), or the largest player (such as a very large retailer). TEI systems usually interface directly with one or more third-party EDI services. Figure 7.4 shows an example of a purchase order moving from customer to manufacturer in EDI.

In this example:

1. The buyer at the customer approves a purchase order release to a manufacturer (pricing, delivery, terms, etc., have already been mutually agreed upon).
2. The customer's computer translates the release into an EDI transaction, addresses it for the selected manufacturer, and sends it to the EDI service provider via direct dial lines. Transmission of transactions from the customer's computer can happen almost immediately, if the customer's computer has full-time access to the EDI service, or in batches once every "x" hours (e.g., once a day, once every 6 hours, etc.).
3. The EDI service provider acts as a central message delivery system, almost like a mailbox for electronic transactions. It receives transactions from thousands of subscribers and routes them to their intended recipient. In this case, the EDI service provider stores the purchase order release in the manufacturer's electronic mailbox.
4. The manufacturer's computer receives the EDI purchase order release from the EDI service via direct dial lines. This can happen

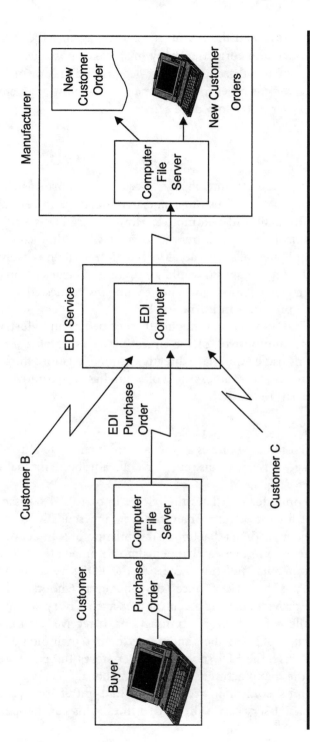

Figure 7.4 EDI Example

almost immediately, if the manufacturer's computer has full-time access to the EDI service, or it can happen in intervals, whenever the manufacturer chooses to access the EDI service.

5. The manufacturer's computer translates the EDI purchase order release into the format accepted by their customer order management system and submits the PO release as a customer order to that system. The customer order management system edits the transaction to ensure accuracy, then processes it as a normal customer order, making it available through the usual inquiries and reports.

Advantages: EDI is the major step in tying customers and manufacturers much more closely together:

- EDI eliminates the printing and rekeying of data; the data from the sending computer electronically updates the receiving computer. The more widely used EDI transactions are shown in Table 7.1.
- Eliminates most time delays. Today's data arrives at the recipient overnight, and usually gets processed at the recipient's computer before the start of the business day tomorrow.

Table 7.1 Common EDI Transaction Types

Trans. Type	Description
810	Invoice
820	Payment Remittance Advice
830	Planning Schedule with Release
840	Request For Quotation (RFQ)
843	Response to Request For Quotation
846	Inventory Inquiry/Advise
850	Purchase Order
855	Purchase Order Acknowledgment
856	Advance Shipping Notification
860	Purchase Order Change
862	Shipping Schedule
865	PO Change Acknowledgment
866	Production Sequence
944	Warehouse Stock Transfer Receipt
947	Warehouse Inventory Adjustment

Disadvantages:

- EDI can be expensive, especially for smaller companies, due primarily to the expense of the EDI service provider.
- While reliability has improved considerably since it was first introduced, it can still have technical difficulties, such as incomplete transmission, data corruption during transmission, and data missing or in the wrong fields.
- It is still basically batch oriented; many manufacturers get orders once a day from the EDI service. This precludes the customer from immediately verifying delivery promise dates and from selecting options and configurations interactively.

E-Commerce

As a first step, e-commerce provides essentially the same capabilities as EDI (electronic transfer of data from computer to computer, rapidly and with minimal errors) very inexpensively by using the Internet. Thus, e-commerce will rapidly become the technology that enables supply chain partnerships. All TEI and some ERP systems are already adapted for e-commerce, with most of the rest following closely behind. This first-stage e-commerce resembles EDI; some companies will communicate through third-party e-commerce message storage services, while others will communicate "directly" with each other (using standard e-mail mailboxes). Both types of communication are illustrated in Figure 7.5. E-commerce can use the same transaction formats as EDI, or two companies can standardize each transaction type between themselves.

The top example in Figure 7.5 is essentially identical to Figure 7.4, EDI. The only major difference is that the two companies are using the Internet (and their local Internet service providers) as a means of communicating data, rather than directly dialing an EDI provider. The bottom example in Figure 7.5 illustrates the following scenario:

1. The buyer at the customer approves a purchase order release to a manufacturer (pricing, delivery, terms, etc., have already been mutually agreed upon).
2. The customer's computer translates the release into an e-commerce transaction (per mutually agreed standard), addresses it for the selected supplier, and sends it to their mail system at their Internet service provider. Transmission of transactions from the customer's

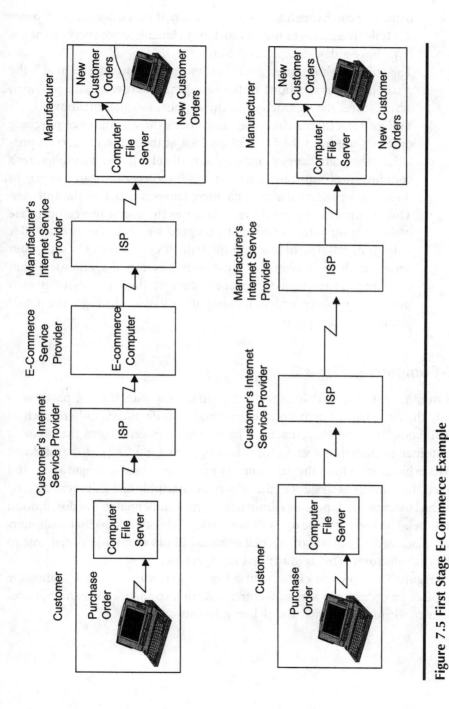

Figure 7.5 First Stage E-Commerce Example

computer can happen almost immediately, if the customer's computer has full-time access to the Internet, or in batches once every "x" hours (e.g., once a day, once every 6 hours, etc.).

3. The customer's Internet service provider transmits the "e-mail" (the e-commerce transaction) to the supplier's Internet service provider, which stores the transaction in the supplier's e-mail mailbox.

4. The manufacturer's computer downloads the e-commerce purchase order release from their e-mail mailbox at their Internet service provider. This can happen almost immediately, if the manufacturer's computer has full-time access to the Internet, or it can happen in intervals, whenever the manufacturer chooses to access the Internet.

5. The manufacturer's computer translates the e-commerce purchase order release into the format accepted by their customer order management system and submits the PO release as a customer order to their system. The customer order management system edits the transaction to insure accuracy, then processes it as a normal customer order, making it available through the usual inquiries and reports.

E-Commerce, Stage 2

However, replacing EDI for specified transactions with trading partners is only the first stage of e-commerce for some manufacturers. Others, such as Dell Computer and Weyerhaeuser, have created Internet sites that allow a customer to directly select features and options for PCs (Dell), and doors (Weyerhaeuser). Once the customer confirms the final configuration and price, the order goes straight to the factory for assembly and shipment directly to the customer. This process eliminates all the middlemen in the distribution channel. The Web sites are open 24 hours/day, 7 days/week, so that customers can place orders outside of normal business hours at no additional cost to the manufacturer. This is illustrated in Figure 7.6.

Figure 7.6 shows an example of a business customer using e-commerce to place an order from a manufacturer, selecting configurations and options, then confirming the price and delivery. In this example:

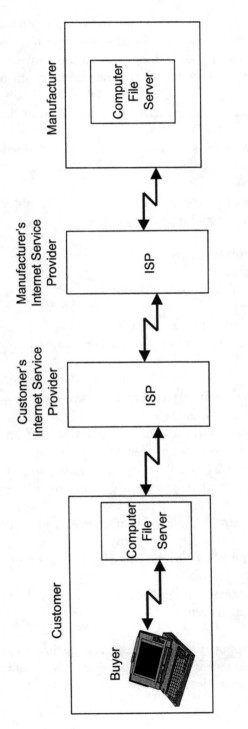

In this model, the buyer is essentially "logged on" to the manufacturer's computer, real time, using the Internet as the data transmission backbone. The buyer has real time access to whatever data the manufacturer wishes to grant access.

Figure 7.6 Second Stage E-Commerce Example

1. A customer logs into the manufacturer's Web site and accesses product information, including configurations, options, delivery dates, and shipping alternatives, with pricing for each option and alternative.
2. The customer selects the desired product configuration and confirms price and delivery.
3. The customer confirms ship-to address and billing information, and enters the PO number for authorization.
4. The manufacturer's computer edits and accepts the entire order, with options and delivery method and date.

This customer-order-entry type of e-commerce requires full TEI system support, 24 hours/day, 7 days/week, including:

- Editing and accepting customer orders
- On-line, real-time credit check
- Very tight and accurate configuration and quoting system
- Extremely accurate inventories
- Extremely accurate promised ship date calculations, based on real capabilities, real work loads, and real inventory availabilities.

Advantages:
- Lowers the manufacturer's cost of receiving a customer order — fully automates the customer quoting and order process.
- Allows customer to create the precise configuration they want, and to understand price differences between alternative configurations.
- Allows customers to order 24 hours per day, 7 days per week (a major advantage when manufacturer sells globally or sells to consumers).
- Directly links of customers' PC and manufacturer's computer, eliminating printing out and re-keying information.
- Less expensive than EDI; available to all companies that have access to the Internet.
- Can eliminate all the middlemen in the distribution channel (with the end customer ordering directly).

Disadvantages:
- Requires Web site and supporting systems (e.g., pricing, inventory availability) to be up 24 hours per day, 7 days per week. Can require substantial initial, investment in a Web site, plus significant on-going support expenses.

- Competitors can determine exact customer pricing by pretending to be customers on a public direct order Web site.

Advanced E-Commerce

Advanced e-commerce uses the capabilities in second-stage e-commerce in a much more tightly integrated manner. This forms the basis for real-time, constraint-based supply chain execution. In this model, the customer's computer and the supplier's computer are so tightly linked that the customer's computer can compute and promise future production and delivery, on-line, using the supplier's computer to determine material and capacity availability (constraint-based) of any necessary items. This is shown in Figure 7.7.

At the level of detail contained in this book, the diagram for advanced e-commerce looks the same as second-stage e-commerce. The difference is in the sophistication of the programming on the two computers, and the timeliness of the response. In advanced e-commerce, the supplier's computer must provide a constraint-based answer within a very few seconds. Furthermore, as the customer's computer receives responses from several suppliers' computers, the customer's system can query each supplier's computer repeatedly until it achieves an optimum result. Thus, the potential processing and transaction load on the supplier's computer can be substantially higher and more intensive.

Finally, there is no technical reason why advanced e-commerce should be limited to a single customer–manufacturer link in the supply chain. Theoretically, it can continue through several links, as long as each customer's computer knows which supplier to query for each needed item. The chain breaks as soon as human intervention is required (for sourcing, pricing, approvals, etc.).

Advantages:
- Enables supply chain execution — can create substantial competitive advantage.
- Timely and accurate linking of customers' and manufacturers' computers, eliminating printing out and rekeying information.
- Inexpensive; available to all companies that have access to the Internet.
- Can eliminate all the middlemen in the distribution channel (with the end customer ordering directly).

Disadvantages:
- Still in early stages of deployment; may not be sufficiently robust or reliable to use as the primary method of exchanging data.

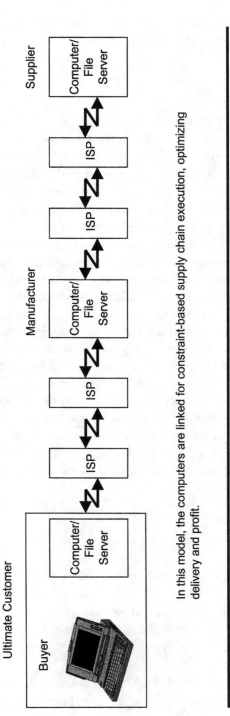

In this model, the computers are linked for constraint-based supply chain execution, optimizing delivery and profit.

Figure 7.7 Advanced E-Commerce Example

- Unless EDI standards are used, the customer and supplier might have to define each e-commerce transaction in complete detail, then program their respective systems to support those transactions, which is expensive, time-consuming, and error-prone.
- Some ERP systems are not yet adapted for e-commerce. All TEI systems currently support e-commerce, and virtually all ERP systems will support e-commerce in the near future.
- Requires accurate pricing and availability data in manufacturer's system.

Data Warehousing

As organizations understand the value of the data that already exists in their databases, decision-makers want the ability to "mine" the data. **OLAP (on-line analytical processing)** is the tool that enables a person to "slice and dice" the data in an almost infinite variety of ways to find relationships that can provide the basis for better decisions. OLAP can provide a high-level, aggregated view of the data by using MDBMS (multidimensional database management) tools. Figure 7.8 shows how routine business transaction data supports OLAP analysis. By 2001, 74% of companies will be using data mining on their customer data to increase revenue, and 34% of companies will be using the data to cut expenses.*

OLTP (On Line Transaction Processing) applications are characterized by many users creating, updating, or retrieving individual records. Therefore, OLTP databases are optimized for transaction updating. OLAP applications are used by analysts and managers who frequently want a higher-level aggregated view of the data, such as total sales by product line, by region, and so forth. The OLAP database is usually updated in batch, often from multiple sources, and OLAP databases are optimized for analysis for multiple user applications.

While relational databases are good at retrieving a small number of records quickly, they are not good at retrieving a large number of records and summarizing them on request. Slow response time and inordinate use of system resources are common characteristics of decision support applications built exclusively on top of relational database technology. Because of

---

* Green, Heather, "The Information Gold Mine," *Business Week e.biz*, July 26, 1999.

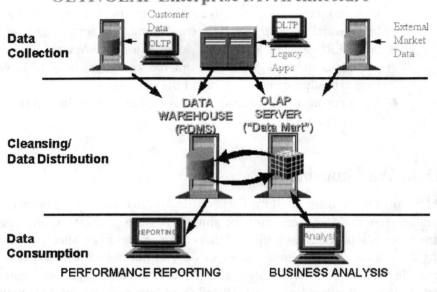

Figure 7.8 Data Warehouse Architecture

the ease with which one can issue a "runaway SQL query," many IT shops do not give users direct access to their relational databases.

Many of the problems that people attempt to solve with relational technology are actually multidimensional in nature. For example, SQL queries to create summaries of product sales by region, region sales by product, and so on, could involve scanning most if not all the records in a marketing database and could take hours of processing. An OLAP server could handle these queries in a few seconds.

OLTP applications tend to deal with atomized "record-at-a-time" data, whereas OLAP applications usually deal with summarized data. While OLTP applications generally do not require historical data, nearly every OLAP application is concerned with viewing trends and therefore requires historical data. Accordingly, OLAP databases need the ability to handle time-series data. Additionally, OLTP applications and databases tend to be organized around specific processes (such as order entry), while OLAP applications tend to be "subject oriented," answering such questions as "What products are selling well?" or "Where are my weakest sales offices?"

Advantages: Data warehouses have the following advantages, when implemented and used properly:

- Speed — well-designed OLAP servers can handle complex queries in seconds, rather than hours for OLTP databases.
- Analytical orientation — ability to answer questions such as "Where are my weakest sales offices?"
- Ability to handle multidimensional data and queries.

Disadvantages: Data warehouses are prone to pitfalls, such as

- Confusion — the real meaning of the data can get lost as the data is being sliced, diced, and analyzed.
- Performance — if a datamart and its analytical tools are not very, very fast, the end user will stop the analysis.
- Ease of use — the analytical tool must be truly intuitive and easy to use for nontechnical people.

Internet

There are two major subtopics in this section:

1. Using the Internet for competitive advantage with customers, suppliers, etc. (with your own Web site and with customer and supplier transactions coming through the Internet),
2. Using TEI software that uses the Web to serve its own applications.

Using the Internet for Competitive Advantage

The World Wide Web itself is a powerful marketing and research tool that can yield competitive advantage to those who use it effectively. Business-to-consumer Internet transaction-based revenue grew from $3 billion in 1997 to $7 billion in 1998, and was expected to approach $20 billion in 1999. Even more significant are business-to-business Web transactions, which grew from $7 billion in 1997 to $24 billion in 1998, and which were expected to exceed $50 billion in 1999.* Just as customers can find a manufacturer on the Web, a manufacturer itself can easily and very cost-effectively research a competitor's offerings, or potential suppliers, or potential customers.

---

* Marshall, Martin, "Application Development: Web Application Servers Give Green Light to ERP — Integration Tools Give ERP a Role in E-commerce," *InformationWeek*, April 5, 1999.

Many manufacturers are creating Web sites to attract potential customers. More advanced manufacturers are also using invitation-only Web sites to provide special attention to selected customers and suppliers. For example, in December 1998, Dell Computer had 8000 private Web areas where customers could display specially configured machines, review recent orders, place and modify orders, check order status, and electronically page their Dell sales representative.* At that time, Dell was adding 1000 new private areas per month! Milacron created one of the Web's most extensive e-commerce sites for selling machine tool supplies, such as cutting tools, grinding wheels, and metal-working fluids to contract manufacturers.**

Other manufacturers have created Web auction sites to sell excess or outdated inventories.

Business Week states that there are ten action items that a CEO must address for the company to survive:

1. Reengineer the company to be Internet-centric.
2. Throw out the old business model; redefine how the company wants to continue to add value to its customers.
3. Understand that the Internet provides the buyer with much more information, giving the buyer an overwhelming advantage.
4. Hold your customer's hand while the customer is on your Web site; provide suggestions for other related items that might be interesting (like amazon.com).
5. Farm out your company's jobs.
6. Integrate your Web site into your non-Web business.
7. Create an online sense of community.
8. Follow the investment money to spot the new competitors.
9. Understand that the Web is now being used routinely by nontechnical people.
10. The CEO must log on and use the Web personally, to fully understand its implications.***

As a personal example, much of the background research for this book was performed on the Web, quite often late at night. The author used three different commercial search services (which often referenced different articles

---

* Thurm, Scott, "Leading the PC Pack," *Wall Street Journal,* December 7, 1998, p. R27.
** Wilder, Clinton, "Old Line Moves Online," *Information Week,* January 11, 1999, pp. 18–20.
*** Hof, Robert D., "What Every CEO Needs to Know about Electronic Business — A Survival Guide," *Business Week e.biz,* March 22, 1999, pp. eb11–12.

on the same topic). The true power of the Web is the links between sites. While researching a topic, the author found links to two other sites. The second site included links to four other organizations (including NIST), each of which had its own search engines and links to still other sites. Access to the wealth of information on the Web reduced the research time for this book by at least 2 to 3 months.

A few companies have bypassed traditional distribution channels, pioneering the end-to-end use of digital networks to communicate with customers, make quotations, take orders, promise shipments, and organize supplies and suppliers. In fact, some executives are starting to use "Dell" (from Dell Computer Corp, one of the leaders in successfully using digital methods) as a verb. To "Dell" is to outflank the competition by cheaper products, by thoroughly using digital technology. "Most executives believe that what Mr. (Michael) Dell has done to the computer industry, someone else will do to autos, chemicals, banking, and plenty of other sectors."*

Advantages:
- 24 hours/day, 7 days/week, 365 days/year sales face in the marketplace.
- Can update information (e.g., add products, change specs, use different target messages) very quickly.
- Can set up customer-specific Web sites for each major customer.
- The size of the market is exploding.
- In many markets, Web capabilities are the expected norm if you are to be viewed as a credible supplier.

Disadvantages:
- Can require extensive up-front investment to create a truly professional site.
- Web-based customers can flood a company with questions and requests for information.
- Competitors can easily access all publicly available information, including pricing and product specifications.

Web-Centric TEI/ERP Systems

The Internet is also the technical basis for another major change: TEI systems are rapidly moving from client/server orientation to Internet-centric designs.

---

* Wysocki, Bernard, Jr., "Corporate Caveat: Dell or be Delled," *Wall Street Journal*, May 10, 1999.

The role of Web application servers as application integration platforms placed in front of TEI systems is only now emerging as a vital element of a company's enterprise strategy.

The Web application server is the means by which IT managers can turn their TEI systems outward to create functions such as bill presentment over the Web, self-service human-resources applications, self-service order tracking, and e-commerce, among others. A Web application server not only brings the ability to add mid-tier business logic to the TEI platform, but can also act as a security screen against sensitive parts of the TEI application, a load-balancer of Web-request traffic, and an integration point of verification systems and databases outside the TEI system.

Where the TEI systems have been able to bridge the departmental barriers to the consolidation of important business data, the addition of Web application servers holds the same consolidation potential for intercompany transactions. Web application server vendors have focused on helping customers build large, scalable e-commerce Web sites. The technologies these middleware packages provide focus on clustering and load balancing in order to support scalable Web applications, by integrating various application development environments such as Microsoft's Component Object Model, CORBA, and Java. Some also support the Extensible Markup Language, which assists users to create more flexible and interactive Web sites.

> Why would IT managers want Web application servers to establish links to TEI systems? After all, the TEI systems were designed to be self-contained, and to generate their own invoices, forms, billing, and human-resources functions without outside interference. And major TEI vendors already have browser interfaces, so that Web-based users can access the TEI systems directly through the Web. The answer lies in the nature of the TEI applications and in the flexibility of adding mid-tier logic to an application via a Web application server. The browser interfaces added by some TEI suppliers allow their applications to be accessed via remote Web browsers, but the functionally they represent is little more than screen-scraping of existing ERP applications.

> Web application servers are increasingly viewed by IT managers as the functional extensions of business TEI data and Internet applications. Web application servers are the mechanism for smoothing the integration of external customer bases and supply-chain vendors into business IT structures. With the mid-tier business logic that can be added on a Web application server, TEI systems are becoming a component of a larger, often multicompany, integration effort.

The business rationale for this movement includes multiple roles of the transaction-capable Web server, including the load balancing of Web-based application requests, the addition of extra logic that ties in all TEI-based business resources, and the simplification of user interfaces with TEI processes for the purpose of customer presentation.

The net result is a variety of self-service applications that, like automated teller machines, reduce the need for support personnel and increase customer satisfaction, directly affecting the bottom line."*

Outsourcing TEI Responsibility

Just as manufacturing operations can be outsourced, so can information technology services. The concept is that the manufacturer does not have to buy a license to the software, provide the hardware or database, pay for software maintenance or upgrade services, or hire and maintain IT staff that is knowledgeable in the TEI package or database. Those services are all covered by the outsourcing services provider. Several ERP and TEI suppliers are starting to provide outsourcing services.

Advantages:
- Predictable, fixed cost for the manufacturer
- Greater operational simplicity
- No initial investment required for TEI system, database software, or server hardware
- Hiring and training of IT staff is eliminated
- TEI package maintenance is performed automatically by experts

Disadvantages:
- Outsourcing was just starting in 1999; the first customers will be early adopters, with the attendant risks
- Manufacturer's confidential and mission-critical data resides off-site, at the outsourcing provider's location — potential security risk
- Can be more costly over the long run
- Outsourcers typically offer little or no support for modifications
- Manufacturer loses some control over selecting the IT staff that will support them

---

* Marshall, Martin, "Application Development: Web Application Servers Give Green Light to ERP — Integration Tools Give ERP a Role in E-commerce," *InformationWeek*, April 5, 1999.

Security

One of the editorial assumptions in this book is that tighter integration throughout the supply chain provides a substantial competitive edge. However, a major requirement for supply chain to function effectively is linking computers between the manufacturer, its customers, and its suppliers. This can create some very real security risks and concerns, such as:

- How can manufacturers share information with business partners without sharing proprietary data?
- Can business partners run reports on data in the manufacturer's computer? Or can they be restricted to "screen-only" viewing? (If they are restricted to screen-only viewing, is there a way to prevent them from printing a screen? If so, does the manufacturer want to try to prevent it, because such a restriction would clearly signal distrust of the business partner).
- Will business partners update information the manufacturer's computer, or merely view it? In fully supply-chain execution mode, a manufacturer must allow a business partner to update the manufacturer's data (for example, by entering or modifying customer orders).
- What is the liability between the manufacturer and a business partner if one party updates data incorrectly:
  - In their own computer, and the other party bases a decision on the incorrect data?
  - In the other party's computer, causing the other party to make incorrect decisions?
- How can the manufacturer allow dial-up access for authorized external users (e.g., remote plants, field salespeople, field service professionals, customers, and suppliers), while preventing hackers or competitors from gaining access to, and potentially changing, sensitive data?
- How can a manufacturer allow customers to see their own pricing without seeing pricing to other customers?
- How can a manufacturer prevent a customer from ordering more than their "fair share" of scarce items, to ensure an adequate supply for other customers?

While there are significant technical ramifications to these questions, they remain, ultimately, business issues that must be directly addressed and resolved as manufacturers open their computers and data to the outside world.

References

Anonymous, *Maximum Security —A Hacker's Guide to Protecting Your Internet Site and Network,* SAMS, 1998.

An Introduction to OLAP (White Paper), Pilot Software, Boston, MA, 1998.

Asbrand, Deborah, "Making Money from Data," *Datamation,* November 1998.

Biggs, Maggie, "Two Views on ERP: Outsourcing Pros and Cons, and Hitching up with E-Commerce," *Infoworld,* January 25, 1999.

Dickeson, Roger, "The Analytical Power of OLAP," *Printing Impressions,* June 1998.

DeMocker, Judy, "Trends — Part 2: Outsourcing: ERP's Future?" *InternetWeek,* March 22, 1999, p. 45.

Ec.com — an E-commerce magazine on the Web.

Green, Heather, "The Information Gold Mine," *Business Week e.biz,* July 26, 1999.

Gunst, Carole and Katzel, Jeanine, "Give Security Measures Top Priority When Implementing Internet Applications," *Plant Engineering,* February 1999.

Hof, Robert D., "What Every CEO Needs to Know about Electronic Business — A Survival Guide," *Business Week e.biz,* March 22, 1999.

Marshall, Martin, "Application Development: Web Application Servers Give Green Light to ERP — Integration Tools Give ERP a Role in E-Commerce," *InformationWeek,* April 5, 1999.

Richards, Bill, "A Total Overhaul," *Wall Street Journal,* December 7, 1998, p. R30.

Thurm, Scott, "Leading the PC Pack," *Wall Street Journal,* December 7, 1998, p. R27.

Walker, Michael and Goff, James, "Using Real-World Benefits of Client/Server Technologies to Achieve Competitive Advantage at OSi Specialities," *1995 Conference Proceedings,* APICS, Falls Church, VA, 1995.

Wilder, Clinton, "E-commerce: Myths & Realities," *Information Week,* December 7, 1998, pp. 52–63.

Wilder, Clinton, "Old Line Moves Online," *Information Week,* January 11, 1999, pp. 18–20.

Wysocki, Bernard, Jr., "Corporate Caveat: Dell or be Delled," *Wall Street Journal,* May 10, 1999.

8 | Other Topics

The original design of MRP II systems, which is still the basic design center for most ERP and TEI systems, was of a discrete manufacturer with one plant, using Bills of Material and routings, and controlling the shop with shop orders. Many ERP and TEI suppliers have since tried to adapt their offerings to other markets, while other suppliers have designed their products specifically for other markets, such as:

- Multi-plant, multi-division, and multinational industries
- "Nontraditional" industries, including
  - Engineer-to-order
  - Repetitive
  - Process
  - Hybrid

Multi-Plant, Multi-Division, Multinational Industries

The terms "multi-plant," "multi-division," and "multinational" can be mutually exclusive. All plants can be in one division and one country. Each division can have only one plant. A company can sell internationally, supplying from only one plant. However, the largest manufacturers (such as automotive assemblers and their direct suppliers, the large oil companies, and the largest consumer package goods manufacturers) are multinational, multi-divisional, and multi-plant. Additionally, as companies become very large, they frequently have multiple product lines, thereby requiring different types of manufacturing processes such as engineer-to-order and process, as well as discrete.

Multi-Plant

If a company has very little in common between separate plants, it can run the operations planning and execution functions of its TEI system as if each plant is a stand-alone, and consolidate only at the financial level. However, if it can make the same products at more than one plant, or if one plant feeds another, or if multiple plants use the same components and raw materials, its TEI package must be inherently designed to support multiple plants from an operational standpoint.

True multi-plant functionality must be designed into an TEI system starting with the item master. An item must be defined according to the plant(s) where it is made or used. However, the same item must be able to have a different BOM, routing, and cost at each different plant where it is made. Master Scheduling must be able to schedule items at any appropriate plant. Yet, they must be interchangeable with respect to customer demand and Master Scheduling to see total production across all plants, and Purchasing must be able to see total demand for common components for all plants.

The implications for the financial software are that costing must be unique to each plant. Each plant must be measured on its contribution to margin and on how well it did compared to its targets. Once an item from any of the plants is received into finished goods, it should carry the company's standard cost. Additionally, each plant should have its own P&L so its management can see the results of their efforts. Balance sheets and cash flow information are not separable by plant.

Multi-Division

Multiple divisions are essentially a superset of multiple plants, except that they usually do not build the same products. Therefore, the materials planning functionality of a single-plant TEI package is sometimes sufficient. However, a division is frequently a stand-alone legal entity. Thus, each division must have its own financial reports, including profit and loss, balance sheet, cash flow, and taxation.

Additionally, the divisions' financials must be able to be easily consolidated into the corporate parent's books. It is not unusual for different divisions to have different TEI or ERP systems (or no TEI or ERP system at all); the corporate parent's financial software needs to be able to accept data from a variety of sources, such as TEI software, PC-based financial packages, and spreadsheets.

Subsidiaries often stand alone, with separate financial statements, taxation, and recognition. However, if the subsidiaries are part of the overall company's material flow or supply chain, the planning and execution systems might need to be integrated.

Multinational

When a company sells products in multiple countries, the complexity increases for manufacturing, materials, engineering, and financial software.

Engineering must accommodate different standards for different countries. Some countries use 110 volt, 60 cycle electricity; others use 220 volt, 50 cycle. In some countries, the power is relatively consistent; in others, it can surge and sag. Even if two countries use the same basic power, they might need different plugs to fit electrical outlets. Most of the world uses metric measurements; the U.S. and a few others still use feet and inches and pounds. The product's packaging must be revised to fit local requirements (such as using the local language on the outside of the box). Operator's manuals must be available in the language(s) that are common in the country being served. And the products themselves might need to be redesigned to fit the unique culture or requirements of the other country, such as right-hand drive cars for Japan and the United Kingdom.

Customer service must understand customs and tariffs implications for each shipment, and should be able to generate the necessary documents in the proper language(s).

If all transactions are in the currency of the company's headquarters, there are few financial implications for selling products internationally. There are credit implications, which might require a Letter of Credit from the buyer.

If the products are sold in the local currency, the accounting and financial modules of the TEI system must support multiple currencies, with currency translations that meet the standards in the company's host country and the other countries.

Manufacturing products in foreign countries increases the requirements on the TEI system in the following areas:

- The accounting system must translate local (and probably other countries') currencies.
- The accounting system must be able to report in dual currencies.
- The costing system must be able to operate in the local currency.

- Payroll must comply with the local taxation laws and standards.
- Human resources must comply with local laws and standards.
- Environmental reporting must comply with local laws and standards.
- The entire system should be multilingual to facilitate communications with local workers.
- Raw materials will probably be purchased from local sources, subject to the laws governing commerce in the foreign country.
- The Bills of Material will need to recognize the characteristics of the foreign raw materials.
- Routings will need to recognize the local work practices and standards. If the local country has a different measurement system (metric vs. English), the standards must be converted, and maintained in both systems.
- Quality standards must also be converted, as appropriate, from English to metric.

Finally, the effects of local customs and regulations will also influence the transferability and comparability of information. Therefore, multinational TEI systems must fully support laws, customs, and work practices, including the trade-off of labor for automation that differs from country to country.

"Nontraditional" Industries

Some TEI suppliers have written packages specifically designed for the "nontraditional" industries; others have adapted their traditional TEI packages to fit these markets. The major differences between "standard" TEI and the functionality required in these industries is outlined below. Figure 8.1 shows the relationship between each of these approaches.

Engineer-to-Order

"Standard" TEI assumes that all production items are specified by item numbers, and that items have specific, unique characteristics. "Standard" TEI centers around material planning of standard items, as shown in Figures 1.3 (showing the evolution of TEI from MRP), and 2.1 (showing the relationships in a TEI package). Figure 8.2 illustrates some of the differences between standard TEI and engineer-to-order.

Variety	**Volume**				
	One of a Kind	Few of a Kind	Many of a Kind	Very High	Commodities Bulk
Project	Project / Engineer to Order				
Job Shop		Discrete / Make to Order			
Small Batch			Repetitive/ Discrete / Assemble to Order		
Large Batch				Repetitive / Make to Stock	
Continuous Flow					Process

Figure 8.1 Volume/Variety Matrix

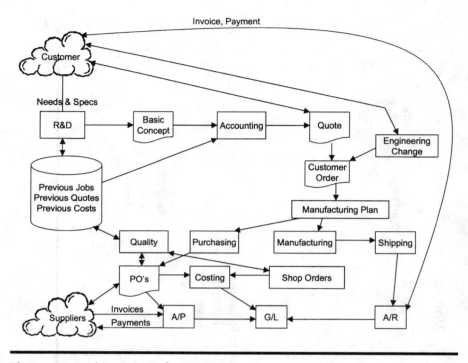

Figure 8.2 Engineer-to-Order System

A true engineer-to-order-oriented TEI system uses a quotation to a customer as the foundation of the entire system, rather than item numbers. Quotations are generated using generic materials (sheets of steel, lengths of pipe, etc.), and estimated engineering standards. When a quote is accepted by the customer, it becomes an order. All activities in the shop are directly attributable to customer orders. The shop does not build work orders identified by part number; it builds specific items for customer orders.

Project-management-based systems, rather than classic MRP/CRP/Shop Floor Control, are required to coordinate all activities involved in designing and building truly complex equipment.

At a minimum, a TEI system must be able to include engineering hours and efforts in both costing a project and managing the project. In a design-intensive company, cost accounting might use engineering hours as the basis for costing, rather than the traditional direct labor hours.

Repetitive

Repetitive manufacturing is defined as:

the repeated production of the same discrete products or families of products. Repetitive methodology minimizes setups, inventory, and manufacturing lead times by using production lines, assembly lines, or cells. Work orders are no longer necessary; production scheduling and control are based on production rates. Products may be standard or assembled from modules. Repetitive is *not* a function of speed or volume.*

Repetitive methodologies organize an entire manufacturing enterprise around the assumption that the company will produce the same items repeatedly. Repetitive methodologies do *not* require continuous production of the same part (e.g., chocolate chip cookies), or high volume. They apply equally well in companies that make many items, even with low volumes.

Repetitive methodologies differ from the two other major manufacturing methodologies, discrete (job shop), and process:

- Discrete manufacturing is organized to build whatever the customer wants. It requires work orders to tell workers what to do on each order, how to set it up, what tools to use, how long it should take, and where to send it when they are finished with their task, or operation. Discrete manufacturers organize their plant floors by the function being performed. They tend to have high work in process and relatively large queues (work waiting to be performed) at each work center.
- Process manufacturing centers on continuous flow, and/or chemical reactions. Process manufacturers tend to have high capital equipment investments and make relatively few end products (except for packaging variations). Process manufacturers organize their plants by the product being made, with raw materials coming in one end and finished goods coming out the other, and the barest minimum of work in process in between.**

Most companies that make products repetitively still use discrete techniques, because those techniques are the commonly accepted practices. However, since products will be made repeatedly, repetitive methodologies suggest organizing material flow into logical (or physical) lines, more like process than discrete. The ramifications of this change in organization are major:

---

* *APICS Dictionary, 9th ed.,* APICS, Falls Church, VA, 1998.
** Langenwalter, Gary A., *White Paper on Repetitive Methodologies for Manufacturing,* APICS, Alexandria, VA, 1999.

- The old model of production is replaced. The old model is making components, putting them into the stockroom until they are needed, then using them in a subassembly, putting it into the stockroom until it is needed, etc. This creates several levels in Bills of Material, considerable material handling and storage, and extensive paperwork. The new model is to handle materials only once — once materials have been started down the line, they should continue until they are finished goods in a box or shippable container. This requires dramatically rethinking the entire manufacturing process, with substantial implications for design engineering. It requires flattening the bills of materials, eliminating storage of components, WIP, and subassemblies.

- Products are grouped into families that use similar processes, and then those families are separated into production lines (logically, if not physically). For production lines to work, the setups inside each of the lines must be absolutely minimized, if not eliminated.

- Since products flow down production lines, work orders are no longer needed, and work order control and reporting can be eliminated. The reason that work orders are required in a discrete environment is that each work order is different, and each work order must contain full instructions on how it is to be made. In a production line environment, those controls are unnecessary (and costly), and instructions can be more effectively communicated by other methods.

- Lead times shrink dramatically, from weeks to days or hours, and WIP shrinks concomitantly.

- Plant scheduling changes from work-order-based to rate-based. "Work orders" are replaced by schedules to make various items each day or week. The Master Scheduler deliberately leaves room in the schedules for "surprises."

- Performance measurements change. By laying the plant out, we create an environment that inherently maximizes efficiency. The new measurements emphasize on-time production and quality.

- Maintenance becomes vital, since unscheduled downtime will stop production.

- Workers become cross-trained and multiskilled to support the flexibility that is a hallmark of repetitive methodologies. This directly impacts the workers themselves, their line supervision, and the human resources function. Longer term, as companies adopt the

repetitive model more fully, they can replace the older command-and-control supervisory paradigm with self-directed work teams or something similar.*
- Accounting systems can change from a focus on direct labor hours or dollars, to advanced costing based on cost drivers.

Appendix A contains a list of software features and functions that are useful in a TEI system for a repetitive manufacturer.

Process

The process industry includes food, beverage, primary metals, paper, plastics, and chemical manufacturers. Process manufacturing uses flow techniques, in which material flows through fixed routings. Flow shops attempt to lay the plant out to make a product, uninterrupted, from beginning to end. Flow shops tend to be capital-intensive, producing high quantities of identical products. Capacity is well-defined and takes a longer time to increase than job shops. Work-in-process inventories are minimized. A flow plant can be shut down by equipment failure or raw material shortage.

Flow shops have great difficulty using traditional MRP II, ERP, or TEI systems. MRP II was used in only 16% of the chemical industry, 83% of pharmaceutical manufacturers, 4% of food and beverage manufacturers, and only 0.1% of other process manufacturers in a 1988 survey conducted by Plant-Wide Research Corp.** The advent of process-oriented ERP and TEI systems has increased those percentages.

Where are the differences? Flow manufacturers are financially driven to keep their equipment operating virtually all the time due to the high capital investment. Raw material scheduling is relatively easy, because they use relatively few feedstocks. Once raw material enters the plant, it is converted to finished goods very quickly. Therefore, the traditional MRP II, ERP, and TEI emphasis on planning discrete work orders, using a multilevel BOM, assuming that capacity is variable, does not fit. Figure 8.3 shows the flow of materials through a flow plant.***

---

* Langenwalter, Gary A., *White Paper on Repetitive Methodologies for Manufacturing*, APICS, Alexandria, VA, 1999.
** Foley, M. J., "Post-MRP II: What Comes Next?" *Datamation*, December 1, 1988.
*** Taylor, Sam G. and Bolander, Steven F., "Can Process Flow Scheduling Help You?" *1996 International Conference Proceedings*, APICS, Falls Church, VA, 1996.

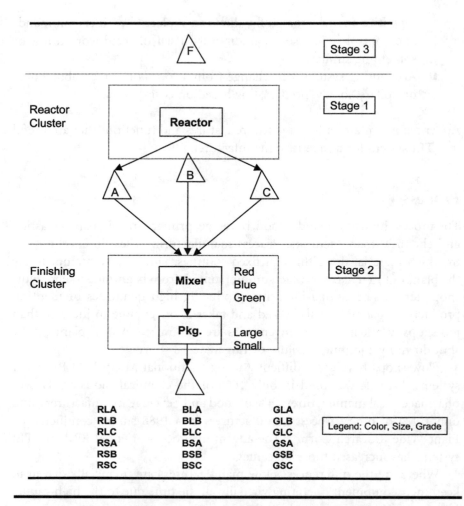

Figure 8.3 Material and Manufacturing Flow — Flow Manufacturing

Process flow scheduling (PFS) uses the following principles to schedule plants:*

1. Scheduling calculations are guided by the process structure. By contrast, typical classic ERP uses product structure (Bills of Materials) to schedule. PFS combines processes into logical clusters, then schedules the most difficult process first.

---

* Taylor, Sam G. and Bolander, Steven F., "Process Flow Scheduling: State of the Art," *1995 International Conference Proceedings,* APICS, Falls Church, VA, 1995.

2. Process clusters are scheduled using processor-dominated scheduling, or material-dominated scheduling. ERP and TEI schedule materials first; PFS allows flexibility to schedule either materials or capacity first, depending on which is the most critical.
3. Process trains are scheduled using reverse flow scheduling, forward flow scheduling, or mixed-flow scheduling. Scheduling begins with the master cluster, and proceeds through the rest of the train.

Using Figure 8.3 as a basis for illustration, the scheduling process starts by identifying the most critical process cluster within a process train. A **process train** is the entire processing line for a product (all the functions in Figure 8.3). For this example, let us assume that it is economically or technically critical to schedule the reactor in a sequence based on some product characteristic, such as molecular weight. It is also important to schedule production runs relatively close to economic run lengths. Because of the dominance of the reactor, we designate the reactor as the master cluster, and the finishing cluster as the support cluster. We schedule the reactor first, then schedule the finishing cluster next.

The finishing cluster contains two process units. Again, they are scheduled in order of difficulty. If color changeovers are more difficult than package changeovers, the mixer is scheduled first, then the packaging operation. The mixer is called the "key unit" in the cluster.

The scheduler then balances the reactor's material push (into the finishing cluster), with the finishing cluster's pull (from the reactor), ensuring that any intermediate storage area capacities are not exceeded.

Figure 8.4 illustrates a different type of flow process cluster.*

Scheduling for process industries can require industry-specific capabilities that some traditional TEI systems do not include, such as the following:

- Storage tanks, permanent, including the time to fill and the time to empty the tanks, plus the ability of a specific tank to safely store the specific substance in question.
- Storage tanks, temporary (with cleaning potentially required before reuse by another substance).
- By-products and co-products.

---

* Taylor, Sam G. and Bolander, Steven F., "Can Process Flow Scheduling Help You?" *1996 International Conference Proceedings*, APICS, Falls Church, VA, 1996.

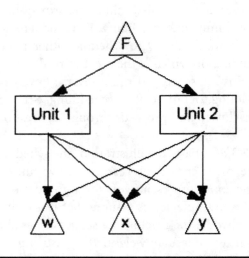

Figure 8.4 Flow Process Cluster, Type 2

Another difference with traditional ERP-oriented manufacturing is that many process manufacturers use natural raw materials (ores, food, wood, petroleum, etc.), which have varying characteristics from one batch to the next, as their feedstocks. Therefore, they have to constantly adjust for acidity, viscosity, color, texture, and a host of other attributes to create a consistent final product. Their manufacturing processes can be designed to continuously measure critical attributes and to adjust the process automatically by using added components, temperature, pressure, or other similar factors.

Traditional ERP/TEI accounting, which uses direct labor hours or dollars as the basis for costing, does not serve process industries well because the bulk of the cost of a product is the usage of the capital equipment, followed by the raw material being consumed. Direct labor is a minute percentage of the total cost of finished goods; one alternative for costing basis might be equipment hours.

Appendix B contains a more detailed list of software features and functions that are useful in an TEI system for a process manufacturer.

Hybrid

Hybrid manufacturers use more than one approach to manufacturing. For example, a caster manufacturer might use process flow techniques for the plant that makes rubber wheels, repetitive techniques for manufacturing and assembling most casters, and engineer-to-order/job shop techniques for engineering samples, proposed new products, and replacement parts for old products.

Some hybrid manufacturers have successfully created several **"plants within a plant,"** or **"focused factories,"** each of which focuses on one type of process. In the ultimate form of a plant within a plant, each miniplant would behave like a stand-alone company, with its own management, support staff (including accounting, purchasing, engineering, IT, and human resources). It would have financial responsibility to its owner (the corporate parent), and would sell to customers (other plants within the same plant and/or outside customers) and buy from suppliers (other plants within the same plant and/or outside suppliers).

A traditional plant layout, organized by manufacturing process, is shown as Figure 8.5.* Figure 8.6 illustrates moving from a traditional layout to focused factories, or plants within a plant, in this case with each plant focused on a specific product line.*

The TEI implications of hybrid plants are extremely straightforward on the surface, but can be relatively difficult to implement. The objective is to have TEI systems that support each of the different operating styles. However, if a manufacturer needs both process and engineer-to-order, it will have great difficulty finding a single software package that supports both functions well. Thus, it will face two alternatives, each of which has at least one major drawback:

1. Buy and implement "best of breed" software for each separate function; integrate at the company financial level (almost like having two separate divisions), and integrate customer service and sales
2. Buy the package that fits the total set of requirements the most closely, and
    - Use manual work-arounds for the areas that do not support the business needs, and/or
    - Modify the package to fit the business needs

Cost accounting in a hybrid organization can be as difficult as TEI package selection and implementation. The basis for costing varies between the different approaches to manufacturing.

---

* APICS Repetitive Manufacturing SIG, *Repetitive Manufacturing Basics Workshop Participant Materials*, APICS, Alexandria, VA, 1999.

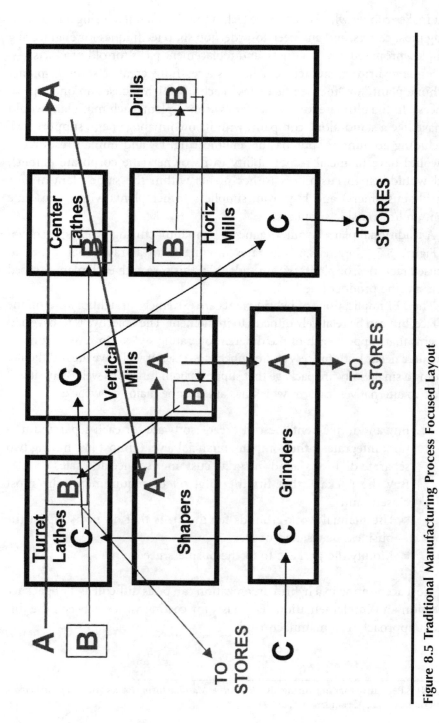

Figure 8.5 Traditional Manufacturing Process Focused Layout

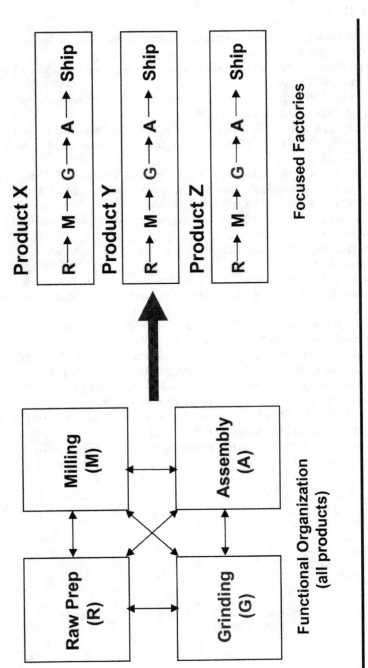

Figure 8.6 Moving to Focused Factories

References:

APICS Repetitive Manufacturing SIG, *Selected Readings in Repetitive Manufacturing*, APICS, Falls Church, VA, 1997.

APICS Repetitive Manufacturing SIG, *Repetitive Manufacturing Basics Workshop Participant Materials*, APICS, Alexandria, VA, 1999.

Funk, Paul N., "Mass Customization of Complex Products," *1998 International Conference Proceedings*, APICS, Falls Church, VA, 1998.

Langenwalter, Gary A., *Repetitive Scheduling Training Aid*, APICS, Falls Church, VA, 1998.

Langenwalter, Gary A., *White Paper on Repetitive Methodologies for Manufacturing*, APICS, Alexandria, VA, 1999.

Massee, Steven J., "Imagine, You CAN Have It Both Ways! A Practitioner's Experience with a Hybrid Manufacturing/Planning System," *1995 International Conference Proceedings*, APICS, Falls Church, VA, 1995.

Process Industry SIG, APICS, Falls Church, VA (access through the APICS Web site at www.apics.org).

Repetitive Manufacturing SIG, APICS, Falls Church, VA (access through the APICS web site at www.apics.org).

Spencer, Michael S. and Cox, James F., III, *Directions in American Production: How Repetitive Manufacturing Occurs*, APICS Educational and Research Foundation, Falls Church, VA, 1996.

Taylor, Sam G. and Bolander, Steven F., *Process Flow Scheduling: A Scheduling Framework for Flow Manufacturing*, APICS, Falls Church, VA, 1994.

Taylor, Sam G. and Bolander, Steven F., "Scheduling Systems for Tomorrow's Factories," *1998 International Conference Proceedings*, APICS, Falls Church, VA, 1998.

Taylor, Sam G. and Bolander, Steven F., "Can Process Flow Scheduling Help You?" *1996 International Conference Proceedings*, APICS, Falls Church, VA, 1996.

Taylor, Sam G. and Bolander, Steven F., "Process Flow Scheduling: State of the Art," *1995 International Conference Proceedings*, APICS, Falls Church, VA, 1995.

Turner, Jeff, "The Unique Requirements of Process Industry ERP," *APICS — The Performance Advantage*, June 1998.

9 System Selection

The system selection process is deceptively difficult. While most ERP and TEI packages have similarities, they also have fundamental design differences, just as motor vehicles have similarities and differences. For example, for a family with three small children, a two-seat sports car is a poor choice as the only vehicle that they own and drive. Similarly, most companies lose 25% to 50% on the final ROI of their entire system investment (software, implementation, and hardware) because they skip or shortchange one or more steps in the process and thus select software that does not fit them very well.

Many TEI suppliers take the position, implicitly or explicitly, that the manufacturer should change its business processes to meet the software supplier's design. Admittedly, the design of the software will probably help the manufacturer simplify and streamline procedures and practices that have evolved through the years. However, the manufacturer must ensure that it is not installing new procedures that undermine its competitive edge or its individual identity in the marketplace. For example, Dell Computer has gained a major competitive advantage with its quick-turn, assemble-to-order strategy and practice.* Should it abandon this practice when it implements a new TEI system? We emphatically insist that each manufacturer should select and intelligently implement a system that accentuates its unique competitive strengths, while helping overcome competitive weaknesses.

---

* Quigley, Phil, "ERP — Are You Going Down the Right Road?" *APICS — The Performance Advantage,* October 1998, p. 78.

How NOT to Select a System

As a classic example of how *not* to select a system, consider the true story of a multi-plant, multinational $100+ million division of a very large corporation. Their products and manufacturing processes are relatively simple, but their systems must tie directly to their customers' systems. Their existing systems, which were not Year 2000 compliant, were more than 10 years old and had been modified so much that upgrading to a current release was not feasible. Their corporate parent told them in 1997 to start ensuring that their systems would be Year 2000 compliant, so they invited one of the large accounting firms to quote on the system selection process. Because the quote was higher than they wanted, they shelved the project.

One of the division's foreign plants implemented a midrange package that was specifically targeted to their industry in early 1998. However, the corporation violated virtually every rule for successful implementations. The corporation had decided to:

- Exclude the division in the package selection process
- Insist on a total implementation in 3 months
- Work no overtime in the plant to bring the new system up
- Insist that the software vendor modify the code extensively (at no charge!) under an extremely tight timetable
- Eliminate virtually all education and consulting assistance

The implementation was a complete disaster; it came very close to shutting the division down. The division blamed the software supplier for the majority of the problems.

In the spring of 1998, the president of the division told the materials manager to look at PC-based systems (since they were a simple business, in the president's eyes, they could run the business with a few PCs at each plant). The materials manager used a questionnaire to narrow the field to three PC-based software packages, and also added one of the packages that is aimed at much larger companies, and the midrange package that had just been implemented in the foreign plant. After a quick review, the materials manager concluded that none of the PC-based packages would suffice, so he invited the large package and midrange package in for demonstrations at the corporate offices in the summer. The large package demo went well; the midrange package was not as flashy and carried the burden of the failed implementation. In September 1998, the materials manager sounded the alarm that their existing system would break on January 1, 1999 because the Year 2000 problem would cripple MPS and MRP logic, which planned a year in advance. So, under increasing pressure from the corporate parent to solve the Year 2000 problem, they chose the large package in mid-September.

What was wrong with this selection process?

- Their selection process did not deliberately position them to realize the maximum ROI on their investment. They treated the system much like a machine on the floor — roll out the old machine, roll in the new machine, and keep running. They ignored the potential strategic advantages that could be gained with a new system. In fact, they refer to the project as "the IS project."
- Only one of the four plants was represented. The one with the most critical information systems requirements was excluded.
- They did not create a clear, compelling vision of how they want to operate in the future; they selected a package based on current operations and habits.
- They chose the package with the sizzle, even though it was substantially more complex. They had no formal list of functional requirements to ensure that the package met their needs.
- They chose a package based on one demo.
- They chose a package that had no real competitors in their selection process. If they had created a proper pool of viable candidates (midrange packages and at least one additional large package), they might have saved more than $500,000 in total implemented cost.

Ten-Step System Selection Process

The ten steps to system selection (Figure 9.1), which deliberately create the foundation for successful implementation and maximum ROI, are as follows:

1. Create the vision (the step most frequently skipped)
2. Create feature/function list
3. Create software candidate list
4. Narrow the field to four to six serious candidates
5. Create RFP; solicit proposals
6. Review proposals
7. Select three finalists

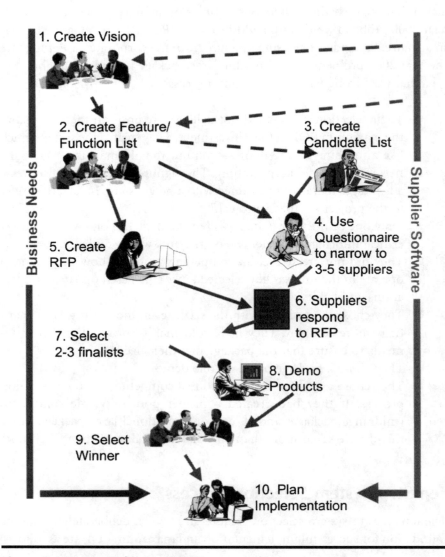

1. Create Vision

2. Create Feature/
   Function List

3. Create
   Candidate List

Business Needs

Supplier Software

4. Use
   Questionnaire
   to narrow to
   3-5 suppliers

5. Create
   RFP

6. Suppliers
   respond
   to RFP

7. Select
   2-3 finalists

8. Demo
   Products

9. Select
   Winner

10. Plan
    Implementation

Figure 9.1 System Selection Steps

8. Demonstrate packages
9. Select the winner
10. Negotiate the contract, run preimplementation pilot, and justify the investment

Step 1: Create the Vision

This is the most important step in an entire selection and implementation process. This vision must describe how the most advanced, most respected company in your industry will delight customers, employees, and suppliers 2, 3, or 5 years into the future. This step accomplishes two vital functions:

- Creates the foundation for achieving the maximum ROI from your system, by empowering the selection and implementation team to think strategically as well as tactically
- Minimizes, if not eliminates, most interdepartmental feuding by focusing the entire team on a cooperative future goal

The vision could be called a "Big, Hairy, Audacious Goal" (BHAG). Boeing Corp. has consistently bet the company on risky ventures, starting with the P-26 pursuit fighter, then the B-17 bomber in the 1930s, then the first commercial passenger jet, the 707, in the 1950s, the 727 mid-range jet in the 1960s. This was a prelude to the decision Boeing made in 1965,

> one of the boldest moves in business history: the decision to go forward with the 747 jumbo jet, a decision that nearly killed the company. At the decisive board of directors meeting, Boeing Chairman William Allen responded to a comment by a board member that "if the [747] program isn't panning out, we can always back out."
>
> "Back out?" stiffened Allen. "If the Boeing Company says we will build this airplane, we will build it even if it takes the resources of the entire company!"
>
> Indeed, as it had with the P-26, B-17, 707, and 727, Boeing became irreversibly committed to the 747 — financially, psychologically, publicly .... As with the DC-8 and DC-9, rival Douglas Aircraft was slow to commit to a jumbo jet project and fell into yet another round of catch-up with Boeing. The DC-10, Douglas' response, never attained the same market position as the 747."*

A successful vision of the company's optimum operating style should be:

---

* Collins, James C. and Porras, Jerry I., *Built to Last: Successful Habits of Visionary Companies*, HarperBusiness, New York, 1994, p. 93.

- **Challenging** — if the vision sounds boring, containing the same old stuff, it fails. A vision must be sufficiently revolutionary, sufficiently challenging, to capture people's imaginations and passion. John Kennedy captured the imagination of the U.S. and the Western world in 1961 when he challenged us to "put a man on the moon before the end of the decade."
- **Compelling** — why will the people and the company benefit from operating in the new way? How will age-old problems finally be eliminated? How will the customers and suppliers benefit? What will the daily operation of a department look like, sound like, feel like? The vision must be so attractive that people *want* to make it happen. The "want" is absolutely indispensable in the middle of the implementation; it is the reason why people will put in the extra time, and solve the problems, and forgive the idiosyncrasies of the new system.
- **Comprehensive** — the vision must incorporate all functions and people in the company, plus customers (and perhaps *their* customers), suppliers (and perhaps *their* suppliers). It must allow for adding future products and plants and discontinuing old products and plants. Many TEI suppliers partner with systems that are outside their areas of focus and expertise, such as transportation and logistics, to offer a complete suite of functionality to their end customers.
- **Clear** — the vision must be simple, direct, and completely clear, so that each interested party can easily read and understand it and its impact on their function.
- **Crisp** — brevity is not only a virtue, it is a necessity. The vision cannot and must not address all possibilities. If it tries to include the details, it fails. The greatest and most enduring documents, such as the Ten Commandments, Declaration of Independence, and the U.S. Constitution are intentionally short, and leave the daily implementation for future interpretation.

The vision must support the mission, vision, and purpose of the organization, as defined by senior management. It must be substantially more detailed, answering the following questions:

- New technology has enabled "mass customization," in which a manufacturer can build one copy of a customized product, cost-effectively and quickly, reducing lead times and cost from the older strategies.

The five categories, which are defined by the amount of influence that a consumer has over the manufacturing process, are:*

- Pure customization, like building a ship or an office building
- Tailored customization, like printing, which uses known processes to create a unique item
- Customized standardization, like making cars or personal computers, which offers predefined features and options at various levels of the Bill of Materials to create a unique item for the final customer
- Segmented standardization, like bread or shoes, which offers variety to various target groups of consumers, without allowing the consumer to select features and options before the product is made
- Pure standardization, like pencils or paper clips, in which the consumer has not been segmented

■ What manufacturing strategy will the company choose? Hayes and Wheelwright created a model of manufacturing strategies, illustrated in Figure 9.2,** that includes:

- Engineer to order (design to order)
- Make to order
- Assemble to order
- Make to stock
- Continuous flow — process

■ Where does the company want to be on the supply chain continuum (shown in Figure 2.16)? How integrated with suppliers and customers?

■ What kinds of new products and services will be offered? Which old products will be discontinued?

■ Will the company be adding or eliminating plants and/or distribution centers? Regionally, nationally, or internationally?

These are but a few of the questions that must be answered before software is selected, or the software will be selected to fit the existing company strategy and tactics, which could severely hamper the company's operations in the future. Vehicles can be divided into categories, including sports cars, small sedans, larger family sedans, luxury automobiles, mini-vans, sports utility vehicles, and trucks. None of these can fit the needs of all consumers.

---

* Lampel, Joseph and Mintzberg, Henry, "Customizing Customization," *Sloan Management Review,* Fall 1996.
** Hayes, R. C. and Wheelwright, S. C., *Restoring Our Competitive Edge: Competing Through Manufacturing,* Wiley, New York, 1984.

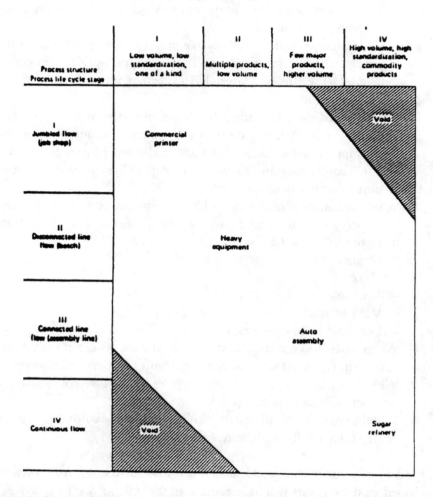

Figure 9.2 Manufacturing Strategies

Similarly, software packages are designed for different target industries and company sizes; none of them can fit all manufacturers equally well.

Creating a vision is not time-consuming or costly. Actually, the vision process truly energizes the rest of the implementation. The six steps to create a radical vision are detailed in the following sections.

Create the Team

Create a radical visioning team, with one participant from each major function (design engineering, sales, marketing, customer service, manufacturing engineering, manufacturing, logistics, materials planning, purchasing, cost accounting, general accounting, human resources, MIS, etc.). This team should include people from the middle level of the organization who know the day-to-day operations. Most importantly, these people should be the informal leaders, the dreamers, the complainers, the people who are not very comfortable with the status quo. Additionally, the team requires an experienced facilitator, generally an outsider. The ideal facilitator has very little political baggage and can challenge the team to create visions that are substantially more radical. At this point, the outside facilitator can be the *de facto* team leader. After the vision is complete, a company employee should become the team leader.

When multiple plants are involved, the visioning process must include participants from all plants, so that each plant has psychological ownership of the resulting vision. Each plant can have its own team, with the resulting vision from each plant being combined into a mega-vision. In this case, it is imperative that each plant's vision remain intact, rather than being edited by a larger committee, so that each plant retains psychological ownership of their vision, which is absolutely essential for a successful implementation.

Start the Creative Process

The facilitator meets with executive management to confirm their vision and strategic objectives, so that these will be included in the middle management vision.

The facilitator gives the team members a sample of a radical vision document to assist them in thinking as creatively as possible.* The facilitator asks each member to bring to the first meeting a page or two that fundamentally restructures the work that flows through their function (and also other areas of the company). For example, if the company is still receiving orders by phone and fax, they could instead envision electronic links with customers' computers, so that orders come in electronically and are promised automatically and instantaneously.

---

* For a complimentary copy of a sample radical vision, contact Manufacturing Consulting Partners International, Bolton, Massachusetts, at (978) 779-6565, or (888) 634-2667, or e-mail them at info@mfgcons.com.

Ensure an Extremely Successful First Meeting

The president of the company welcomes the team members, emphasizes the importance of the team's mission, and pledges wholehearted support. If the team members do not know each other well, or are truly skeptical, they can work jointly with a team-based creative exercise (such as the "Great American Egg Drop,"* which features raw eggs being dropped 8 feet onto a hard and unforgiving surface).

Then each team member reads aloud their vision for their department (and the rest of the company). Some initial visions are more radical than others; sometimes the person changes the vision as they read it based on a document that has just been read. The facilitator ensures that each person is heard, that each contribution is valued by the team, and that critical judgment is suspended for the time being. The facilitator also ensures that the initial visions are sufficiently radical.

If one person's vision is so radical that existing technology cannot currently support it, the facilitator thanks the person for their work and informs them that required technology will probably be available in the future, and that the company will be ready to use the technology to gain a competitive edge when it becomes available and reliable.

Synthesize and Distribute the First-Draft Vision

The facilitator collects each written vision, synthesizes those visions into one collective document, and distributes that document to the team members as quickly as possible. Team members read the section(s) pertaining to their functions, plus any other sections they wish to read. They create suggested revisions, comments, and questions for the whole document, but especially their areas.

The synthesis process is key to the eventual success of the vision. The facilitator must ensure that:

- Each person's vision is retained in sufficiently original form that they feel valued.
- The various departmental visions can indeed support each other holistically.
- The resultant vision is sufficiently radical.

---

* For a complimentary copy of the instructions, contact Manufacturing Consulting Partners International, Bolton, Massachusetts, at (978) 779-6565, or (888) 634-2667, or e-mail them at info@mfgcons.com.

Revise the Vision

At the second meeting, team members share their suggested revisions, comments, questions, etc. The facilitator ensures that the team reaches reasonable consensus. Most importantly, the facilitator also ensures that team members refrain from thinking that only one style of operation can be included in the vision. If, for example, the company can best support its customers by operating in make-to-stock, assemble-to-order, and make-to-order modes, the facilitator includes all three modes in the vision. If a third or fourth meeting is required, the team schedules those meetings. After each meeting, the facilitator quickly issues a revised version of the collective vision.

Broadcast the Vision to the Entire Company

The team presents the vision to top management for their official approval, then schedules meetings of all employees to share the vision. Let the team's excitement show! This passion is one of the benefits of the vision; it provides the power required to successfully change.

Long-term employees of some companies have endured so many management fads and programs that they will probably view this vision and the resulting system with skepticism. Sometimes organization change experts can help these valuable individuals; other times, they have to see commitment (the new system arriving, management providing resources and education, etc.) to allow themselves to hope again.

Step 2: Create Feature/Function List

The feature and function lists evolve directly from the vision created in Step 1 and from the list of TEI functions in Figure 1.2. A person who is knowledgeable about software packages and the industry should review Figure 1.2, with the committee to ensure that the vision is sufficiently comprehensive. The person then increases the size of the vision document by a factor of 2, 3, or 4, by adding features and functions required for software to effectively support the vision for the company and for each individual area. This "translator" can be one or more employees and/or an outside facilitator. In times past, some companies created detailed function and feature requirements documents; in fact, the specifications sometimes exceeded 100 pages. The following approach will create the most effective dialogue with software suppliers:

- Keep the document short (35 to 50 pages for a single plant).
- For each major function, describe, in one or two paragraphs, how the department will ideally function.
- For each major function, follow up with features and functions that are important to your company, but not necessarily found in software packages. Exclude features that are in most software (e.g., "The Bill of Materials must support effective dates"); they do not help differentiate between proposals.

Step 3: Create the Software Candidate List

Where do companies find out about software suppliers? From ads in trade publications, from friends at other companies, from attending regional and international conferences, from cold calls by suppliers. But with over 300 TEI/ERP providers on the market, where does a company start? Three major criteria can potentially be used to initially narrow the field:

1. Industry (both manufacturing processes and customers). The company must determine its unique characteristics based on its industry, vision statement, and feature/function lists, and use those characteristics to narrow the field. From a manufacturing process standpoint, repetitive *is* different from job shop/discrete; plastic film *is* different from vacuum cleaners. Each package targets one or more industries; no package fits all industries equally well. Likewise, from a customer standpoint, selling to the large retailers *is* different from selling to machinery manufacturers, which is different from selling to the government.
2. Manufacturer size. Some packages are designed for very large companies; others, for midsized companies, and others for small companies. Even if the initial software cost of a package designed for a large company is the same as one designed for a midsized company, the implementation cost will probably be higher for the large company package, because it will have more features and functions to be considered during the implementation. And its complexity will probably lengthen the elapsed implementation time and increase the effort required by key individuals throughout the company.
3. Technical platform. This can include operating system, and/or database, and/or coding language(s). If a company has a major investment in one or more of these, the search can be limited to those packages

that operate on the specified platform. Changing platforms can involve major technical and financial costs and risks. However, we strongly suggest that the selection process include packages that fit the platform, and packages which do not. During the final decision, the committee can decide whether the best software for the business, without restriction, is sufficiently better than the best software that resides on the specified technical platform to be worth the additional time, expense, and risks to change platforms.

This step creates a potential candidate list of approximately 12 software packages that apparently fit the major criteria reasonably well.

Step 4: Narrow the Field to Four to Six Serious Candidates

Suppliers talk among themselves. The software supplier community is generally aware of the manufacturers that are starting to look for new software. They also quickly find out how many suppliers have received an RFP, and who those suppliers are. Most software suppliers do not have the time or interest in responding to all the RFPs they receive; the more popular suppliers are particularly interested in prioritizing their efforts. When suppliers receive an RFP that has been sent to many other suppliers, they frequently choose to not respond. When a manufacturer sends an RFP to suppliers whose solutions sell for $100,000 and those whose solutions sell for $1,000,000, the suppliers will assume that the manufacturer does not understand what it really needs. An RFP must provide the supplier enough specific information that they can determine what it will take to win the business, and their probability of winning. This step is essential for a company to identify those software suppliers who fit the company's needs the best, and to ensure that these suppliers will indeed respond to the RFP.

Software suppliers are also aware that some selection processes are only a "show," or front — the actual selection has already been made behind the scenes, and the public selection process is being staged to satisfy corporate or legal requirements. Suppliers are also aware that some consulting firms have favorite packages, which they usually convince their clients to accept. A neutral consulting firm or other outside source whose integrity is widely known and respected in the area can provide assurances of impartiality to the suppliers.

The feature and function list should be condensed into 1 ½ to 2 pages of difficult questions that will effectively separate the final candidates from the also-rans. No single supplier should be able to answer "yes" to all these questions. The chairman or facilitator:

- Calls each of the suppliers to arrange a 1-hour phone interview.
- Faxes them the questions so they can be prepared.
- Calls them to discuss their answers to the questions; the discussion should take about an hour. The supplier will frequently have both a salesperson and pre-sales technical support specialist on the phone call.

The chairman or facilitator summarizes the strengths and weaknesses of each package and supplier, and recommends to the selection committee which packages should be included and which should be excluded, identifying those that are difficult to classify. The committee meets to discuss the recommendations and to vote on the final list of four to five suppliers that will receive the RFP. The chairman or facilitator should call each supplier immediately to let them know the outcome. The suppliers who have been eliminated will have spent only 3 to 4 hours; the ones who remain should be interested in investing more time, because their chances of winning are reasonably good.

If the pre-RFP questions contain sensitive company information, the company might require each software supplier to sign a nondisclosure or confidentiality agreement prior to receiving the fax.

Step 5: Create the Request For Proposal

A Request For Proposal (RFP) typically contains two major sections:

1. The feature and functions list, which describes how the company wants each department or function to operate
2. The "outer wrapper," consisting of instructions to the supplier, the terms and conditions, supplier response forms, etc.

The feature and function list forms the central core of the Request For Proposal (RFP). It is the final output of Step 2, above. The "outer wrapper" is absolutely essential for software suppliers to take your RFP seriously. One standard format includes the following sections:

I. Introduction
   A. The Business (two to three pages)

   B. Scope of the RFP
   C. System Objectives
 II. Proposal Guidelines
   A. Proposed selection and implementation schedule
   B. Selection criteria
   C. Contact person (name, address, phone)
 III. Intended Business Model — the features and functions, starting with an overall company vision (this is from Step 2, above)
 IV. Supplier Response Forms
  V. Hardware and Software Environment, current and envisioned
 VI. Attachments

To many suppliers, the RFP represents the company's level of interest in the process. Sloppy RFPs are less likely to be treated seriously. A well-designed RFP makes it as easy as possible for a supplier to respond. Some companies include a disk containing the RFP in a popular word processing format, so the supplier can easily incorporate their answers into a professionally formatted document.

One key ingredient in a successful RFP is the clear statement to suppliers that the RFP represents the company's best understanding as to how the company can achieve its objectives, and that the supplier is encouraged to propose alternative methods to accomplish the company's objectives. This attitude must be supported when the supplier meets with the selection team.

The team must decide at this point whether it is willing to entertain a consortium of suppliers whose combined software will meet the company's needs. When this book was written, there were no software packages available that encompassed all the functions discussed in this book. And rather than trying to write each TEI module themselves, many software providers are teaming with other providers of complementary software to fill a customer's entire TEI needs. For example, a TEI supplier might use additional "third party" software for EDI, transportation and logistics, payroll and human resources, sales force automation, maintenance management, and product engineering. In our opinion, selecting software from a well-established consortium of partners is as good a choice as a "single-source" provider, because many of the single-source providers have merely purchased smaller firms to include their software (but the technical integration of the purchased software might be no better than a consortium).

Step 6: Review Proposals

Suppliers require 3 to 4 weeks to review the RFP and respond appropriately. Most suppliers will not write a proposal unless they have visited the company, toured the plant, and met with many of the selection team members. Each supplier's visit should be separate.

Trying to keep the suppliers' identities secret from each other is an exercise in futility; they will eventually find out anyhow. (One rather standard technique is glancing through the visitor's log while signing in at the front desk, which gives the last visitors a competitive advantage.) Letting each supplier know who their competitors are has two advantages:

1. Some will self-select out based on their knowledge of the competition and your company; they do not want to invest their time and effort if they have a low probability of eventually winning. This leaves the stronger suppliers in place.
2. Those who remain sometimes provide insights about their competitors' weaknesses. These alleged weaknesses should be investigated (from a somewhat skeptical viewpoint); they can sometimes prove invaluable in the final decision. They can also indicate the veracity and professionalism of the supplier who is providing the insights.

Each selection committee member should read each proposal, concentrating on their functional areas(s). They are also invited to read any other areas that they find interesting. As they read, they should take notes on the following:

- Areas of special strength (and how important they are to the company)
- Areas of perceived weakness (and how important they are to the company)
- Areas that require more clarification, in which they did not understand what the supplier was trying to communicate
- Areas of doubt, in which they have difficulty believing the supplier's claims

They bring these notes to the selection discussion and share them with the committee. They also bring these notes to the demonstrations, to probe:

- Weaknesses — how does the supplier propose to work around them?
- Clarification — what did the supplier mean?
- Doubt — can the supplier demonstrate what they claimed?

Step 7: Select Three Finalists

The committee meets to discuss strengths and weaknesses and decide on three finalists who will be invited to demonstrate their packages. A person with extensive industry experience can be invaluable in interpreting suppliers' answers — one supplier's "maybe" might be more solid than another supplier's "yes." The experienced person should also provide additional insight into the potential weaknesses of each proposed package and supplier.

This is the first time that the committee is forced to make real compromises — package "x" is stronger in the financial areas, but package "y" has better support, and package "z" excels in the customer service function. There are several methods, including forced ranking, giving each person one positive vote and one negative vote, and numeric analysis. Numeric analysis consists of scoring each response numerically by section, weighting each section, then adding up the final scores. Numeric analysis is not as objective as it might sound; we have seen committees perform numeric analysis, then change weightings and even responses until their favorite candidates rose to the top. Thus, "how" the consensus is finally reached is not as important as reaching a solid consensus. If a substantial minority of the committee disagrees with the majority, the committee members should decide what issues need further clarification, then postpone the final decision until that clarification is available.

Three is the desired number of demonstrations. More than three demonstrations tends to confuse and numb the selection committee. Sometimes supplier demonstrations convince a committee beyond any reasonable doubt that they do *not* want to buy this package, or from this supplier. If there are only two demonstrations and one of them elicits a strong negative response, the committee suddenly has only one alternative, and much less negotiating leverage.

If the committee cannot find three strong finalists in the proposals, they should not move forward into the demonstrations, but should instead consider inviting one or more additional suppliers to write proposals as quickly as possible. Bringing the additional suppliers up to an equivalent position takes substantially less time here than after the demonstrations.

Before the demonstration, selection committee members call each finalist's references using a reference checksheet. Each committee member needs to learn how to ask questions in a neutral manner, and to listen not only for the words but for the tone and implications of the response. For example, if the answer to the question, "would you recommend this package to a friend?"

is a long pause, followed by a somewhat hesitant, "yes, I guess so," the committee member needs to record that hesitancy, rather than an unqualified "yes." The reference checks should ask:

- How the reference site runs its business
- How the reference site is using the software (as an integrated planning tool, or to supplement the informal systems that are really running their company)
- The ease of implementation (compared to the supplier's promises)
- The excellence (or lack thereof) of supplier support:
  - Locally
  - Nationally
- Quality of the software:
  - Functional completeness
  - Quantity and severity of "bugs," and how quickly they were resolved
- Quality of the documentation
- Quality, appropriateness, and availability of supplier education
- Which other packages the reference site considered, and why they chose the one they chose
- Would they buy the package again, knowing what they know now?
- Would they recommend the package to a friend, and if so, with what words of caution or warning?

Step 8: Demonstrate Packages

The selection team will be able to relate to their own product lines and customers much more easily than whatever standard demo data (e.g., a PC, a bicycle, a camera) each supplier uses. Well in advance of the demonstrations, the committee should provide each finalist with a demonstration package that includes the following:

- Demo data:
  - 20 to 30 item numbers, descriptions, etc., from three to four different product lines, with BOMs and routings
  - 3 to 5 customers
  - 3 to 5 suppliers
  - "Sanitized" cost information

- Demo script — "a day in the life of our company," with customer orders and changes, engineering changes, shop orders, purchase orders, cash coming in, bills being paid, etc. The script must not be detailed, but should guide the finalist in preparing the demo.

During the demo, the outside facilitator is absolutely invaluable in keeping the finalist focused on the company's actual needs, rather than the finalist's strengths. The outside facilitator also prevents the finalist from obfuscating weaknesses and ensures that the tough questions are asked and answered squarely. The facilitator also ensures that the committee members have made the reference phone calls, and that they are prepared to ask questions based on the information from those calls.

Before each demo, the committee chairman and/or the outside facilitator prepare the committee by reviewing the supplier's perceived strengths and weaknesses. The demo should take place in the company's conference room. A full demo will take 2 days. All selection team members should participate in all sections of the demo, so that they will fully understand the tradeoffs when it is time for the final selection. A demo is *not* entertainment! Team members will work at least as hard as the presenting software supplier, focusing on how well the system fits their department's needs and their company's future vision. After *each* day of demonstration, the team chairman should collect strength/weakness comment sheets from each selection team member; they should actually be filled out during each demo day.

After each supplier finishes its second day of demos, the committee meets briefly to share observations and create an initial consensus to the question, "could we run our company well with the software we just saw?" After the second supplier finishes, the committee can take a straw vote to determine which of the two packages they would prefer.

Step 9: Select the Winner

This is not always as easy as it sounds. Sometimes the choice is extremely difficult, such as between an established company that has not yet implemented new technologies (with the very real risk that they may not survive on the new technologies) vs. a much smaller company that has already successfully embraced the new technology, but still lacks a large installed base and some functionality.

An outside facilitator can help in the following ways:

- Minimize the "halo effect," which gives the most recent supplier an unfair advantage. People tend to assume that the supplier that demonstrates last is generally capable of most of the good attributes of the previous suppliers. If the last supplier performs well in one or two key areas in which previous suppliers had problems, the last supplier tends to win. The committee fails to diligently examine the last supplier for weakness in one or two key areas where the previous suppliers were strong. This is why experienced suppliers will maneuver to obtain the last demonstration time.
- Prioritize and bring additional insight to some of the intangibles, such as technological risk, or the probability of a newer software package surviving.
- Separate the presentation skills and style of the supplier salespeople from the day-to-day functionality of the system. Suppliers know that "glitz" sells systems; experienced buyers know that software "glitz" does not usually delight a company's customers.

When companies select their first system, price is frequently a major factor. However, the second and subsequent times, other criteria become more important:

- Supplier support:
  - Education
  - Technical support
- Ease of implementation
- Closeness of fit to the company's business
- Flexibility to easily change as the company's business changes
- Technological risk
- Value (total implemented cost vs. total benefit to the company).

If the team cannot select a winner, it should schedule a meeting with each finalist to discuss its concerns. It can also request additional demonstration of specific functions and features, visit installed references, etc., to help the final decision process. If, after all the research, the team is still uncomfortable with each of the packages, it should *not* pick one and move forward. It should consider reviewing other packages (the suppliers that did not make the finals, or those that were winnowed out in Step 4). It takes courage to *not* select a package at this point, but the team (and the executives) must remember that whatever package they select they will live with for the next 10 years.

We suggest that after selecting a winner and a second-place supplier, the team invite the two suppliers to separate meetings. The team should inform each supplier of their perceptions about strengths, weaknesses, and concerns, and invite the supplier to respond within a few days. They can also request a "Best and Final Offer," which allows the suppliers to revise their proposals to more closely fit the needs of the company.

The team should visit at least one reference site of the winning software, to see the software in actual use in a company. The software vendor should remain discreetly at a distance while the team and the reference company discuss the software's capabilities.

Step 10: Negotiate the Contract, Run Preimplementation Pilot, and Justify the Investment

Once a winner has been selected, take time to celebrate. Then the team should create the first draft implementation plan. (A high-level implementation plan is shown in Figure 10.1 in the next chapter.)

Negotiate the Contract

The negotiating committee finalizes the terms, conditions, and financial arrangements with the suppliers of software (there can be multiple software suppliers), hardware, technical support, documentation, and implementation services. The committee must remember during the negotiations that the company will need the supplier's good will when circumstances become difficult; at that time, the final $10,000 savings negotiated by using every tactic in the book will be insignificant compared to the value of "extra-mile" support from the supplier. Unlike machines, which have no emotions or memory, software support and implementation support are provided by people.

Run the Preimplementation Pilot

Very few companies run a preimplementation pilot due to the psychological pressure to "move forward decisively," and the general euphoria surrounding the final decision. However, a preimplementation pilot can be the least expensive career insurance available to the system champion and other decision makers.

The purpose of the preimplementation pilot is to uncover major surprises (good and bad) about the software as quickly as possible, so that the selection decision may be reversed, if necessary, with minimal loss of time and investment. The selected software supplier(s) provide a full trial copy of their software, which the company loads on hardware in a conference or training room. During the preimplementation pilot, each selection committee members try to closely simulate a typical day in their department, using unmodified software. To do this, the committee members must accomplish the following:

- Create a test database, which can be based on the demo database, with:
  - Human resources
  - Items, Bills of Material (recipes), and routings
  - Customers, orders and quotations
  - Suppliers and orders
  - The Chart of Accounts
  - Work centers, machines, cells, and lines
- Enter a sales and operations plan and/or some forecasts to drive demand into the system
- Enter and print quotations (ignore electronic linking to suppliers and customers for this first test)
- Enter new customer orders, including converting a quotation or two
- Run the planning system (MPS and MRP, or APS)
- Release purchase orders (or releases) to suppliers
- Release work orders (or schedules) to the shop
- Track and complete shop orders, with desired shop floor reporting and inquiries
- Take a machine or line down for unscheduled maintenance; understand the implications on the schedule
- Respond to customer inquiries, "When will my order ship? Where is it now?"
- Accept customer changes to quantities, dates, specifications, and line items in customer orders; reschedule purchased items
- Receive purchased items
- Perform quality assurance, where applicable
- Run a Payroll run
- Ship finished goods to customers; invoice the customers correctly and easily
- Run Accounts Receivable
- Receive customer payments
- Receive supplier invoices

- Run Accounts Payable
- Pay suppliers
- Answer an executive's question, "Should I try to win business for product 'y'? At what price? When could we deliver?"
- Run a monthly financial and operations closing; review the analysis reports — are they useful, informative, and accurate?

This type of pilot will require 12 to 16 hours from each person on the selection team for each iteration; they should bring other key individuals as well. The company should be willing to pay the software suppliers to provide on-site consultants to help the team use the system; otherwise, the pilot might very easily fail due to lack of understanding of how to use the system, rather than because the system did not fit. Additionally, the selection team must be aware that there is no such thing as a "perfect TEI system."

Based on the preimplementation pilot, the team will create an implementation plan that includes the following items:

- Missing functionality, and how that will be overcome:
  - Manual workarounds
  - In-house customization
  - Purchased customization
- Throughput and software reliability
- Capabilities of supplier support professionals
- High-level backup and disaster recovery plans

This implementation plan must be realistic in the amount of resources that will be available.

Justify the System

Using the implementation plan, the committee can time-phase the anticipated costs and benefits and create a final justification for the capital appropriation request. Each member of the team signs up for the savings in their department. These savings should not be from head-count reduction (or the people who will lose their jobs will probably ensure the failure of the new system); instead, they should be from eliminating wasted effort and materials, with the resulting freed-up time being invested in growing the company and improving processes and profitability. For the company to streamline operations and take advantage of the capabilities of the new system, individuals

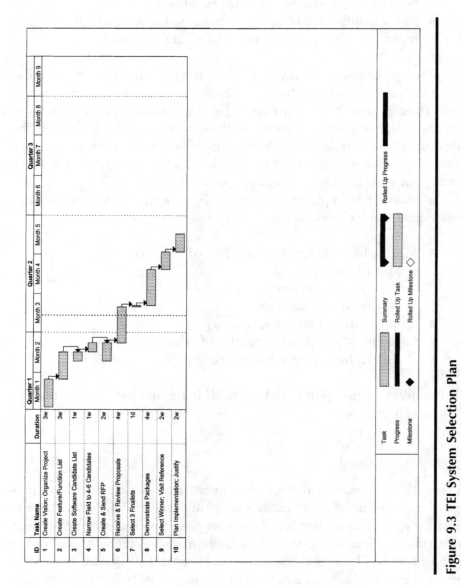

Figure 9.3 TEI System Selection Plan

must be willing to perform different tasks, although their pay should be guaranteed by the company (assuming certain business volumes).

Wherever possible, the new system should be justified on "hard" or "semi-hard" benefits. However, our experience indicates that the intangible benefits will probably equal the tangible benefits.

Selection Project Management

For a single plant, or multiple plants with one committee, the entire selection process can take 3 to 4 months, as shown in the Gantt chart in Figure 9.3. Larger organizations with multiple committees will require more time.

The project must be managed and led by a committed project leader, guided by an outside facilitator, and supported by an executive champion, or it will probably produce a selection that does not fit the company's future needs nearly as well as possible.

References

Collins, James C. and Porras, Jerry I., *Built to Last: Successful Habits of Visionary Companies*, HarperBusiness, New York, 1994.

Gilmore, James and Pine, Joseph, "The Four Faces of Customization," *Harvard Business Review*, Jan.-Feb. 1997.

Hayes, R. C. and Wheelwright, S. C., *Restoring Our Competitive Edge: Competing through Manufacturing*, Wiley, New York, 1984.

Lampel, Joseph and Mintzberg, Henry, "Customizing Customization," *Sloan Management Review*, Fall 1996.

Pannesi, Ronald T. and O'Brien, Helene J., *Systems and Technologies Certification Review Course Student Guide*, APICS, Falls Church, VA, 1995.

Quigley, Phil, "ERP — Are You Going Down the Right Road?" *APICS — The Performance Advantage*, October 1998.

10 Successful Implementation

The *way* a company implements its new TEI system determines its return on investment. Most companies realize a return on investment (ROI) in the 25% to 50% range. But they probably could have achieved 50% to 100% or higher if they had implemented with high ROI as their constant goal. Realistic ROIs for TEI systems range from 25% to 100%, depending on the company's current practices and the amount that a company is willing to streamline its business processes.

System implementations are times of opportunity to dramatically improve how the company operates on a day-to-day basis, by taking advantage of the capabilities in the new system. TEI systems, because of their increased power and integration, can be more complex and more difficult to implement. This chapter outlines the 12 steps that will maximize the ROI of the implemented system. With all the incentive to succeed, why do implementations continue to fail? Because an implementation is not a technical project, like installing a new machine. Implementations are people projects; successful implementations require that people and departments and organizations change. Successful implementations realize that people don't resist change as much as they resist *being* changed. Chapter 11 focuses on the "people" side of a company. In this chapter, we discuss the most common reasons for failure, and close with the ten roadblocks to a successful implementation.

Twelve Steps to Successful Implementation

The 12 steps to a successful TEI system implementation, illustrated in the Gantt chart in Figure 10.1, are:

1. Organize the project.
2. Define the vision-based performance measures for the new system.
3. Create the initial detailed project plan. Hold the project kick-off meeting.
4. Educate the project team and other key individuals.
5. Assess the integrity of the existing database; plan to address any vital problems.
6. Install any new hardware.
7. Install the software; perform the computer room pilot.
8. Educate the critical mass.
9. Define and refine procedures for the new system in the conference room pilot.
10. Ensure that all data bridges are sufficiently robust and that data is sufficiently accurate.
11. Bring the first module/product/plant live; refine and adjust. Repeat for other modules/products/plants.
12. Improve continually.

Step 1: Organize the Project

Assuming that each major function or department was represented on the selection team, most of the selection team members will probably remain on the implementation team. However, this is an excellent time to bring in new members who have greater ability to lead the implementation in their departments.

Steering Committee

Midsized manufacturers usually have a steering committee, comprised of senior executives and the project team leader. Larger manufacturers will have this same structure for each plant, but will have additional coordinating committees across the various plants and divisions. In smaller manufacturers, the steering committee and project team might be combined into one group.

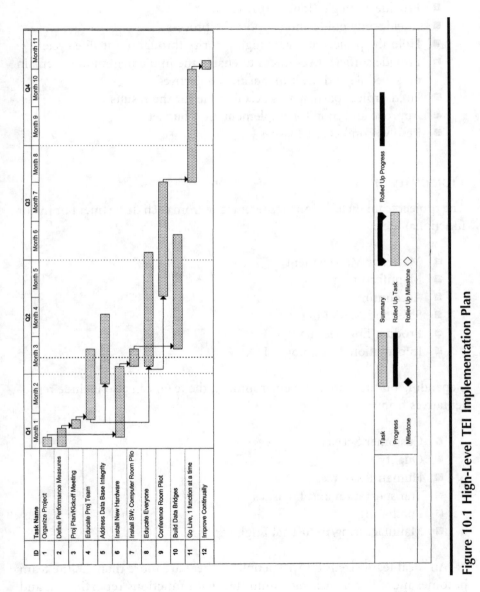

Figure 10.1 High-Level TEI Implementation Plan

The steering committee meets at least monthly (and more frequently, such as weekly, during the critical phases) to:

- Provide strategic (long-term) vision
- Intelligently guide and support the process
- Hold the project at a very high priority throughout its life cycle
- Provide sufficient resources to enable the implementation to remain on schedule and meet its business objectives
- Hold project participants accountable for the results
- Approve and monitor implementation budgets
- Resolve conflicts and issues.

Project Team

The project team includes one representative from each department or major functional area:

- Materials Management
- Manufacturing
- Accounting
- Sales and Marketing
- Product Engineering
- Information Technology (IT).

Depending on the company's environment, the team can also include representatives from:

- Customer Service
- Quality
- Human Resources
- Transportation and Logistics
- Purchasing
- Manufacturing/Industrial Engineering.

An ideal team size is 8 to 10 people; if there are more than 12, the team becomes more like a steering committee, with functions reporting in, and informal subteams tend to develop to accomplish the day-to-day work. If there are less than 6, the team might lack representation from at least one critical area.

The most successful teams are comprised of members who are discontent with the status quo, and who are not afraid to be creative, think new thoughts, and try new ideas. Some companies deliberately place skeptics in the project team with the intent to co-opt the skeptic into becoming a champion. This is risky; the skeptic can also dampen the enthusiasm of other team members sufficiently to substantially diminish the final results.

Team Leader

The team leader leads the team on a day-to-day basis. Ideally, the team leaders should be from materials or manufacturing or customer Service, because those are the departments that will be affected the most by the new system. However, leadership skills and a holistic viewpoint are more important than the department that the leader comes from. The team might have an additional representative from the team leader's department, to focus on that department. The team leader should *not* be from Information Technology, because the system should not be perceived as an "IT project," and the department that is usually stretched the most during an implementation is IT.

The "how-to implement successfully" guides usually insist that the team leader work full-time on the project. In most smaller companies and many midsized companies, that requirement ignores the business realities of a very small professional staff. While full-time is ideal, part-time is often reality.

If most of the team members have not been through an TEI implementation before, the team can benefit from having an outside consultant who has implemented similar systems. The outside consultant can accomplish the following:

- Help keep the team focused on the important issues.
- Provide a "reality check" concerning potential issues with the software supplier.
- Serve as a sounding board for the team leader.
- Provide encouragement during the difficult times.
- Advise the steering committee.

Step 2: Define the Vision-Based Performance Measures

What activities and results need to be measured so that the implementation provides an ROI of more than 100%? What goals need to be set for those measurements? How should those goals be time-phased?

As the first step in the selection process, the selection team created a clear, crisp, compelling, comprehensive, challenging vision about how the company could become the benchmark in its industry. Now that the system has been selected, the implementation team should revisit that initial vision and revise it to reflect decisions that have been made and new information that has been learned. The team might be able to make the vision even more aggressive in some areas due to the capabilities of the new system, and might have to reduce goals in other areas.

The overriding question is, "how must we operate to become *the* benchmark in our industry, to become *the* manufacturer that our customers and suppliers use as the benchmark for products and service and value?" Some attributes that might be appropriate to measure include:

- On-time deliveries (to customer request date) — 99.5+%
- Gross profit margin — varies by industry, but 50% is very aggressive in most industries
- Customer order-to-ship time — 2 to 4 hours is achievable in many industries
- Inventory turns (or "spins") — varies by industry, but some have hit 50 and are still climbing
- Velocity (total elapsed time in manufacturing divided by value-added time) — less than 2 is excellent
- Defects — should be heading toward parts per million

Defining the new goals and measurements assumes that the implementation team has proper awareness of the capabilities of the new TEI system.

As the measurements are defined, take a snapshot of current operations (with the promise that nobody will lose their job!) to use as the benchmark. Then create a chart for each measurement showing current performance and desired future performance by week or month, with realistic improvements at appropriate times. Finally, plot actuals against the desired performance, as illustrated in Figure 10.2. The implementation team and the steering committee must continually remind themselves that the goal is not just implementing the system so that it replaces the old system — the goal is implementing the system to achieve the business objective of becoming the benchmark in the industry.

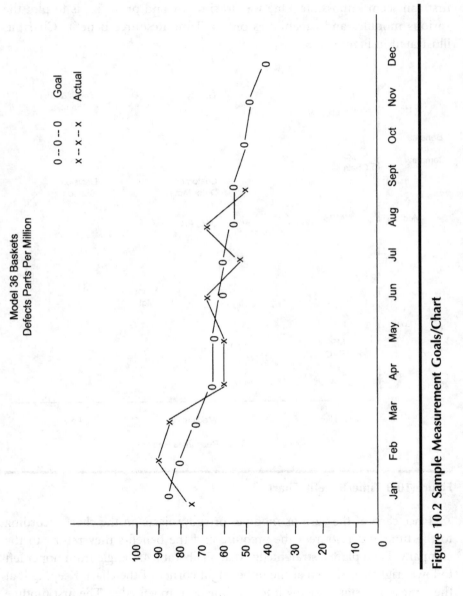

Figure 10.2 Sample Measurement Goals/Chart

Step 3: Create the Initial Detailed Project Plan

"How do you eat an elephant? One bite at a time." A full TEI system has so many modules and so much capability that deciding what to implement first can seem impossible. One way to simplify and prioritize is to plot the various modules and capabilities onto a Time-Resource/Benefits Chart, as illustrated in Figure 10.3.

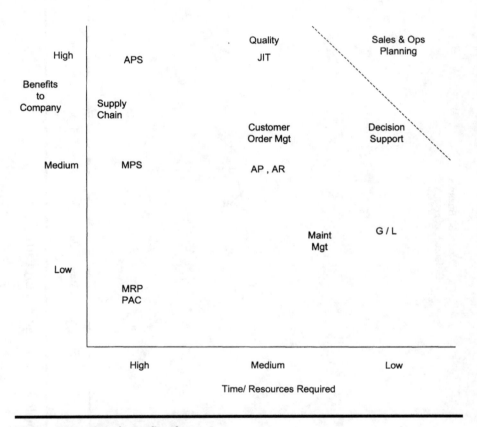

Figure 10.3 Time/Benefit Chart

Place each of the various modules or subprojects on the chart according to the time and resources they require and the benefits they return to the company. Then place a straightedge diagonally (at a 45° angle from upper left to lower right), as shown at the upper right corner of the chart. Keeping it at the same angle, start moving it toward the bottom left edge. The first module or subproject that it reaches is the highest priority — it returns the greatest benefit for the lowest organizational cost. In Figure 10.3, the module with the highest return for the lowest resources required is Sales and Operations Planning. The next three are Decision Support, Quality Management, and JIT.

Some of the subprojects on the chart may have technical requirements for other modules or functions to precede them — for example, a chart of accounts before any inventory functions, or the item master as the prerequisite for all functions and processes which use items.

To create this initial detailed project plan, add substantial detail to the initial plan from Step 10 of the selection process. Add the resources required for each task; ensure that no resources are overcommitted. Creating a detailed project plan normally involves several iterations:

- Adding the detailed steps and resources to the high-level project plan
- Running the plan assuming finite resources, which causes the projected completion date to be much too late
- Reviewing the resource requirements, and offloading tasks from critical resources to other resources
- Rerunning the plan, with a projected due date still too late
- (Optional) Creating a justification for using outside resources in the most critical areas
- (If the resources are denied) Reviewing the estimates of actual time required for key sections to see if the project can be scheduled to complete somewhat close to the desired due date
- (If the resources are denied) Trying to figure out how to make the project fit the unrealistically small time estimates

Kick-Off Meeting

The most successful projects start with an official kick-off meeting that includes the entire company. The most critical part of the meeting is the speech by the CEO or president that includes the following points:

- The company's vision, mission, and strategies.
- The business reasons for the new system — the goals that senior management wants to achieve, and how the new system is vital to achieving those goals.
- Senior management's complete commitment to the success of the implementation.
- The promise that no one will lose their paycheck due to the implementation as long as business remains at the current levels; however,

the day-to-day tasks and responsibilities of many people will change so that the company can gain the benefits that the new system offers. Any person who will have difficulty wholeheartedly supporting the new system should meet privately with an executive to receive a transfer to a noncritical area, with no penalty or repercussions. After the project has started, failure to cooperate wholeheartedly will be viewed as a direct impediment to the progress of the company, and can be reason for termination.

- Request that each person help create an exciting company that will be the benchmark for the industry, fully understanding that the process of creating means that there will be some "failures," which should be viewed as learning experiences.
- Introduction of the project team and the project team leader.

The project team leader outlines the project plan, showing how and when each department will implement major functions in the system. The project team leader highlights the most critical resources (e.g., IT) and asks for help in minimizing the load on those resources.

Step 4: Educate the Project Team and Other Key Individuals

"If you think education is expensive, try ignorance."

The project team and key individuals attend education and training classes. Education can be defined as teaching concepts and understanding of "why"; training can be defined as teaching detailed day-to-day operation and "how to." A company can educate its team on the concepts of TEI; they can have the software supplier train their people on the functionality of each module.

Education is absolutely vital to enable the project team to effectively apply the capabilities of the new system to achieve the company's business objectives. Without extensive education, the team will almost invariably design a "new operating style" that will basically replicate the existing methods, thereby squandering the best opportunity in a decade to truly improve company operations and profitability.

An ideal education program uses construction toys and other "games" to help the project team design how the company can operate with the new tools. It helps the team add detail to the vision that they originally created at the start of the system selection process.

Once the education is complete, the team starts training on the various functions and features of the software. This training is frequently offered by the software supplier, either at their education centers or in-house. The advantages to going to their education centers are:

- Lower cost for a few participants
- Team members learn from other companies
- No distractions from the plant during the class

The advantages to having a dedicated class on site are:

- Lower cost per participant for many participants
- Participants can focus strictly on the company and its issues
- The instructors can provide guidance on company issues and problems.

Step 5: Assess the Integrity of the Existing Database

If the company has been operating from an informal system and merely tolerating the existing MRP II system, the basic data in the MRP II system is probably incorrect. Some counselors advise correcting the data *before* starting to implement, while others advise starting to implement, then correcting the data as the errors become apparent. We recommend the middle ground:

- Separate the items into three groups:
  - A — items made frequently
  - B — items made sometimes
  - C — items that are made infrequently, if at all

Perform these next steps on the A items only; save the B and C items for review the next time they are scheduled to be built:

- Review and correct basic data that would cause serious errors if incorrect, such as the components themselves, BOM quantities, and possibly scrap factors.
- Whenever an item is built, have manufacturing review the paperwork closely, coordinating any needed changes with engineering. Engineering should make the changes on the spot, and scheduling should reissue the work order.

While this approach will catch errors before an item is built incorrectly, those errors will have been used for planning, so there will be shortages for some parts and excesses for other parts. The alternative, reviewing and fixing the records before starting the implementation, generally delays implementations for several months, which can threaten the eventual success of the implementation.

Step 6: Install any New Hardware

If the new system can function well on the existing computer network, this step is relatively quick, easy, and inexpensive. However, if a company is changing from a mainframe-based system to a PC network-based system, new network wiring and hardware might be required.

Most systems require a PC for each user. However, the PC that is already on a user's desk might lack sufficient power to run the new software properly. Fortunately, powerful new PCs are now inexpensive and continue to drop in price and increase in performance.

Step 7: Install the Software; Perform the Computer Room Pilot

A technical support person from the software supplier will often install the software and run a few tests to make sure that it is installed correctly. "Installed" should not be confused with "implemented." "Installed" merely means that the software is now available to be used by the company.

During the computer room pilot, the software supplier's technician tests the standard version of the software to ensure that it all functions. This process takes a day or so. At that point, the hardware is ready; the software is loaded, and the implementation team frequently starts feeling panic. There are no longer any technical obstacles or excuses between them and using the new system effectively. The team can also start feeling overwhelmed, due to the myriad interdependent tasks that must all be completed. An experienced consultant can provide valuable reassurance at this point.

Step 8: Educate and Train the Critical Mass

"Expecting someone who knows how to use Windows to automatically know how to operate an TEI system is like thinking that someone with a license to drive a car can fly a jet fighter … in combat … and win a dogfight … and return safely to base."*

The "critical mass" that must be educated and trained includes everyone who will use the new system, and everyone whose job will be directly affected by it. In our opinion, *everyone* should receive at least an overview education of the new system, explaining how it is going to change the way the business operates, and how the company, the customers, the shareholders, the employees, and the suppliers will each benefit (and what each of those groups might have to give up).

Education is absolutely critical. It forms the foundation for individuals and groups to change habits, procedures, and culture. Studies in the 1980s conclusively found that investments in education paid for themselves many times over in improved use of the system (and increased ROI for the entire system investment). This probably still holds true, because human nature changes very slowly.

It is very time-sensitive; education and training that is not used is quickly forgotten. Therefore, each group must be educated and trained immediately prior to their participation in the conference room pilot, which should be immediately prior to that group starting to use the system in their work area on a daily basis.

The company should offer basic PC/Windows training to all participants as the first course; many people are not sufficiently skilled in those fundamentals. The large number of people to be trained, and the large number of modules of training that are available, require the education and training effort to be tracked formally. One method is a table, which lists the course offerings across the top and the employees down the side. If an employee needs to take a specific course, the date of the course can be filled in. Once the course is taken, the box can be filled in with a color, such as green. The format of such a course-tracking chart is illustrated in Figure 10.4.

Given the quantities of people to be trained, the training courses should probably be offered "in-house." The project team members might lead some of the courses if they are very familiar with the concepts and have had a chance to learn the applications fairly well on the test system. Otherwise, investing in a qualified trainer is the best alternative.

One of the best ways to minimize learning and retention is to have a boring format, such as a person lecturing, using an overhead projector with Power-Point slides and screen samples from the software. By contrast, the presentation

---

* Turbide, David A., "Penny Wise, Pound Foolish," *Midrange ERP,* February 1999, p. 88.

	ERP Overview	PC/Windows Overview	Inventory	Chart of Accounts	Cash Receipts	Quality Mgt	Order Entry
Anandapurna	8/14	8/21		8/28			9/5
Bradley	8/14	8/21				8/28	9/5
Carlos	6/10	6/17	6/26			8/28	
DeStasi	4/3	4/10		4/17	4/19	4/24	4/30
Espinoza	6/30	7/7		7/14			7/21
Fujyama	4/3	4/10	4/17	4/19		4/26	4/30
Gorbachev	8/14	8/21		8/28		9/25	
Hunter	6/30	7/7		7/14	7/17		
Isaacson	6/10	6/17	6/19	6/26			
Jacobsen	4/3	4/10		4/19	4/24	4/26	4/30
Korhaczka	6/30	7/7		7/14	7/17		7/21
Langenwalter	4/5	4/12	4/17	4/19	4/24	4/26	4/30

Figure 10.4 Education and Training Tracking Chart

format should change every 20 to 30 minutes. These training courses can be supplemented with videotapes, hands-on exercises, games, homework, etc.

After the initial education and training effort, the training coordinator should design curricula for new employees so that they can also learn the system well enough to use it effectively. The employee on site (or even worse, the employee who is leaving) cannot be expected to have the skills, materials, or knowledge to train the new employee properly.

Step 9: Train on the Conference Room Pilot

The conference room pilot is the TEI equivalent of a flight simulator for pilots. Its purposes are to serve as a:

- Safe training ground for each person in the company to learn how to use the system to perform their job with the new system.
- Forgiving environment for participants to learn what causes mistakes and how to recover from them (because it is not "live" data, and can therefore be reloaded after a problem).
- Test bed for revising policies and procedures to incorporate the new system's capabilities.

A company that skips or minimizes this step reduces its ROI on its entire investment by 25% to 50%, because the people implementing the new system will make it support the way that they are accustomed to working (thereby minimizing substantive changes).

The conference room pilot must be housed in its own separate room, with dedicated PCs. If there is no suitable space in the company's existing buildings, an office trailer can be rented for the 6 months that the room is required.

The conference room pilot process follows these steps; time estimates are for a medium-sized, single plant manufacturer:

1. The project team creates a skeletal business case test environment. This can start with the test database that the company furnished each of its software suppliers for their demonstrations, with additional data and functions to round out the basic test environment. This can require 1 to 2 weeks.

2. The project team creates business processing scenarios for each basic function (such as receiving a customer order through shipping the requested items), so that the function implements the vision of best practices that the selection team created as the first step in the selection process, and as detailed in the second implementation step. The team can flowchart these functions on brown paper, lining the conference room, or they can use flowcharting and process simulation software. The objective is to understand the total elapsed time required for each function, and to design the process to minimize places where the process waits, and the time the process waits at those places. This can require 4 to 6 weeks.

3. The team refines those scenarios for each basic function until they flow relatively smoothly. This can require 4 to 6 weeks.

4. The team documents the scenarios and creates basic policies and procedures that reinforce them (this can involve revising existing

policies and procedures, or completely rewriting them). This can require 4 to 6 weeks, and can overlap Step 3, above.

5. The team then creates "bad" scenarios (for example, missing data in the incoming EDI) to test the software and their procedures. When the new system and procedures have been strengthened to survive typical mistakes, the team tries to deliberately "crash" the system, and to learn how to recover from unexpected systems halts. The team can also create and test manual backup procedures, to be used in case the system becomes unavailable for a period of time. Finally, the team documents a rudimentary disaster recovery plan so that the company can continue operations if the central file server is destroyed. This step can require 2 to 4 weeks.

6. Simultaneously, the team sets up and tests security, to ensure that authorized persons can indeed access all transactions and inquiries that they need, and that unauthorized persons cannot reach any of their transactions and inquiries. This can require 1 to 2 weeks.

7. When the team is satisfied that the software, policies, and procedures are sound, they present the entire package to upper management for approval. (They should have been keeping upper management informed during the process, and obtaining interim approvals on important policy matters or substantive changes in operating processes.) The presentation should include comparisons between current business practices and the proposed practices, with respect to elapsed time, number of manual intervention steps, and error handling. This presentation (including preparation time) can require 1 to 2 weeks.

8. A "department team" is the implementation team in a specific department. The project team helps the department team from the first department or function that is going to use the software design its learning and test process. This process should basically replicate Steps 1 to 6, above, building on the foundation that the project team has created. This can require 1 week.

9. The department team trains on the software and revises policies and procedures for its department, following its learning and test process design. When complete, it presents its policies, procedures, and operating methodologies to its management for approval. The entire process can involve 2 to 6 weeks, depending on the additional amount of detail required.

10. As the department team writes more detailed procedures and tests functions, it will probably uncover errors and areas of potential

improvement in the project team's flow and procedures. The project team then revises its overall design and procedures.

11.   When the first department team's design is complete, the new system can theoretically be brought live in that function. We say "theoretically," because a single function cannot operate independently from the rest of the company. If the cost and risk of building data bridges is sufficiently low, the department can indeed "go live" when the data bridges are complete and tested. Otherwise, they will need to wait until enough other departments and functions are ready to start using the new software.

12.   If the first department starts using the software "live," future change requests from subsequent departments can be much more difficult to implement. However, if the first department has to wait for several months to start using the new system in its department, its enthusiasm will probably wane substantially during the waiting period. And the people might forget how they were going to use the new system, to the degree that a quick refresher might be required just before they go "live."

13.   This process repeats until all departments and functions are finished.

Step 10: Ensure Data Bridge Robustness and Data Accuracy

The difficulty of bringing the new system up in stages increases with the degree of integration of the old system and the degree of integration of the new system. When the old and new systems are each integrated, building automated and manual data bridges is basically the only alternative to a "big bang" implementation, in which the entire new system is turned on all at once.

Although these data bridges will only be used for a few months, they must be treated as mission-critical, because they can seriously compromise the integrity of the new system (to the ultimate extent of causing complete system failure) if they introduce errors into the database. Thus, they must go through the entire development and testing process, with the exception of detailed user documentation:

■   Design the basic functionality, by comparing the new system data layout to the old. Decide what to do in each case when the new system needs data that the old system does not provide.

■   Code the bridge program(s).

- Create a comprehensive test database, including both good data and bad (and missing) data.
- Test the programs until they work flawlessly under all conditions.
- Document the design, the tests run, and test results.

The data being brought across must be sufficiently accurate for people to start trusting the new system. If the company has been operating with an informal system until this point, critical data will almost inevitably be missing, out-of-date, or incorrect. The incorrect data will cause the new system to plan incorrectly, which can seriously impact on-time shipments and profitability.* Critical data includes:

- On-hand and on-order inventory balances, by location
- Bills of Materials/recipes
- Routings/process sheets
- Customer profiles and information
- Critical accounting data

Step 11: Bring the First Module/Product/Plant Live; Refine and Adjust. Repeat For Other Modules/Products/Plants

Which department/product line should be implemented first? The one that is a guaranteed success. If the first implementation effort fails, no matter what the reason, the rest of the implementation will be much, much more difficult, because the people will not be as willing to risk their careers or invest their personal time for a project that is a "loser." The first success should be deliberately designed to easily attain benefits that are visible to much of the company.

Once the first department(s) to use the new system have been trained, the new procedures written, security established, and all data bridges written and tested, the new system is ready to start being used in real production. Celebrations are appropriate as each department starts using the new software effectively.

However, in spite of all the training and testing, the first few days or weeks of actual use will probably uncover some difficulties. Appropriate representatives from the project team, IT department, software supplier, and the outside consulting firm should be present or available when needed to ensure that these difficulties are swiftly resolved (and the underlying causes

---

* Stedman, Craig, "ERP Can Magnify Errors," *Computerworld*, October 19, 1998, pp. 1, 14.

fixed permanently). If some of the earlier steps have not been completed properly, the number and magnitude of problems encountered at this point can be sufficiently overwhelming that the company should fall back to using the old system until the problems with the new system can be fully addressed. Failure to address problems can cause catastrophic system failure later, or can debilitate the integrity of the database to such an extent that people ignore the new system, choosing to use informal systems instead.

In its initial implementation, one large manufacturer's new system was creating a set of exception reports over 2 feet tall for each planner each week! Instead of listening to the planners, who were protesting that the new system was completely unworkable in its current form, top management chose to discontinue the old system to "force those change-resistant planners to use the new system anyhow."

The alternative to the phased, or departmental/functional approach, is the "big bang", or "cold turkey" approach. In this scenario, the company prepares thoroughly for the cutover date, which should be at least a long weekend, and might preferably be during a plant shutdown of 1 to 2 weeks.

Step 12: Improve Continually

When the new TEI system is running reasonably well, or they are too tired to continue, most companies "declare victory," participants agree that the implementation was a success, and they move on to other projects.

Unfortunately, this practice ignores the reality that a company can only absorb a certain amount of change during a finite time period. The truly successful companies understand this and encourage their practitioners to use the system to continue to improve. For example, after the new system is operational, management can request that the materials planners run an inventory turns report monthly and track the improvement from month to month. Another department can run a monthly report on total time from receipt of customer order until the truck departs with that order.

Why Implementations Fail

The percentage of ERP (and presumably TEI, although TEI is still very new) implementations that can be classified as "failures" ranges from 40% to 60% and higher. Yet, companies continue to try to implement these systems because they are absolutely essential to responsive planning and communication. If a company understands the basic reasons why most implementations fail, it can substantially increase its chances of success by planning to recognize, and to avoid or overcome those issues. We categorize the reasons for failure as follows:

1. People don't want the new system to succeed.
2. People are comfortable, and don't see the need for the new system.
3. People have unrealistic expectations of the new system.
4. People don't understand the basic concepts of the system.
5. The basic data is inaccurate.
6. The system has technical difficulties.

Underlying all these is the *people* side of TEI, because TEI is much more than just a technical system. Chapter 11 discusses this concept in greater detail.

People Don't Want the New System to Succeed

If people don't want the new system to succeed, it probably won't. But why would people want the new system to fail?

1. **Loss of jobs** — They might be afraid that they (or their friends) will lose their jobs. Some companies actually plan to lay off unneeded people as soon as the new system is in. The president of one company intended to lay off half the implementation project team! (The president was under the impression that the people were not aware of his intentions. However, the people knew it when they started the implementation.) One way to overcome this fear is to assure everyone in the entire company, both during the project kickoff meeting and in written communications, that no person will lose their paycheck because of the new system, as long as business holds steady or improves. Some options include filling other positions, creating new positions, and early retirement. The steering committee must address this issue, directly and openly, or people will make their own assumptions.
2. **Measurement/reward system has not been changed** — The measurement and reward system has not been adjusted to reflect the new system. For the new system to succeed, the compensation system must support it directly. If the new system requires accurate inventories, include accurate inventories as a major factor in performance reviews.

3. **New system makes job more difficult** — The new system might make a person's job more difficult. This could be due to reorganizing the responsibilities of each function and department. At the very minimum, management must recognize that some jobs will become more difficult and address those issues squarely.

4. **Fear of failure** — People are afraid to fail, especially in public. If the new system changes a person's functions and responsibilities, the person might fear that he or she will not be able to perform the new tasks well. In some respects, that is absolutely correct, because they cannot be as skilled in the new tasks as they are in the ones they have been routinely performing for years. This issue can be mitigated by insisting on each person spending time with the conference room pilot until they are relatively comfortable with the new system.

   Perhaps even more important is the culture in some companies that failure can lead to punishment or loss of job. Management must make it absolutely clear that it understands that people will make honest mistakes as they learn the new system, and that these mistakes will be not only tolerated, but even welcomed. People must understand that the goals for the new system cannot be accomplished with the old approaches and that any learning requires failure. The analogy of a child learning to walk, or a youth learning to ride a bicycle, can be helpful in communicating these concepts to the workforce. Additionally, management can create a "Most Creative Mistake" award, to be given every 3 months to the person whose attempt to improve was the most creative. Only by celebrating the learning process, and the mistakes included in that process, can the company attain the potential benefits from the new system.

5. **Reduced social importance** — The new system might reduce the social importance of key individuals. The new system might automate the communications that key individuals had previously provided, such as the actual status of a customer order or work order, or determining a ship date, or contacting a supplier with a requested reschedule. Many people at all levels of the company come to work more because of the social contacts than the money. They will struggle to retain these social rewards.

People are Comfortable, and Don't See the Need for a New System

When people do not see the need for a new system, they will not expend the effort required to assure its success, thereby virtually assuring failure. Companies that are comfortably profitable are frequently highly resistant to change. This is one reason why some of the best candidates for the implementation team are those who chronically complain about the status quo.

The two approaches to encouraging people to change are:

1. **Avoided pain** — This is the possibility that the company will lose sales and lay off people, which can occur if a competitor is capable of gaining competitive advantage, or the customer demands that the company implement new systems to support them (such as VMI or EDI).
2. **Increased pleasure** — This is the promise of a person's job becoming easier, more rewarding, or providing greater social status. In the 1980s, when one company implemented a new MRP II system, some of the shop floor workers wanted to be trained to operate the computer terminals so that they could increase their job skills and marketability.

People Have Unrealistic Expectations of the New System

It is easy to have unrealistic expectations of the new system. In fact, the sales environment for acquiring a new system almost guarantees that some expectations will be out of line with reality. The following sections explain the most common ones.

Unrealistic Expectations

During the sales cycle, software suppliers are sometimes tempted to embellish on the benefits and to minimize the actual difficulty of implementation and the ongoing cost of operation of the system. Additionally, the internal champion or other key individuals might be tempted to promise whatever people want to hear to ensure that the new system will be selected and purchased. The best way to minimize this behavior is to visit actual reference sites and to listen between the lines when people are describing how to implement and use the new system.

Unrealistic expectations include unrealistically low estimates of resources required (time, people, and cash). One type of unrealistic time estimate is an implementation date that is unrealistically soon. This condition is exacerbated if the deadline is due to external circumstances (e.g., spin-off from the old parent company and loss of its IT system, a move to a new building, summer plant shutdown).

Implementing a new system is somewhat analogous to raising a child or starting a new business. People have heard stories about how difficult it will be. However, midway through the process, those who have not been through it before will admit that they did not imagine that it would be *this* difficult. The project leader is primarily responsible for setting realistic expectations about the amount of effort and time required. If the expectations of the amount of work and difficulty have been set too low, the project team and others can become discouraged when they begin to realize the full scope of the effort and the inadequate resources that are available. The project is at risk of failure at this point. An objective outside assessment can be invaluable to reset expectations realistically.

Companies also tend to underestimate the amount of outside assistance that they will require, both technical (for example, for building bridges between the old system and the new system and for integrating the new system into existing systems that will remain), and project (project management).

"Aircraft Carrier" Syndrome

Both management and workers frequently assume that operations will starting improving immediately once the new system is implemented,* as illustrated in Figure 10.5a. However, a more realistic expectation is that productivity will initially drop as the new system is implemented, then start improving, similar to the path of a jet taking off from an aircraft carrier. When the jet leaves the carrier deck it can dip toward the ocean before it has sufficient airspeed to start climbing, as illustrated in Figure 10.5b.

During an implementation, this phenomenon is caused by the fact that people are not as familiar with the new system as they are with the old, and therefore will not be immediately as productive. If management does not understand and expect this phenomenon, it can incorrectly decide that the new system is a failure, and cancel the entire project shortly after

---

* Chew, W. Bruce, Leonard-Barton, Dorothy, and Bohn, Roger E., "Beating Murphy's Law," *Sloan Management Review,* Vol. 32, No. 3, 1991.

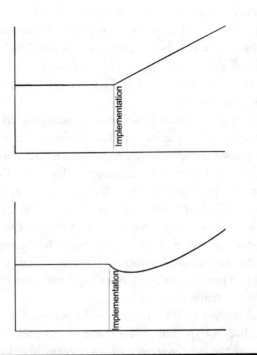

Figure 10.5 "Aircraft Carrier" Syndrome of Expectations vs. Reality

implementation. Management must also direct the project closely enough during the critical early days after implementation to ensure that the productivity curve turns upward quickly.

Poor Implementation Project Management

The project leader must treat the implementation as the very large, complex, and critical project that it is. He or she must know how to run a large project, including:

- Communicating, communicating, communicating, and then communicating some more
- Setting realistic expectations for time and resource requirements
- Ensuring that sufficient resources are available for each task
- Monitoring the status of the project, and continually updating the project plan
- Ensuring that each project participant meets deadlines

If the project leader has not successfully run a project of this magnitude before, providing an outside coach to assist in managing the project can be an excellent investment.

"It's an IT Project"

It's a supply chain project, including customers and suppliers. IT provides the technical foundation. It's not an "IT project," any more than making parts in the factory is a "maintenance project." If the company considers the implementation to be an IT project, failure is virtually assured. To avoid this stigma, the project leader and most project team members should be from non-IT departments, and should focus on business issues.

People Don't Understand the Basic Concepts of the System

The fundamental concepts of TEI systems have been implemented since the late 1970s, with the early MRP II systems. Those systems integrated planning and communications across several departments and functions. However, some people are not yet aware of the basic concepts of these systems. The best way to address this issue is extensive education, followed by lots of hands-on training in the conference room pilot setting. The project leader must understand the extent and depth of education and training required for those people who have never used such a system before, and even for those who have used a system (but who still lack understanding of the basic concepts).

The Basic Data is Inaccurate

A front-page article in *Computerworld* in October, 1998, highlighted the problems of data inaccuracy at a company that had just implemented a new ERP system.

> Three months after [a manufacturer] went live with [an ERP system] last year, a curious thing happened: the [manufacturer] began running out of screws, fasteners, and other manufacturing materials. The culprit turned out to be incorrect bills of material that were entered into the software for production uses and then passed along to inventory managers.*

---

* Stedman, Craig, "ERP Can Magnify Errors," *Computerworld*, October 19, 1998, pp. 1, 14.

The article continues,

> other users are learning a similar hard truth about ERP applications: Although the integrated nature of the software is tying companies together like never before, it can become a double-edged sword when errors are instantaneously spread around the system. That's a big change for workers used to stovepipe applications that keep mistakes to themselves. *

Before the integrated system was implemented, the incorrect bills of material didn't affect production, because the shop floor workers knew and used the right quantities of components to be used for each assembly. The shortages occurred because the new system relied on the inventory data, which was based on incorrect BOMs. After the material shortages surfaced, the manufacturer put on a mandatory, 2-day training class to show all of its employees how transactions flow through an integrated TEI suite.

The article identifies five operations that can be affected by errors in a bill of materials entered into an integrated applications suite:

1. Preparation of production work orders
2. Assembly of raw materials
3. Routing of products through manufacturing plants
4. Tracking of materials and component inventories
5. Logging of components in case of recall

Geoff Griebel, director of IT at Penwest Pharmaceuticals, states, "No matter what you do now, it impacts somebody else. And if you make a mistake, it gets sent out in real time."*

The System has Technical Difficulties

In the late 1980s and early 1990s, systems were technically robust and reliable. However, the advent of client/server systems has increased the level of technical risk. Software manufacturers with existing systems spent millions of dollars to redesign and recode their systems to operate in a client/server environment. Some of those new systems did not work in the field; they failed to operate successfully in actual manufacturing companies, leading to failed implementations. It is not unusual for a software supplier

---

* Stedman, Craig, "ERP Can Magnify Errors," *Computerworld,* October 19, 1998, pp. 14.

to fail in their first few attempts to create an object-oriented foundation for their systems.

Even if the software supplier's system is technically robust, day-to-day operation of a client/server environment is much more difficult and much less reliable than the old legacy systems. In a legacy system, turning a terminal off while an application was running did not affect the integrity of the system. Legacy systems were designed to be restarted, with integrity, in the event that the main computer halted midstream. And the best of the main computers were legendary in their reliability — IT professionals would brag about their computer running for years without any unplanned stoppages. PC networks are by their very nature much more fragile, and PC operating systems are much less reliable than the central computer operating systems. PC-network-based systems have many potential points of failure, which can make recovery extremely difficult. For example, if a PC hangs up while an application, such as master scheduling, is running on it, what happens to the master schedule data when the PC is rebooted? Has some of the data been updated on the file server?

Ten Roadblocks to Successful Implementation

In his presentation to the 1995 APICS International Conference, Paul Wojciak lists ten pitfalls to successful implementation, in the form of characters or personality types:*

1. **The Evil Naysayer** — This is the person who is negative about the project, and everyone and everything associated with it. What the company has right now works just fine for him or her. *Suggested solution:* The Naysayer can come from one of two places — fear of loss of social importance, and fear of failure with the new system. If the Naysayer can be coached through their fears, they can become a powerful ally.
2. **The Yes Man** — This person agrees with everything that anyone says, without contributing original ideas of their own. *Suggested solution:* the Yes Man is usually a junior member of the team who lacks confidence to speak his or her own opinion. Project team members are generally senior, experienced people. The Yes Man can begin to par-

---

* Wojciak, Paul J. "So You're the Project Leader! 10 Roadblocks to Watch Out For," *1995 International Conference Proceedings*, APICS, Falls Church, VA, 1995.

ticipate more actively through coaching and encouragement, both off-line and in meetings.

3. **The Clueless Wonder** — How this person ever got into the company, or why this person was appointed to the project team, is a complete mystery. Unfortunately, this person can represent a department that is critical to the success of the project. *Suggested solution:* Replace them with a more competent person, even if it's politically difficult. The alternative is to leave them on the team with the probability that they can cause the entire project to fail.

4. **The Invisible Man** – This person has the knack for being somewhere else when the project team needs him, and for not delivering what was promised. He or she attended the initial high-level meetings, but disappeared when the workload started getting heavy. This is frequently a person with high stature in the company. Unfortunately, their behavior undermines the morale of the rest of the group — if this person doesn't have to contribute, why should the others? *Suggested solution:* Recognize the Invisible Man's hot buttons (wasting the company's money, creating a bad image, etc.) and appeal to those. Let the Invisible Man know what's going on and give them the choice to either start delivering results or step aside.

5. **The Moray Eel** — This is a very senior person (who has chosen to limit participation) who vetoes a couple months of work with no warning. They have said, "I don't care how you structure things, as long as everything works and we don't shut the plant down." However, they *do* care, and they won't let the team continue on the path the team has selected. They want the team to change things to fit their very limited understanding of the system, which can have catastrophic results. *Suggested solution:* Have a private conversation with the Eel, telling them what their actions are costing. This can be an excellent task for the outside consultant. The best long-term solution is to get the Eel more involved; at worst, they will come to accept the team's judgment, and at best, they will become a true ally.

6. **The Underlying Reasoner** — This person is a cousin, twice removed, to the Yes Man. The person will constantly attempt to slant each decision and discussion toward their personal agenda. While this is a common human trait, this person becomes a burden to the rest of the team because he or she does not understand that the team can accomplish much more as a group than as individuals only if they give up their personal agendas. *Suggested solution:* The

Underlying Reasoner can be coming from a place of fear (losing control over their empire, or that the system might be used to spy on them), or ignorance (not understanding how their department and the company can gain from a truly integrated system). From the start, emphasize that the team will be forced to make compromises to succeed, and how the entire company and each department will benefit with the new system.

7. **Roger Dodger** — Roger has a lot of great input, and is enthusiastic. However, Roger misses deadlines regularly, with a litany of excuses that all appear legitimate. He has actual expertise to contribute, if he would only perform. *Suggested solution:* Communicate with Roger what his actions are doing to the team and the successful implementation. The Rogers of the world often have trouble seeing the big picture and believe that their role is not as critical as it really is. Help Roger understand his role and the importance of it; help him track his assignments and progress. He is worth saving if he can be turned around; otherwise, he must be replaced.

8. **Wendy Whiner** — "I haven't got time for this stuff. I have a job to do." Wendy is a long-time employee who is used to doing things the old way and has seen many other projects come and go. She is not usually part of the formal project team, but she gets heard (and believed) by a lot of people, and can therefore kill the project's momentum. *Suggested solution:* The project time line, and the first success, will provide the leverage in a discussion with Wendy. Help her understand that on date "x" the new system will be live in her department. The key is to help her want the change and the new system. People don't resist change as much as they resist *being* changed. Help Wendy understand what the new system can do *for* her and her department and the company. There are many Wendys in any company; each team member needs to learn how to deal successfully with them.

9. **Harry Kari and Carla Kazi** — If their enthusiasm could be bottled, the project could be implemented without any more difficulties. They are the real key players; there is nothing they can't do (except implement the system by themselves). This is a problem in reverse — Harry and Carla are so good, the other team members think that Harry and Carla will take care of everything. In reality, they will burn out before the system is implemented unless the team contributes its fair share. *Suggested solution:* Find out why the team is willing to let Harry and

Carla do most of the work. Possible root cause — fear of making mistakes and being blamed for them.

10. **Person in the Mirror** — Yes, you. Confidence levels can be like a yo-yo as the wins and losses occur. Energy levels will probably wane, because the project leader normally feels completely underappreciated for much of the implementation. *Suggested solution:* Remember that there was a reason you were selected; others have confidence that you can do it. Know your strengths and use them heavily; know your weaknesses, and have others supplement you. Confide in your executive champion; get support from other sympathetic people. Realize that being leader means helping the other people succeed. And reward yourself and the team for the successes.

Summary

System implementations are times of opportunity to dramatically improve how the company operates on a day-to-day basis, by taking advantage of the capabilities in the new system. A new TEI system, properly implemented, could be capable of returning 100% or more of the entire investment. We have outlined a field-proven path for successfully implementing a new system. We have pointed out the most common areas in which companies have had difficulty, under the premise that prior knowledge of these pitfalls will help companies avoid them. TEI systems, because of their increased power and integration, can be more complex and more difficult to implement.

References

R. F. Alban Associates, *MRP II Implementation and Operations Handbook* (five volume set).

Allen, Dan J., "Multisite Implementation: Special Strategies," *1997 International Conference Proceedings*, APICS, Falls Church, VA, 1997.

Chew, W. Bruce, Leonard-Barton, Dorothy, and Bohn, Roger E., "Beating Murphy's Law," *Sloan Management Review*, Vol. 32, No. 3, 1991.

Hanekamp, Jim, McGowan, Tim, and Mather, Jim, "Don't Let a Rapid Implementation Short-Change Long-Term Value," *Midrange ERP*, February 1999.

Hutchins, Henry Alex, "7 Key Elements of a Successful Implementation, and 8 Mistakes You Will Make Anyway," *1998 International Conference Proceedings*, APICS, Falls Church, VA, 1998.

Krupp, James A.G., "Transition to ERP Implementation," *APICS — The Performance Advantage*, October 1998.

Oden, Howard W., Langenwalter, Gary, and Lucier, Raymond, *Handbook of Material and Capacity Requirements Planning*, McGraw-Hill, New York, 1993, Chapter 11.

Stedman, Craig, "ERP can magnify errors," *Computerworld*, October 19, 1998, pp. 1, 14.

Tincher, Michael G. and Sheldon, Donald H. Jr., *The Road to Class A Manufacturing Resource Planning (MRP II)*, 1995.

Turbide, David A., "Penny Wise, Pound Foolish," *Midrange ERP*, February 1999.

Wallace, Thomas F., *MRP II: Making It Happen*, Oliver Wight Publications, 1990.

Wojciak, Paul J., "So You're the Project Leader! 10 Roadblocks to Watch Out For," *1995 International Conference Proceedings*, APICS, Falls Church, VA, 1995.

11 The People Side of TEI

When I was a graduate teaching assistant in the Department of Management at Michigan State University in the late 1960s, I was enamored with existing and emerging technologies. One afternoon I was talking with the chairman of the department, Dalton McFarland, about my opinion that the new technologies could provide a forward-thinking company with an unstoppable competitive edge. Professor McFarland responded with great wisdom, "Let's assume that there are two identical companies, one of which has the latest technology, and one of which doesn't. If the people in the first company don't want to make the new technology win, it won't. If the people in the second company use the technology they have to the best of their ability, they will win." At the time, I was completely convinced that Professor McFarland was wrong. Now, I am completely convinced that he was right. Therefore, although the topic might seem totally out of place in a technical book, I have chosen to include this chapter in the hope that the people involved in any TEI (Total Enterprise Integration) system appreciate and support each other for who they truly are: gifted, unique, awesome, creative, wonderful individuals. Such an environment will substantially increase the success of a TEI system, both during implementation and daily operation.

James Collins and Jerry Porras researched 18 pairs of large, successful companies from various industries. In each pair, the two companies were selected to be as similar as possible. The only difference was that one company in each the pair focused exclusively on maximizing profits; the other company in the pair had at least one other, nonfinancial goal. Collins and Porras discovered that in 17 of the 18 pairs, the company that was more successful was "more ideologically driven and less purely profit-driven than the comparison companies. ... Profit maximization does not rule, but the vision-ary companies pursue their aims profitably. They do *both*."*

One example of a company that understands the importance of spirit is Merck & Co. As part of their centennial celebration, Roy Vagelos, the CEO, stated,

> Imagine that all of us were suddenly transported to the year 2091. Much [of our strategy and methods] would have been changed by develop-ments we cannot anticipate. But no matter what changes might have occurred in the Company, I know we would find one thing had remained the same — and the thing that matters most: the ... spirit of Merck people. ... A century from now, I believe we would feel the same *esprit de corps.* ... I believe this, above all, because Merck's dedication to fight-ing disease, relieving suffering, and helping people is a righteous cause — one that inspires people to dream of doing great things.**

Peter Drucker agrees when he compares Ford to General Motors,

> The failure of GM as an institution — for failure it is — is to a large extent the result of an attitude that one might call "technocratic" best exemplified in Alfred P. Sloan's own book, *My Years with General Motors.* It focuses exclusively on policies, business decisions, and structure. It is perhaps the most impersonal book of memoirs ever written — and this was clearly intentional. Sloan's book knows only one dimension: that of managing a business so that it can ... generate profits. Business in the community; business as a life rather than a livelihood; business as a neighbor ... — these are all absent in Sloan's world.***

A second company with clear vision of a purpose larger than making profits is Hewlett-Packard. David Packard's address to a group of managers who were launching the management development program that was a key to HP's success describes that vision.

> I want to discuss *why* a company exists in the first place. In other words, why are we here? I think many people assume, wrongly, that a company exists simply to make money. While this is an important result of a company's existence, we have to go deeper and find the real reasons for

---

* Collins, James C. and Porras, Jerry I., *Built to Last: Successful Habits of Visionary Companies,* HarperBusiness, New York, 1994, p. 55.
** *Values and Visions: A Merck Century,* Merck, Rahway, NJ, 1993, p. 173.
*** Drucker, Peter F., *Concept of the Corporation,* John Day, New York, 1972, p. 305.

our being. ... The real reason for our existence is that we provide something which is unique [that makes a contribution].*

Why do 80% of the working people dislike their work?** Because it does not feed their spirit, or soul. Tom Hanks parodied the workplace as entirely devoid of joy in the movie, *Joe vs. the Volcano*. Efficiency and productivity and profits are essential for continued existence of corporations, but they, and the economic model they represent, cannot provide an answer to the most basic question of all — the reason for living. In industrialized countries most people have found their meaning and their satisfaction in life from activities outside their workplaces, far removed from any concern with efficiency and profits. We need to escape from our cultural belief that only the things with a monetary price are worth having or doing. In our hearts, we know that is not true.

Thus, if organizations view TEI systems as *only* systems and try to implement them and operate them with standard technologically oriented approaches (e.g., project management, return on investment or assets), the organizations ignore a fundamental truth, thereby causing results to fall far short of expectations. This truth is that **all** organizations necessarily have a spiritual basis. The essence of that spirituality is that each of us is deeply and irrevocably connected with all others and with the ultimate source of life.

Unleashed spirit is the most powerful force in business today, even when compared to all our modern technology. Spirit is the genius that creates technology. Spirit is the power that causes groups to dream the impossible dream and then achieve it. Spirit is the glue that holds organizations together when the going gets tough. However, we can't demand, we can't command, and we can't control spirit.

Organizations thrive on predictability; they sacrifice virtually anything and everything else to be predictable, so that they can be "in control." Organizations are a mirror of ourselves; we want to be in control to avoid being controlled or taken advantage of. Can we imagine a CIO saying in an executive staff meeting, "We've empowered our people to unleash their creative spirit. I don't know when the TEI implementation project will be finished."

---

* Packard, David, speech given to HP's training group March 8, 1960, courtesy of Hewlett-Packard Co. archives, as quoted in Collins, James C. and Porras, Jerry I., *Built to Last: Successful Habits of Visionary Companies,* HarperBusiness, New York, 1994, p. 56.

** Secretan, Lance H. K., *Reclaiming Higher Ground, Creating Organizations That Inspire the Soul,* McGraw-Hill, New York, 1997, flyleaf.

The paradox is this: the power, creativity, and passion that is required for an organization to excel, and even to survive long-term, is that very power that organizations are typically unwilling to embrace and release, because they fear losing control. We propose that the unspeakable topic inside organizations today is not sex, or drugs, or felonies, or politics, or integrity, or even ethics; instead, the unspeakable topic seems to be spirituality — the very essence of humanity.

Carol Pearson suggests that there are actually five different spiritual and organizational systems (Table 11.1), which are constantly interacting with each other:*

Table 11.1 Spiritual and Organizational Systems

System	When present, helps people to:	When present, Leads to:	When lacking, Leads to:
Meaning	Find meaning and value from the work they do	Self-esteem	Demoralization, cynicism
Learning	Synthesize and apply information for the good of the enterprise	Wisdom	Boredom, inertia
Production	Get organized to produce a product in an efficient way	Quality of product or service	Shoddy products or service
Human community	Work well together	Sense of mutual and respect	Turf battles, infighting, alienation
Material	Enjoy material comforts, including equipment, comfortable surroundings, benefits, and financial security	Atmosphere of stability and ease	Atmosphere of chaos and rising anxiety

So how do we start acknowledging the spirit and helping it flourish in our organizations? We can use the TEI or ERP system as an excuse to let people redesign their work so that it meets their spiritual as well as economic needs. Some potential ways include:

---

* Pearson, Carol, *Thinking about Business Differently,* Inner Edge, Aliso Viejo, CA, 1998.

- Spirit — recognizing that spirit is the underlying fabric of any business, and being willing to articulate that vision and the possibilities it can create.
- Joy — deliberately designing our jobs to create joy in the job-holder.
- Creativity — imbuing each person with not only the right, but the urgency, to be fully creative at work.
- Organizing — organizing for cultivation of spirit.
- Learning — creating an environment that supports continual learning.
- Integrity — being in integrity.
- Respecting — respecting each individual.

Spirit

Matthew Fox states,

> Work comes from inside out; work is the expression of our soul, our inner being. It is unique to the individual; it is creative. Work is an expression of the Spirit at work in the world through us. Work is that which puts us in touch with others, not so much at the level of personal interaction, but at the level of service in the community.*

Studs Terkel has observed that for work to be authentically human, it must be "about a search, too, for daily meaning as well as daily bread, for recognition as well as cash, for astonishment rather than torpor; in short, for a sort of life rather than a Monday through Friday sort of dying."**

Companies should

> design their organizations artistically, rather than mechanically — in a way that is soulful rather than Newtonian. This requires them to change their thinking in a fundamental way. It is uncomfortable for many traditional managers to abandon their commitment to goal-setting because they depend on personal and corporate goals to navigate through life. These navigational beacons take the form of strategic plans, marketing plans, sales objectives, budgets. ... [However,] corrosion of the soul results.***

---

* Fox, Matthew, *The Reinvention of Work: A New Vision of Livelihood for Our Time*, Harper-Collins, New York, 1994, p. 5.
** Terkel, Studs, *Working*, Ballantine, New York, 1985, xiii.
***Secretan, Lance H.K., *Reclaiming Higher Ground: Creating Organizations That Inspire the Soul*, McGraw-Hill, New York, 1997.

In the 1960s, Tom Chappell and his wife Kate moved to Kennebunk, Maine, where they founded Tom's of Maine, a maker of all-natural toothpaste and similar products. Chappell left a sales position at Aetna Insurance, and recalled later,

> In my darkest days, I was working for aims that were too narrow for me. I was working for market share, sales growth, and profits. It was a sense of emptiness. I was to some degree depressed, undirected, unconnected to myself. I felt like an actor because what I was doing was not authentic. I was a phony to myself because I wasn't living up to what I cared about.*

Living a goal-directed life is unnatural. It isn't fun; and it isn't fulfilling. We are not arguing that goal-setting should be abandoned, but instead that the nature of the goals and how we measure them should be changed. We propose thinking of the activities of life — personal and organizational — as art. The fundamental reason that we create art is to express our innate creative genius and to inspire the soul. Can't our work be the same? Isn't the real purpose of our work to inspire the soul? Should we not ask, "How does this task inspire my soul and the souls of others?" each time we embark on a work activity?

The *Wall Street Journal* accused Henry Ford of "economic blunders if not crimes" which would soon "return to plague him and the industry he represents as well as organized society." In a naive wish for social improvement, declared the newspaper, Ford had injected "spiritual principles into a field where they do not belong" — a heinous crime."** This was because Ford had said,

> I don't believe we should make such an awful profit on our cars. A reasonable profit is right, but not too much. I hold that it is better to sell a large number of cars at a reasonably small profit ... I hold this because it enables a larger number of people to buy and enjoy the use of a car, and because it gives a larger number of men employment at good wages. Those are the two aims I have in life."***

He accomplished his goals, by reducing prices on the Model T 58% from 1908 to 1916, in spite of the fact that orders exceeded capacity which would have permitted him to raise prices. This action spurred a shareholder suit.

---

* Dumaine, Brian, "Why Do We Work," *Fortune*, November 26, 1994, pp. 196–204.
** Lacey, Robert, *Ford — The Man and the Machine*, Ballantine Books, New York, 1986, p. 179.
*** *Detroit News*, November 14, 1916, cited in Lacey, Robert, *Ford — The Man and the Machine*, Ballantine Books, New York, 1986, p. 179.

He also introduced the $5 per day wage for his factory workers, double the normal rate, which outraged the business community. Henry Ford apparently embarked upon "the most foolish thing ever attempted in the industrial world" partly under the influence of the highly idealistic philosopher Ralph Waldo Emerson and, in particular, his essay, "Compensation."*

Joy

> We have a right to and a need for joy in our work. If joy is good enough for God and powerful enough to have been the cause of the universe, then clearly joy is integral in our work too. "There can be no joy in living without joy in work," Aquinas warns us, for clearly much of our living is about work. There is no creation without some joy. Love draws us to work. … Love assures us that our work will be voluntary, ready, pleasurable, and firm. In addition, the pleasure we take in work ensures that we do better work."** Thus we see that pleasure blesses the work, not just the worker.***

Play, surprise, and praise — these are all the true elements of work. When we play at work, we become creative, and create more than we ever imagined possible. When we open ourselves to the element of surprise, we allow our Creator to speak to us, to guide us, to provide greater joy and power, which we in turn invest back into our work. When we give our work away as praise, it returns, as Spirit, as strength, as creation itself.

Ed Simon, president of Herman Miller, said,

> Why can't work be one of those wonderful things in life? Why can't we cherish and praise it, versus seeing work as a necessity? Why can't it be a cornerstone in people's lifelong process of developing ethics, values, and in expressing the humanities and the arts? Why can't people learn through the process that there's something about the beauties of design, of building something to last, something of value? I believe that this potential is inherent in work, more so than in many other places.****

---

* Collins, James C. and Porras, Jerry I., *Built to Last: Successful Habits of Visionary Companies,* HarperBusiness, New York, 1994, p. 53.
** Fox, Matthew, *Sheer Joy,* Harper, San Francisco, 1992, p. 295.
*** Fox, Matthew, *The Reinvention of Work,* HarperCollins, New York, 1994, p. 95.
**** Senge, Peter, *The Fifth Discipline,* Doubleday Currency, New York, 1990, p. 144.

How can we redesign the jobs and tasks in our workplaces to foster joy on the part of the workers? It might be very, very difficult, perhaps even impossible in some situations. However, the simple, straightforward approach is to ask the people who are doing the jobs what gives them joy now, and what they would like to change to increase their joy. And then implement every one of those suggestions!

Creativity

People are inherently creative. Watch any group of children at play; they continually create: new games, new rules to old games, "make-believe." Some even create imaginary playmates. The creative process is both simple and absolutely awesome: from nothing, the creator forms something.

"In the beginning, God created the heavens and the earth," are the very first words in the Bible and the Torah. They define God as a powerful, creative force. Genesis 1:26 continues, "Then God said, 'Let us make humans in our image, in our likeness,'" thereby making humans creators as well, by our very nature. Artists create their art, usually not because of the monetary rewards, but because their creative spirit compels them to. Craftspeople create at work, when they are allowed to by the organization structure.

The reason people create is simple: they want the creation to exist.

> In fact, I love the creation enough that I will take whatever actions are necessary to bring the creation into the world. This is how it is for all creators, although we have been taught not to admit it, for when we talk like that, we can be accused of being elitists, mystics, or fools.
>
> Love is what creating is all about. ... When you are creating, the love comes first, and the situation later. *In the creative process, love is generative rather than simply responsive.* ... The creator is able to love something that does not yet exist — even in the imagination — and bring it into existence."*

Creating generates a powerful, positive experience on the part of the creator, one which accesses the deepest recesses of the psyche. Creating is a truly spiritual experience.

There are at least three factors in most corporations which, individually and collectively, decrease creativity:

---

*   Fritz, Robert, *Creating,* Fawcett Books, New York, 1993, pp. 15–16 .

1. **The quality movement,** which has been creating rigid structure around all processes to ensure that the product meets quality standards. While this has indeed ensured that all products meet quality specifications, it has also removed much of the artistry and creation from the workplace, reducing the people involved to a highly mechanical existence.

2. The relentless focus on **increased productivity and efficiency** (to reduce product cost) has forced people to work harder and faster, eliminating any time they might have available to think about improvement opportunities. Is it not possible to ask workers to use their inherent creativity to reduce product cost, rather than just insisting that they work harder and faster? One of Just-In-Time's major contributions in this area was the practice of scheduling a cell for 7 hours of production, rather than 8, leaving the last hour for catching up (if necessary), routine maintenance, and continuous improvement (which is creativity by a different name).

3. **Accounting systems,** which view labor as an expense to be reduced, rather than an asset to be nurtured. The people in an organization are the well-spring of new ideas which can ensure that the company thrives both short-term and long-term. How many ideas for improvement have your machines contributed recently? And yet they are listed as "assets" on the balance sheet!

In his Pulitzer-prize-winning book, *The Soul of a New Machine,* Tracy Kidder tells the story of a product development team at Data General that was challenged to create an ambitious new computer.

> Against a business atmosphere of urgency bordering on crisis, the team turned out a ground-breaking computer in remarkable time. Visiting with the team manager Tom West and team members several years later, I learned just how remarkable their feat was. They told me of a stage in their project where certain critical software was several months behind schedule. The three engineers responsible came into the office one evening and left the next morning. By all accounts they accomplished two to three months of work that evening — and no one could explain how.*

---

* Senge, Peter, *The Fifth Discipline,* Doubleday Currency, New York, 1990, p. 221.

Failure

If there are no failures, people are not being creative. Thomas Edison tried more than 1000 filaments that could potentially create light in a light bulb before he finally found one that produced the results he wanted. The average life span of a Fortune 500 company is a mere 40 years. The only way for an organization to survive long term is to create an atmosphere that not only tolerates "failure," but rejoices in it. We encourage companies to give an award quarterly which celebrates the most innovative and audacious attempt that ended in "failure."

In a broader sense, there are no failures except inaction. When a person or group tries something new, they get some sort of result. They have one more data point than they had before; therefore, they have succeeded, because the reason for trying something new is to learn what the results will be. If the results are different than what they had hoped for, they can adjust the experiment and try again.

One palpable difference between Japanese and U.S. cultures in the 1980s and 1990s was the Japanese would be glad when a mistake happened, because that provided one more opportunity to learn and improve. U.S. companies still viewed mistakes and failures as "bad."

Knowing that humans will continue to make mistakes, Martin Luther said, "Go and sin boldly." We wholeheartedly agree; that is the only way to be truly alive and creative.

Destruction

Creativity intrinsically requires destroying what was there before. Something that has existed must give way, or even die, so that the new creation can exist. That something is not only physical; it frequently includes belief systems, organization structures, and values. William Bridges has outlined three stages for a person or organization to transition from the old to the new:*

1. Letting go of the old
2. Creating a new understanding in the intervening chaos and uncertainty
3. Moving toward the new.

---

* Bridges, William, *Managing Transitions: Making the Most of Change*, Addison-Wesley, Reading, MA, 1991.

Some of the difficulty in successfully implementing successful change arises from the pain of destruction, or letting go, of the old.

Organization

Humans are, by nature, social. We spend time with each other because it meets a basic need. Many studies, including the Tavistock studies in England, have clearly demonstrated the negative effect that the destruction of social structure has on productivity.

Dictatorships have long recognized (and feared) the inherent power of groups. That is why the U.S. Constitution expressly includes a clause that protects the right of the people to assemble.

TEI implementations require teamwork across the entire organization. The teams are the most important factor in successfully implementing a new system. What can an ideal team do? It can:

- Create a collective vision that is greater than the sum of the individual visions.
- Encourage creativity from each participant.
- Provide ideas that overcome obstacles.
- Hold individuals accountable and responsible for performing as they promised.
- Encourage authenticity on the part of its members.
- Engender trust internally, between participants, and externally. between participants and other individuals and groups.
- Provide autonomy to its members, and be autonomous within the larger organization.

> If a business is now, in its essentials, a collection of people, it will make more sense to think of it as a town or village rather than a piece of machinery. This will eventually change the way we think about businesses. It is already changing the way we talk about them. The language of political theory — leadership, constituencies, alliances, power, and influence — is replacing the old engineering and property language of structure, planning, control, and even management. Talented individuals don't like to be "human resources," or to be managed. They prefer to be led by someone they respect. Try calling a pop star or a leading actor a "resource" and wait for the response — it won't be polite.*

---

* Handy, Charles, *The Hungry Spirit*, Broadway Books, New York, 1998, p. 154.

Citizenship and Herding Cats

Charles Handy describes a new type of organization, one in which individuals are equal citizens in a company.

> Citizenship is about autonomy, the freedom to run your own life. In return for this freedom, the corporate state can demand little, but hope for much. Citizens in a democracy are free to emigrate. You cannot stop anyone leaving. Nor can you demand commitment, only hope for it. Combining this freedom and these rights with the aims of the organization is the real challenge of the citizen company. Many managers would prefer not to accept the challenge, because organizing talented people is akin to the proverbial herding of cats — difficult by definition. We have to manage people whom we can't totally control. Instead we have to trust them, and they have to trust us. The principle is simple. The practicalities mean that it seldom happens.*

Learning

Peter Senge, in his landmark book *The Fifth Discipline,* created the phrase "the learning organization." A learning organization has six key characteristics:

1. Personal Mastery, including the spirit of the organization and personal vision.
2. Mental Models, which describes how people and companies view their organization, their competition, and their opportunities.
3. Shared Vision, in which participants are enrolled in the possibilities that the new vision creates, and want to achieve those possibilities.
4. Team Learning, describing how a team can create a synergy that is almost magic, which jazz musicians call "being in the groove."
5. Openness, in which teams and companies can transcend internal politics and game playing that characterizes most organizations.
6. Localness, which describes how to achieve control without controlling.

---

* Handy, Charles, *The Hungry Spirit,* Broadway Books, New York, 1998, p. 178.

Being in Integrity

Integrity and the ability to trust another person's word are a cornerstones of society. We have to trust that other drivers will stay on their side of the road and stop at stop signs. We have to trust that the contents of a box of breakfast cereal are indeed wholesome food.

Unfortunately, half-truths, misrepresentations, and out-and-out lying permeate much of our business culture and conversations today. "Of course you'll have a job waiting for you when you get back from this overseas assignment." "Yes, if you'll partner with us, we'll share all the prospects." From the voice of an automated attendant, while you are on hold for 10 minutes or longer waiting to speak to a human being, "Your call is very important to us. We apologize for the delay. Customer service is our Number One priority!" "Yes, of course this product will perform that function!" "Hi, this is the voice mail of XXX; I'm not here right now, but I'll get right back to you, so please leave a message." "I personally guarantee that we'll complete that job by Friday." "Send us your information (or proposal); we'll call you next Tuesday morning." "I'll have that on your desk first thing in the morning." Or the ancient classic, "The check is in the mail."

Some companies have built their reputations on integrity. Their word is stronger than most legal contracts. IBM, Hewlett-Packard, Shaklee Corp., Bayer Pharmaceuticals, and McDonald's, to name but a few, have built reputations of integrity in the marketplace. What they promise, they deliver.

Truly being in integrity requires people to make commitments and then to fulfill them. It requires people to be honest and to take responsibility for their actions and their results. Integrity requires people to admit when they made mistakes, even when those mistakes were costly. But for people to admit mistakes, they must expect the company to have integrity and to treat them fairly and ethically.

Where integrity has been compromised, the people wither inside. Where integrity is valued and honored, people flourish. It's that simple. And it's *very* difficult to practice.

Respecting Each Individual

No matter what their function in a company, each individual needs to feel respected for their contribution. This respect stems from the fact that all humans beings are truly equal in the eyes of our Creator. Each person is endowed with a special mix of talents, gifts, and shortcomings, strengths and weaknesses, insights and blindnesses.

Scott Adams has a unique talent for capturing the essence of corporate life in his comic strip, Dilbert. A Sunday strip had the following dialogue:

> Dilbert: "There's Ted. He never sent me the information he promised."
>
> Dilbert: "Why have you ignored my request, Ted?"
>
> Ted: "I was killed by a squadron of giant military squirrels."
>
> Wally: "He doesn't respect you enough to tell a plausible lie."
>
> Dilbert: "I DEMAND A PLAUSIBLE LIE!"
>
> Ted: "Okay, maybe I *wasn't* killed by giant military squirrels, but I *was* imprisoned in their secret lair at the center of the earth."
>
> Wally: "You can't prove that one either way."
>
> Dilbert: "He did say it was a "secret" lair."*

True respect requires humility; it levels the playing field and eliminates arrogance. It ignores differences in financial compensation, style of clothes, size of office, race, gender, culture, and other perceived differentiators. It allows each person to be a valuable member of the team, and to contribute all they are capable of.

Case Study — KEEPER® Corp.

"People think we're crazy," says Doris Obsharsky, plant manager at KEEPER® Corp. "When I presented how we operate at a seminar four years ago, one person predicted that I'd be dead in a year, but I'm still here."

KEEPER® Corp., a manufacturer of tie-down straps and bungee cords, was experiencing typical growing pains. After more than 10 years of dedication and hard work, they had finally landed the top retailers as customers. Communications was becoming more fragmented as they added people throughout the organization to keep up with the increased customer orders,

---

* DILBERT© United Feature Syndicate. Reprinted by Permission.

and frustration levels and tension in the office and the plant were increasing. Additionally, the error rates in the shipping department, while still somewhat acceptable, needed improvement. Ken Porter, the president and owner, invited my consulting firm to study the shipping department and recommend the actions they could take to decrease error rates.

We studied the actual errors, interviewed each person in the shipping department and other key individuals, identified several causes, then created recommendations to address the causes. Our primary recommendation, however, was that KEEPER® implement a self-directed work team in the shipping department so that the people would personally assume responsibility for continually improving their performance. Ken, who had earned a liberal arts degree, liked the idea. He agreed, as long as Doris Obsharsky, the plant manager, would become the facilitator and coach. Doris was extremely nervous but was willing to try. She had been one of the earliest associates in the company.

Even at the beginning, KEEPER® was much more open and human-centered than most other companies in the area because of the culture that Ken fostered. A relatively new associate told the consultant about his first day on the job. The new associate was in the break room that morning when another man walked in, introduced himself as "Ken," and asked, "What do you think of your new job?" The new associate told Ken that the job and company seemed fine, but that there were some areas that could be improved. Ken asked what they were. The new associate told him. Ken thanked him and left. The associate's supervisor walked into the break room and said, "Oh, I see you've met the president." The associate was afraid that he was going to be fired for having spoken his opinions. The supervisor assured him that Ken valued associates' honest and constructive opinions, and would think more highly of the associate.

So we led the formation of a self-directed work team (SDWT) for the shippers. Simultaneously, we started coaching Doris to change from a benevolent command-and-control style of management to a coaching/facilitative style of leadership, using the shipping department SDWT as the learning laboratory. The most difficult transition was for the floor supervisors, who were used to directing activities on the shop floor and in shipping, in a detailed manner. Doris started showing the supervisors how to be coaches, rather than bosses.

The shippers were a little confused a first; they were not used to making their own decisions, even about little things. One of our recommendations was that the shipping SDWT be given a budget of $100/year to be used for improving the department, on their decision alone. No other approvals were required. The underlying message was this: "We trust you; we trust your judgment to use these resources wisely." They bought hand-held calculators and some other small items that they needed. Morale and spirits in the shipping department soared; they were really excited about coming to work.

We showed the shippers how to track errors on statistical charts and how to use fishbone diagrams to identify potential causes. They posted the charts in their areas, and were excited when the numbers improved, and concerned when the numbers fell back.

The genie of magic and empowerment was out of the bottle. The news of the shipping department's SDWT spread quickly throughout the plant; other workers started asking if they could form teams also, because they "wanted to have fun, too." Within 6 months, all workers throughout the plant had formed teams, except for six very independent individuals who didn't want to be part of any group. Those six finally became their own team of "nonteam players." And the supervisors formed their own team.

Three months after the start, Jay McCue, a shipper, came up to us and said proudly, "Come on out to my area. I have something I'd like to show you." We smiled inwardly, contrasting Jay's ownership of "his" area to the initial visit, in which the shippers had no psychological ownership in the area, the process, or the results.

Doris blossomed into a superb coach. A few months after the change started, we asked her opinion of the old way and the new way. Doris responded, "The new way is much, much easier on me. Whenever anyone would bring me a problem before, I used to think I had to have the answer. Now, I can tell them, 'I don't know. What do you think?' and let them solve it. Their answers are often better than the ones I would have come up with. And it takes a lot of pressure off of me. I don't have to be 'right' all the time."

The teams of production workers started deciding which teams would assemble each of the products each day, removing a scheduling chore from Sally Cosgrove, a supervisor. They started focusing on continuous improvement, challenging themselves to do better. One weekend, they even changed the layout of the production floor to improve throughput. The teams routinely change team members, recruiting new members from other teams, and letting current members join other teams. The most frequent reason for changing team members is for a team to improve, to learn something new from the new member.

KEEPER® had been known as a good place to work before this started; afterward, it became known as the best place to work in the area. The wage structure remained the same, but the attitudes had gotten even better. A year after the program started, KEEPER® had become so different from the other major employers in the area that the supervisory team created an informal program to help new hires understand their special culture. Not everyone who joins can adapt to the culture of freedom and its concomitant responsibility.

Some go back to the more familiar command-and-control culture of other employers. Several associates who have left KEEPER® for other companies have returned to KEEPER®. For those who work at KEEPER®, it is by far the best place to work. It has freed their spirits and captured their hearts.

Summary

The following quotation from Marianne Williamson was used by Nelson Mandela during his inaugural address as President of South Africa. His was a message of hope, of reconciliation, of inviting each person to embrace the goodness and greatness within themselves and others.

> *Our deepest fear is not that*
> *we are inadequate.*
> *Our deepest fear is that we are*
> *powerful beyond measure.*
> *It is our light, not our darkness, that frightens us.*
> *We ask ourselves, "Who am I to be brilliant,*
> *gorgeous, talented, and fabulous?"*
> *Actually, who are we **not** to be?*
> *You are a child of God. Your playing small*
> *doesn't serve the world.*
> *There's nothing enlightened about*
> *shrinking so that other people*
> *won't feel insecure around you.*
> *We were born to make manifest the*
> *glory of God that is within us.*
> *It's not just in some of us, it's in everyone.*
> *And as we let our own light shine,*
> *we unconsciously give other people*
> *permission to do the same.*
> *As we are liberated from our own fears,*
> *our presence automatically*
> *liberates others.**

---

* Williamson, Marianne, *A Return to Love: Reflections on the Principles of a Course in Miracles,* HarperCollins, New York, 1996 (reissue).

References

Barger, Nancy J. and Kirby, Linda K., *The Challenge of Change in Organizations: Helping Employees Thrive in the New Frontier,* Davies-Black, Palo Alto, CA, 1995.

Bolman, Lee G. and Deal, Terrence E., *Leading with Soul,* Jossey-Bass, San Francisco, 1995.

Bracey, Hyler, Rosenblum, Jack, Sanford, Aubrey, and Trueblood, Roy, Dell Trade, New York, 1990.

Bridges, William, *Managing Transitions: Making the Most of Changes,* Addison-Wesley, Reading, MA, 1991.

Chappell, Tom, *The Soul of a Business: Managing for Profit and the Common Good,* Bantam, New York, 1993.

Collins, James C., and Porras, Jerry I., *Built to Last: Successful Habits of Visionary Companies,* HarperBusiness, New York, 1994.

Covey, Stephen R., *Principle-Centered Leadership,* Simon and Schuster, New York, 1990.

DePree, Max, *Leadership Jazz,* Doubleday, New York, 1992.

Drucker, Peter F., *Concept of the Corporation,* John Day, New York, 1972.

Dumaine, Brian, "Why Do We Work," *Fortune,* November 26, 1994.

Fox, Matthew, *Sheer Joy,* Harper, San Francisco, 1992.

Fox, Matthew, *The Reinvention of Work: A New Vision of Livelihood For Our Time,* Harper-Collins, New York, 1994.

Fritz, Robert, *Creating,* Fawcett Books, New York, 1993.

Green, Alan, *A Company Discovers Its Soul: A Year in the Life of a Transforming Organization,* Berrett-Koehler, San Francisco, 1996.

Handy, Charles, *The Hungry Spirit,* Broadway Books, New York, 1998.

Jones, Laurie Beth, *Jesus CEO: Using Ancient Wisdom for Visionary Leadership,* Hyperion, New York, 1995.

Lacey, Robert, *Ford — The Man and the Machine,* Ballantine Books, New York, 1986.

Lulic, Margaret A., *Who We Could Be at Work,* Blue Edge Publishing, Minneapolis, 1994.

McCarthy, Dennis G., *The Loyalty Link: How Loyal Employees Create Loyal Customers,* Wiley, New York, 1997.

McKnight, Richard, "Spirituality in the Workplace," in John D. Adams, ed., *Transforming Work,* Miles River Press, Alexandria, VA, 1984.

Pasmore, William A., *Designing Effective Organizations: The Sociotechnical Systems Perspective,* Wiley, New York, 1988.

Pearson, Carol, *Thinking about Business Differently,* Inner Edge, Aliso Viejo, CA, 1998.

Peck, M. Scott, *The Different Drum: Community Making and Peace,* Touchstone, New York, 1998.

Pergamit, Gayle and Peterson, Chris, *Leaping the Abyss: Putting Group Genius to Work,* Knowhere Press, Palo Alto, CA, 1997.

Peters, Tom, *The Pursuit of WOW!,* Vintage, New York, 1994.

Quinn, Robert E., *Deep Change: Discovering the Leader Within,* Jossey-Bass, San Francisco, 1996.

Renesh, John, Ed., *New Traditions in Business: Spirit and Leadership in the 21st Century,* New Leaders Press/Sterling & Stone, San Francisco, 1991.

Rucci, Anthony J., Kirn, Steven P., and Quinn, Richard T., "The Employee-Customer-Profit Chain at Sears," *Harvard Business Review,* January-February 1998.

Secretan, Lance H. K., *Reclaiming Higher Ground: Creating Organizations That Inspire the Soul*, McGraw-Hill, New York, 1997.

Semler, Ricardo, *Maverick : The Success Story behind the World's Most Unusual Workplace*, Warner Books, 1995.

Senge, Peter, *The Fifth Discipline*, Doubleday Currency, New York, 1990.

Senge, Peter, *The Fifth Discipline Fieldbook: Strategies and Tools for Building a Learning Organization*, Doubleday, New York, 1994.

Terkel, Studs, *Working*, Ballantine, New York, 1985.

Weisbord, Marvin R., *Productive Workplaces: Organizing and Managing for Dignity, Meaning, and Community*, Jossey-Bass, San Francisco, 1987.

Wheatley, Margaret J., *Leadership and the New Science*, Berrett-Koehler, San Francisco, 1992.

Williamson, Marianne, *A Return to Love: Reflections on the Principles of a Course in Miracles*, HarperCollins, New York, 1996 (reissue).

Appendix A:
Features and Functions for
Repetitive Manufacturing

T he following ERP/TEI features and functions were identified by the Repetitive Manufacturing Specific Industry Group of APICS as helpful for a repetitive manufacturer.*

Scheduling/Orders

- Flexible scheduling without the use of work orders; scheduling should include shift, daily, and weekly options.
- Rate-based forward scheduling.
- Identify production lines with products and rates per period; ability to schedule a product on more than one production line.
- Overlap unit scheduling.
- Mixed model scheduling for each product line.
- Transfer units between repetitive lines; all costs are automatically transferred with units.
- Work order BOM and routings created for the specific repetitive schedule from master BOMs and routings; ability to modify for a specific schedule.

---

* APICS Repetitive Manufacturing SIG Committee, *Basics of Repetitive Manufacturing Workshop*, APICS, Alexandria, VA, 1999.

- Cumulative or continuous schedule for labor, burden, and material cost; charges must be traceable to the repetitive schedule.
- Close the continuous order for the financial reporting period and reestablish the order for the next period.
- Set independent shop calendars for each production line.

Simulation Workbench

- Workbench or simulation capability to level load production lines with repetitive schedules.
- Graphical line/load representation for workbench. Ability to manipulate the load directly from graphical screen.
- Sequencing algorithms to minimize setups.

Reporting

- Option to report backflush quantities at yielded or perfection component quantities.
- Milestone and nonmilestone operations; automatic reporting of completions to interim nonmilestone operations.
- Report rejected units and route for rework; record rework charges separately from initial work.
- Report scrap units with or without backflush of labor and materials.
- Backflush from multiple point-of-use floor stock locations.
- Backflush materials and labor to repetitive schedule.
- Performance reporting to include efficiency, productivity, WIP cost, labor cost, burden, reject, and scrap.
- Control files to allow completions to consume schedule in stated periods forward and/or backward.

Integration

- Repetitive picklist and transfer from primary stockroom to point-of-use floor stock locations.

- Compatibility with *kanban* system for demand and material replenishments for production lines.
- Directly tied to material requirements planning system for development of exception and action messages.
- Include provisions for subcontract operations tied to purchasing system.

Appendix B:
Features and Functions
for Process Manufacturing

The following ERP/TEI features and functions can be required by a process manufacturer.

Enterprise System Requirements

- Enterprise supply chain, linking suppliers, the manufacturer, and customers
- Multiple plants
- Multiple warehouses
- Multiple branches
- Centralized management features

Items, Formulas, and Units of Measure

- Item — formula architecture
- Items are developed from one or more formulas
- Items can have grades, determined by quality specifications

- Formula or recipe is fully integrated:
  - Process
  - Materials
  - Labor
  - Equipment
  - Utilities and water
- Complex unit of measure conversion, including specific gravity
- Alternative quantities:
  - "Catch weight" of item or package
  - Potency
- Container type(s)
- Formulas, rather than Bills of Materials:
  - Unpredictable quantity (yield)
  - Unpredictable quality
  - Property calculations (e.g., nutrition, for food)
  - Alternate raw materials
  - Specification-oriented

Process and Quality Specifications

- Ability to support all three major manufacturing styles:
  1. Bulk refining
  2. Additional refining
  3. Packaging:
     - Intermediate containers
     - Wide variety of brands, styles, and sizes
     - Ability to mix different packages onto the same pallet for shipping
- Quality:
  - Tests and specifications must be specified with the item itself, by grade
  - Determines which customers are willing to buy a specific lot
  - Potency by batch
- Process control:
  - Real-time monitors linked to quality and lot tracking systems:
  - Physical — Temperature, pressure, viscosity, etc.
  - Chemical – pH
  - Other
- Process control automatically adjusts inputs, both material and environmental, to keep outputs in specified range

Planning and Scheduling

- Forward and backward scheduling from critical resource
- Constraint-based, with user's choice of constraint orientations:
  - Capacity
  - Materials
  - Both
- Ability to manage and prioritize materials in bulk and packs
- Sequencing of products and batches
- By-products and co-products
- Lot traceability:
  - Complete forward and backward traceability
  - Automatic interface with quality measurement systems
  - Ability to mix or not mix lots in a batch or to a customer
  - Ability to support a recall or quarantine
  - Across entire supply/distribution chain
- Shelf life
- "Soft allocation" of lots in various stages of production or storage to specific customer orders or forecasts, by quality specifications and delivery dates
- Adjustments for quantity usage variances due to humidity, temperature, acidity, and other factors
- Intermediate storage requirements:
  - Tanks or vessels, of specific types:
    - Clean-out, before use, after use, or both
    - Size
  - Storage times, minimum and maximum
- Recycling scrap back into the process:
  - Maximum or minimum percentages allowable
  - Shelf life of scrap

Supply Chain Order Management

- Ability to manage a mix of customer types, both domestic and international, including:
  - Retailers
  - Distributors
  - Manufacturers

- Industrial customers
- Institutions
- Governments
■ Complex pricing and promotions:
  - Adjusted automatically for changes in raw materials costs
  - Including freight costs
  - Including minimum and maximum volume requirements
  - Hierarchical promotions

Simulation Workbench

■ Workbench or simulation capability to level load production lines with flow or batch schedules.
■ Graphical line/load representation for workbench. Ability to manipulate the load directly from graphical screen.
■ Sequencing algorithms to minimize setups.
■ Optimizing capabilities to achieve maximum profits and customer service:
  - Formula blend of raw materials:
    - Cost
    - Properties
  - Multiple simultaneous constraints

Accounting and Costing

■ Costing not based on direct labor hours — uses equipment hours or raw material units as basis.

Reporting

■ Yields — actual vs. planned
■ Variances from specifications:
  - Process
  - Material

References

Klappich, Dwight, "Your Best Defense for Managing Recalls, Improving Quality Control," *Process Supplement, Midrange ERP,* January/February 1999.

Klappich, Dwight, "Ten Issues For Food and Beverage ERP," *Midrange ERP,* March 1999.

Lippmann, Carol, "Controlling Quality in the Process Environment," *Process Supplement, Midrange ERP,* January/February 1999.

Phelan, Stephan D., "Enterprise Formula Management," *Midrange ERP,* March 1999.

Thompson, Olin, "What Makes Process Process?" *Process Supplement, Midrange ERP,* January/February 1999.

Turner, Jeff, "The Unique Requirements of Process Industry ERP," *APICS — The Performance Advantage,* June 1998.

Appendix C:
Professional Associations

AIAG — Automotive Industry Action Group

http://www.aiag.org

... Improving the productivity of the North American automotive industry.
AIAG is a not-for-profit trade association of North American vehicle
manufacturers and suppliers. These member organizations come together
under the auspices of AIAG to tackle a wide range of industry issues. The
result of this work is the development of new technologies and the standards
that govern their usage.

AME — the Association for Manufacturing Excellence

http://www.ame.org

The Association for Manufacturing Excellence enables members' companies to achieve excellence and competitive advantage. This is accomplished
through education, documentation, research and experience sharing. AME
membership provides a forum for all functions of manufacturing enterprises.

APICS — Educational Society for Resource Management

http://www.apics.org

APICS is a not-for-profit international educational organization respected
throughout the world for its education and professional certification programs. With more than 70,000 individual and corporate members in 20,000
companies worldwide, APICS is dedicated to using education to improve the
business bottom line.

APICS is recognized globally as:

- The source of knowledge and expertise for manufacturing and service industries across the entire supply chain — in such areas as materials management, information services, purchasing and quality.
- The leading provider of high-quality, cutting-edge educational programs that advance organizational success in a changing, competitive marketplace.
- A successful developer of two internationally recognized certification programs, Certified in Production and Inventory Management (CPIM) and Certified in Integrated Resource Management (CIRM).
- A distribution center for hundreds of business management publications and educational materials.
- A source of solutions, support, and networking local chapters, workshops, symposia, and the annual APICS International Conference and Exposition.

CLM — Council of Logistics Management

http://www.clm1.org

The mission of the Council of Logistics Management is to serve the evolving logistics profession by developing advancing and disseminating logistics knowledge. The Council of Logistics Management is a not-for-profit professional organization that provides:

- Leadership in developing, defining, understanding, and enhancing the logistics process on a worldwide basis.
- Forums for the timely exchange of concepts and best practices among logistics professionals.
- Research that advances knowledge and leads to enhanced customer value and logistics performance within the supply chain.
- Education and career development programs that enhance career opportunities in logistics management.
- Promotes involvement of individuals with the broadest possible backgrounds in its programs and activities, thereby assuring that the organization benefits from and develops the diversity of its members.

NAPM — National Association of Purchasing Management

http://www.napm.org

NAPM is a not-for-profit association that provides national and international leadership in purchasing and supply management research and education. NAPM provides its 180 affiliated associations and its more than 46,000 members opportunities to expand their professional skills and knowledge.

AICPA — American Institute of Certified Public Accountants

http://aicpa.org

The American Institute of Certified Public Accountants is the national, professional organization for all Certified Public Accountants. Its mission is to provide members with the resources, information, and leadership that enable them to provide valuable services in the highest professional manner to benefit the public as well as employers and clients.

In fulfilling its mission, the AICPA works with state CPA organizations and gives priority to those areas where public reliance on CPA skills is most significant.

CAM-I — Computer-Aided Manufacturing, International

http://cam-i.org

CAM-I is an international consortium of companies, consultancies and academics who have elected to work cooperatively in a precompetitive environment to solve problems that are common to the group.

CAM-I's Participative Model produces value for members through

- Participative Research — by working together the participants understand the journey — the best practice path.
- Targeted Intellectual Efforts — each program targets results and produces implementable deliverables by our sponsors.
- Human Networks — Develop and continue to share, challenge ideas, and learn long beyond the end date of the specific result.

IIE — Institute of Industrial Engineers

http://www.iie.org

Founded in 1948, the Institute of Industrial Engineers is the society dedicated to serving the professional needs of industrial engineers and all individuals involved with improving quality and productivity.

MESA — Manufacturing Execution Systems Association

http://www.mesa.org

MESA was formed in the fall of 1992 by the leading manufacturing execution system (MES) software vendors. MESA is a not-for-profit trade association providing a legal forum for competitors to work together to expand awareness and use of manufacturing technology ... particularly MES and all the related products and services required by the modern manufacturing enterprise.

NAEP — National Association of Environmental Professionals

http://www.naep.org

The National Association of Environmental Professionals is the multidisciplinary association dedicated to the advancement of the environmental professions in the U.S. and abroad; a forum for state-of-the-art information on environmental planning, research and management. It is a network of professional contacts and exchange on information among colleagues in industry, government, academe, and the private sector; a resource for structured career development from student membership to certification as an environmental professional.

SCC — Supply Chain Council

http://www.scc.org

The Supply Chain Council was formed in 1996–1997 as a grass roots initiative by forward-thinking individuals representing companies including Advanced Manufacturing Research (AMR), Bayer, Compaq Computer, Pittiglio Rabin Todd & McGrath (PRTM), Procter & Gamble, Lockheed Martin, Nortel, Rockwell Semiconductor, and Texas Instruments.

SME — Society of Manufacturing Engineers

http://www.sme.org

SME, headquartered in Dearborn, Michigan, U.S. is an international professional society dedicated to serving its members and the manufacturing community through the advancement of professionalism, knowledge, and learning. Founded in 1932, SME has nearly 65,000 members in 70 countries. The society also sponsors some 275 chapters, districts, and regions, as well as 240 student chapters worldwide.

Index